With Lincoln
in the White House

With Lincoln in the White House

LETTERS, MEMORANDA, AND OTHER WRITINGS OF JOHN G. NICOLAY, 1860–1865

Edited by Michael Burlingame

Southern Illinois University Press
Carbondale and Edwardsville

Frontispiece: Photograph of John G. Nicolay by Matthew Brady.
Courtesy of the Illinois State Historical Library, Springfield.

Library of Congress Cataloging-in-Publication Data

Nicolay, John G. (John George), 1832–1901.
   With Lincoln in the White House : letters, memoranda, and
other writings of John G. Nicolay, 1860–1865 / edited by Michael
Burlingame.
      p. cm.
   Includes bibliographical references and index.
      1. Nicolay, John G. (John George), 1832–1901—Correspon-
dence. 2. Private secretaries—United States—Correspondence.
3. Lincoln, Abraham, 1809–1865—Friends and associates—
Correspondence. 4. Lincoln, Abraham, 1809–1865. 5. United
States—History—Civil War, 1861–1865—Personal narratives.
6. United States—Politics and government—1861–1865.
I. Burlingame, Michael, 1941– II. Title.
E467.1.N5 A4 2000
973.7'092—dc21   99-086598
ISBN 0-8093-2332-X (alk. paper)

For Wayne C. Temple,
scholar and friend

Contents

Acknowledgments

Wayne C. Temple, chief deputy director of the Illinois State Archives, is a legendary Lincoln scholar who generously shared with me his discoveries and helped me solve innumerable puzzles as I conducted research on this volume and its siblings.

Thomas F. Schwartz, the Illinois state historian, kindly read the manuscript and gave me the benefit of his vast knowledge of Lincoln and his times.

I am grateful to John Y. Simon, dean of documentary editing in American history, for his encouragement over the years.

Librarians across the country also provided invaluable assistance, especially at Brown University's John Hay Library, where Mary Jo Kline, Samuel Streit, Jean Rainwater, Andrew Moel, Pat Soris, and their colleagues have been warmly hospitable as well as efficiently helpful. At the Library of Congress, I have over the years enjoyed the friendship and able assistance of Mary Wolfskill, Fred Bauman, Jeff Flannery, John Sellers, Clark Evans, and many others. Their counterparts at the Pike County Historical Society in Pittsfield, Illinois, the National Archives, the J. P. Morgan Library, the Huntington Library, the New York Public Library, the New-York Historical Society, the Lincoln Museum in Fort Wayne, Indiana, the Illinois State Historical Library in Springfield, and Connecticut College in New London have also offered welcome aid as I pursued my scholarly quarry. Connecticut College's R. Francis Johnson Faculty Development Fund helped defray some of the expenses involved in the research and writing of this volume.

My brother, Lloyd, and my sister, Sue, have been emotional rocks of Gibraltar as well as generous hosts who make research visits to New York and Washington, D.C., not only enjoyable but affordable.

Sarah Thomas similarly facilitated extended research binges in Springfield, for which I am most grateful.

As an undergraduate at Princeton University and as a graduate student at Johns Hopkins University, I was fortunate to have the guidance and support of David Herbert Donald.

Acknowledgments

At Connecticut College, I have had the cheerful and efficient assistance of Gina Foster and Anita Allen in preparing the manuscript.

Lois McDonald has helped more than she knows to make this book and the others possible.

Introduction

John G. Nicolay, Lincoln's chief personal secretary from the time of his nomination for the presidency until his assassination, claimed that "in the five years during which he [Lincoln] gave me his confidence and intimacy, I learned to know him perhaps better than any other person, except the members of his own family."[1] Unlike his assistant in the White House, John Hay, Nicolay failed to keep a diary, though occasionally he recorded his observations of Lincoln's activities. He did, however, write several memoranda of his chief's conversations that shed direct light on Lincoln; indirect light on him is cast by Nicolay's many letters to Hay and to his fiancée, Therena Bates,[2] describing events and the mood in the White House as well as expressing opinions that may have been shaped by the president. Referring to both Nicolay and Hay, one scholar concluded that they "seem generally to have adopted Lincoln's opinions as their own; and it may be surmised that the observations in their Letters, Diary, and Notes, were not far out of line with what Lincoln thought at the time, even when they do not quote him directly."[3] This hypothesis is difficult to prove, but it seems plausible, for Nicolay and Hay were young men who admired the president extravagantly and regarded him as a benevolent father figure.[4] Thus, from Nicolay's letters one may glean what Lincoln perhaps thought about people and events.

As literature, Nicolay's correspondence and memoranda are less scintillating than John Hay's diary and letters. Nicolay was, in the words of his daughter, "very reserved, even when writing to those nearest him."[5] She reported that her father's "manner was so quiet and grave that one had to know him long before finding out the vein of humor that lay close under the surface. He showed this real self more often to his daughter's friends than to men or women of his own age, and he would talk interestingly and charmingly to children about Mr. Lincoln, when at a question from an adult he would instantly cease. I think the four years' experience of trying to shield his chief made him skeptical of the genuine interest and ulterior motives of most grown-ups."[6]

Nicolay was too discreet to share inside information with his fiancée, whom he told in December 1860, "I have no news of importance since my last letter. . . . I mean, of course, news that interests you and which I am at liberty to communicate. In my position, I necessarily hear something new almost every day, that would be of infinite interest sometimes to one and sometimes to another, but about which my duty is to say nothing."[7]

This volume contains all the "memoranda of conversations," all the journal entries describing Lincoln's activities, and excerpts from most of the nearly three hundred letters Nicolay wrote to Therena Bates between 1860 and 1865. I have included those letters and portions of letters that describe Lincoln or the mood in the White House or that give Nicolay's opinions, which may reflect Lincoln's views. Also included are letters Nicolay wrote while on presidential troubleshooting missions. In a garbled, occasionally inaccurate form, some of these items appeared in Helen Nicolay's biography of her father.[8] Others are quoted in the ten-volume life of Lincoln by Nicolay and Hay, who were not always careful transcribers.[9] A few of the memoranda are included in Charles M. Segal's *Conversations with Lincoln*[10] and in *Recollected Words of Abraham Lincoln,* compiled and edited by Don E. Fehrenbacher and Virginia Fehrenbacher.[11] In addition, I have reproduced official business letters by Nicolay that supplement Roy P. Basler's edition of Lincoln's collected works[12] as well as the more revealing letters to John Hay and other friends.

Born near Landau in Rhenish Bavaria on 26 February 1832, Nicolay at the age of six came to the United States with his parents and older siblings.[13] After landing in New Orleans, they settled first in Cincinnati, then moved to Indiana, then to Missouri, and finally to Illinois. Nicolay evidently led a hard life. As his daughter noted: "Being the youngest member of his family, he found little companionship in his own home. Physically frail and mentally of a different calibre, there was little in common between himself and the scuffling young ruffians of the log schoolhouse." (Nicolay remained frail throughout his life; he grew to five feet, ten inches tall and never weighed more than 125 pounds.) His mother, Helena, died around 1842, shortly after the family had settled in Pike County, Illinois.[14] His illiterate father, who established a mill on Bee Creek, passed away in 1846. The orphaned Nicolay went to live with relatives in White Hall, Illinois, where in 1847 the bookish youth attracted the attention of his Sunday school teacher, Joel Pennington. That gentleman recommended the lad to a merchant, who hired him as a clerk.[15] When in 1848 Pennington moved to Pittsfield, Nicolay asked his help in obtaining a job there in the office of the *Pike County Free Press;* Pennington did so.[16]

Another version of this story was told by Zachariah N. Garbutt, editor of the *Pike County Free Press,* who recalled hearing young Nicolay howling in pain as he was being punished severely by a woman. When asked what had prompted her to thrash him, Nicolay replied that "he had done nothing but that licking him was a habit" of this woman "and he 'reckoned she done it 'cause she liked it, but he did not.'" Garbutt then, in effect, adopted the "freckle-faced, red-headed boy in bed-ticking trousers and straw hat." So the seventeen-year-old Nicolay settled in Pittsfield with Garbutt and his wife, who "brought him up as tenderly as they could have done had the child been their own."[17] In old age, Nicolay recalled that Mrs. Garbutt "always welcomed me as one of 'her boys'—for I was not the only youth she thus befriended—and I have ever felt that had I been her own son she could not have taken a deeper interest in my welfare and success than she did."[18]

Nicolay's daughter offered a variant on these narratives: Discouraged because he earned but four dollars per month as a clerk in White Hall and was unable to save more than two dollars after a full year's work, he "heard through a friend that the Free Press, published in Pike county, was in need of a printer's devil. Walking to Pittsfield to apply for the job, he slept, the first night, on sacks of wool in the carding mill—got the job—and made a record for speed and accuracy in his first attempt at typesetting that he was not always able to live up to, even after he became more expert." He also earned money as a church organist.[19]

Nicolay's formal education was limited to about two years in St. Louis and Cincinnati studying in bilingual schools, primitive log structures "where slates, pencils, pens, paper, and ink were unknown."[20] He described life on the Illinois frontier as "irregular and somewhat spasmodic, with quick fluctuations, vibrating between plenty and want,—from fullness to hunger, from hot to cold, from dry to wet, from comfort to misery. Nothing was steady but ignorance and solitude."[21] In a third-person autobiographical sketch, he recalled that schools were "very scarce," offering "only primary instruction, and that for very limited periods. At seventeen he became a printer's apprentice in a country newspaper office, in which during his stay of eight years he educated himself, rising through all the grades of employment to those of proprietor, publisher, and editor."[22] Among the subjects he studied were the arts. Eventually he became "a recognized connoisseur in art matters and a warm patron of music" as well as "a linguist of much ability" with "a poetic strain which found outlet in many graceful verses."[23]

In Pittsfield, he befriended Thomas Wesley Shastid, a boy his own age who remembered that Nicolay was "always a modest, perhaps even diffident" person. When they would walk about the little town together at night, the "very, very painfully shy" Nicolay would "shun the streets whereon the élite of the village were most likely to be passing."[24] Another friend recalled that Nicolay was "a man of reticent and unassuming manners."[25] He may have been embarrassed by his poverty, for "he was a poorly dressed youth who could barely make ends meet." Nicolay also grew close to the baker Joseph Heck and his wife, who did the boy's washing as well as some cooking for him.[26] Nicolay became a boon companion to John Hay, who was attending a local private school. When Hay left Illinois to attend Brown University, Nicolay longed to join him, but poor health and a lack of funds made that dream impossible to realize.[27]

One day during the 1856 presidential campaign, when Abraham Lincoln asked Shastid where he could have a printing job done quickly, the young man led him to the *Free Press* office and introduced him to Nicolay.[28] Many years later, Nicolay described this memorable encounter to an interviewer, who recorded that a "big meeting [political rally] had been arranged, and Nicolay was on the committee having it in charge. There were two notable speakers in the state—Lincoln and [U.S. Senator Lyman] Trumbull—and as there were 100 counties to be covered, it was agreed that both should not appear in any one county, but that one of them should speak in each. The Pittsfield committee knew this, but it was a crafty committee . . . and, while it knew it might consider itself lucky if it secured one of the great men, it widely advertised that both would surely address the meeting." The day of the rally, Nicolay, who was clerking in a store to earn extra money, "watched with admiration" as Trumbull strolled along the sidewalk. When the senator encountered Lincoln, Nicolay "was all anxiety to get near to the great men," but the store was too busy to allow him to leave his post. That evening, as a member of the Republican committee, Nicolay "was presented to Trumbull and Lincoln before the speechmaking began. When the first brief handshake and word of greeting on the speakers' platform was over, Nicolay was an ardent personal follower of Abraham Lincoln. The rugged features, lighted by a kindly smile, the earnest eyes, the hearty grip, the simple, sincere words of one man of the plain people speaking to another, won the young politician's heart and soul. Later, during and after the speech, the wonderful magnetism of the orator held Nicolay spellbound and cemented his devotion."[29]

The following year, after applying unsuccessfully for work as a *Chicago Press and Tribune* correspondent,[30] Nicolay managed to win such a post with the *Missouri Democrat* of St. Louis when Lincoln and half a dozen other Illinois Republican leaders agreed to pay him five hundred dollars to help increase the paper's influence in southern and western Illinois.[31] As the paper's "authorized correspondent and business agent for the State of Illinois,"[32] Nicolay traveled to Springfield, where he covered the state fair, as well as to Belleville and Peoria. The newspaper's proprietors, he explained to Senator Trumbull, grew angry at him because "I had not devoted my time to canvassing for subscribers instead of writing letters about the fair. I was considerably annoyed at this—as well as at several other occasions where I thought I did not receive the courtesies at their hands to which I was entitled—but I have so far kept my temper." He returned to his home territory, Pike County, where, because of the financial panic of 1857, he was able to sign up only two dozen subscribers in three weeks. He therefore suspended operations until "the first fright of the 'hard times' among the people should be over." He complained about such "hard and rather uninviting work," yet he was prepared to continue it the following spring. In St. Louis he met with the publishers of the *Missouri Democrat,* who approved of his decision.[33]

Although Trumbull was pleased with Nicolay's work,[34] the publishers were not; in December 1857, they complained that the young German lacked "the mental force" and "the requisite enterprise & activity" to continue as the *Democrat*'s Springfield correspondent: "We want an intelligent, active young man, one who is, or may immediately become, familiar with the policy of our party in Illinois, who can write a sprightly and comprehensive letter and who will be particular to see that his correspondence is duly placed in the hands of the Express company so that we may *never be behind the [Missouri] Republican.*"[35]

Nicolay was reassigned to clerk in Springfield for Ozias M. Hatch, secretary of state for Illinois and a friend of Lincoln.[36] When Nicolay explained to Hatch that he wanted to study law, his Pike County friend hired him with the understanding that he could read law books in the office.[37] At that office, which served as a kind of Republican party headquarters, young Nicolay often saw Lincoln. "All election records were kept by the Secretary of State, and I, as Mr. Hatch's principal clerk, had frequent occasion to show Mr. Lincoln, who was an assiduous student of election tables, the latest returns or the completed record books," he later recalled.[38] There, Lincoln and Nicolay often played chess.[39]

While in Springfield, Nicolay wrote a column of "Capitol News" for the Pike County paper he had edited.[40] In his leisure hours, he and John Hay socialized with the family of Nicholas H. Ridgely, a prominent banker whose home was "the center of musical culture in town" and whose autocratic manner earned him the sobriquet "Czar Nicholas."[41] Nicolay spent much time at Ridgely's, known as "the centre of Springfield social life for the younger set—a center where music and jollity reigned, tempered by the Czar's rather rigorous ruling, where there were earnest if rather youthful efforts at improving the mind, and where foreign languages were the fashion."[42] There he met Anna Ridgely, who later described him as "of plain appearance" but "attractive from his intellectual acquirements, for if ever there was a man who worked, John Nicolay was that man, self-made and industrious." Nicolay, she added, "was no mean musician and used to sing a book of duets with my sister in one evening."[43]

Lincoln came to regard the young man highly. In 1858, he recommended Nicolay to Horace Greeley as a correspondent, calling him "entirely trust-worthy." A year later, he had Nicolay deliver to a publisher in Ohio his carefully prepared scrapbook of the 1858 debates with Stephen A. Douglas.[44] In early 1860, Nicolay visited Pittsfield to see his sweetheart, Therena Bates, "the only girl in town who smiled at him when he was poor and ragged."[45] (In 1869, she was described by a Springfield woman as "a cultivated lady quite stylish looking and seems to have good sense.")[46] While there, Nicolay called on the editor of the *Pike County Journal,* Col. Daniel B. Bush, who asked him to write an editorial. Nicolay penned an enthusiastic presidential endorsement of Lincoln, which Bush ran on 9 February.[47]

When Lincoln won the presidential nomination in May 1860, Nicolay was looking for a job.[48] He recalled:

> [I]t occurred to me that I might write the campaign biography. . . . Full of this purpose, and having no idea that any one would dispute my right to do the work, I began to prepare for the task at once. A week after the nomination, however, a newspaper man [William Dean Howells] from Columbus, O., appeared at the capital and announced his intention of writing the life of Lincoln. I was instantly filled with jealous rage, and hastened to a friendly official [William Butler], who was closely attached to Mr. Lincoln, to complain of what I considered to be a usurpation of my just prerogative. I shall never forget that complaint nor his answer to it. The official heard me out in silence—he was a quiet, dignified man—and I was very bitter. After I had finished he looked down at me smilingly. "Never mind, Nicolay," he said; "you are to be Mr. Lincoln's private secretary."

Lincoln had told Hatch: "I wish I could find some young man to help me with my correspondence. It is getting so heavy I can't handle it. I can't afford to pay much, but the practice is worth something." When Hatch mentioned Nicolay, Lincoln accepted the suggestion. After the election, the president-elect kept him on as his principal White House secretary.[49]

Lincoln may have chosen Nicolay as a compromise candidate for the job.

Following the 1860 election, William O. Stoddard, editor of the *Central Illinois Gazette,* expressed interest in joining the White House staff; Lincoln asked him to put his request in writing and said that he would see to it.[50] Also lobbying for the secretary's post was another journalist, Benjamin F. James, who had helped Lincoln in his quest for a congressional seat in 1846.[51] In September 1860, James applied for the job.[52] Lincoln's friend and colleague at the bar Henry C. Whitney alleged that both Stoddard and James told him "that Lincoln entertained with favor the idea of appointing one but not wishing to offend the other, he concluded to keep Nicolay."[53]

Not everyone approved of the choice. Herman Kreismann, a Republican leader in Chicago, thought it "ridiculous" because Nicolay lacked the necessary polish and savoir faire: "It wants a man of refinement and culture and thoroughly at home in fine society. He arranges the President's dinners and parties and all that and a great deal depends on that appointment whether our republican [administration] will make itself ridiculous or not. The idea of Nicolay being fit for such a place[!] I have heard men like [Massachusetts Senator Charles] Sumner, [Charles Francis] Adams and others express more solicitude about that place than any other."[54] In November 1861, Henry Martin Smith, city editor of the *Chicago Tribune,* lamented that "Mr. Lincoln has no private secretary that fills the bill and the loss is a national one."[55] Henry C. Whitney expressed surprise that the president would appoint a "nobody" like Nicolay to be his secretary.[56] To Lincoln's law partner, William H. Herndon, Whitney declared: "it is astonishing that he took Nicolay—a mere clerk—and did not have a confidential friend of astuteness & affection like you."[57]

At the White House, Nicolay became known as "the bulldog in the anteroom" with a disposition "sour and crusty."[58] A New Yorker complained to the president early in his first term: "If the stories I hear about Nicolay . . . are true, you ought to dismiss him. If he is sick, he has a right to be cross and ungentlemanly in his deportment, but not otherwise. People say he is very disagreeable and uncivil."[59] Alexander K. McClure, who in 1891 quarreled with Nicolay about the history of the nomination of Andrew Johnson as vice president, described Lincoln's principal secretary as "a good mechanical, routine clerk" but whose "removal was earnestly pressed upon Lincoln on more than one occasion because of his want of tact and fitness for his trust." McClure claimed that "only the proverbial kindness of Lincoln saved him from dismissal."[60] Though his assistant John Hay became a lifelong friend, Nicolay was occasionally jealous of his younger colleague. When the diary of the English journalist William Howard Russell was published in 1863, with favorable allusions to Hay, it gave Nicolay "ill feelings . . . as he is never named in it." Hay tactfully removed the offending volume from the Executive Mansion.[61]

Noah Brooks, a California journalist, deemed Nicolay a "grim Cerberus of Teutonic descent who guards the last door which opens into the awful presence." Nicolay, in Brooks's view, "has a very unhappy time of it answering the impatient demands of the gathering, growing crowd of applicants which obstructs passage, hall and ante-room." Brooks recommended that "an inside guardian of affable address, as well as flintiness of face," be "placed on duty . . . where the people come almost in actual contact with the great man within, whom they learn to love or dislike, according to their treatment by his underlings." Lincoln, Brooks noted, "is affable and kind, but his immediate subordinates are snobby and unpopular."[62] Thurlow Weed thought Nicolay had "a bilious temperament."[63]

Other observers were more charitable. According to John Russell Young, who frequently observed Nicolay during the Civil War, the young man from Pike County "had the close, methodical, silent German way about him. Scrupulous, polite, calm, obliging, with the gift of hearing other people talk; coming and going about the Capitol like a shadow; with the soft, sad smile that seemed to come only from the eyes; prompt as lightning to take a hint or an idea; one upon whom a suggestion was never lost, and if it meant a personal service, sure of the prompt, spontaneous return." Young thought Nicolay had "great powers of application" and "endurance." Withal, he was a "man without excitements or emotions, never saying anything worth quoting, and in that regard invaluable as a private secretary; absorbed in the President, and seeing that the Executive business was well done."[64] Similarly, John McWilliams recalled that Nicolay was "a methodical, studious man, very quiet and unassuming."[65]

William O. Stoddard, who served as an assistant to the two presidential secretaries during the Civil War, gave a balanced assessment of Nicolay in the White House: "A fair French and German scholar, with some ability as a writer and much natural acuteness, he nevertheless—thanks to a dyspeptic tendency—had developed an artificial manner the reverse of 'popular,' and could say 'no' about as disagreeably as any man I ever knew." But, Stoddard added, Nicolay served Lincoln well: "That . . . for which we all respected him, which was his chief qualification for the very important post he occupied, was his devotion to the President and his incorruptible honesty Lincoln-ward." Nicolay "measured all things and all men by their relations to the President, and was of incalculable service in fending off much that would have been unnecessary labor and exhaustion to his overworked patron." Stoddard believed that Nicolay "deserves the thanks of all who loved

Mr. Lincoln" and observed that "[p]eople who do not like him—because they cannot use him, perhaps—say he is sour and crusty, and it is a grand good thing, then, that he is. If you will sit in that chair [Nicolay's] a month or so, you will see what has become of any easy good-nature you sat down with."[66]

Recalling his days as Nicolay's assistant, John Hay complained that "contact with the greed and selfishness of office-seekers and the bull-dozing Congressmen is unspeakably repulsive." He could not abide the "constant contact with envy, meanness, ignorance and the swinish selfishness which ignorance breeds."[67] In 1865, the *Albany Evening Journal* described satirically those "White House bores" that Hay complained of:

> They cannot be driven off; they cannot be bluffed. Bars and bolts will not shut them out. The frowns of janitors have no terrors for them. They are proof against the snubbings of secretaries. It is in vain the President sends word that he "cannot be seen." He must be seen; he shall be seen. Has not the Honorable Jonathan Swellhead come all the way from Wisconsin to consult him about the quota of his town? Has not the Reverend Dr. Blowhard travelled a thousand miles to impress upon him the necessity of increasing the number of fast days? Has not Christopher Carbuncle, Esq., travelled two days and nights in order to arrange with him the vexed question of the post office in Grabtown? Has not Mr. Samuel Shoddy come expressly from Boston to get him to endorse an application for a blanket contract? Has not a committee from the synod of the Seek-No-Further church come to implore him to open cabinet meetings with prayer and inaugurate his Wednesday evening levees with the singing of a psalm? Nor can these clamorous patriots be dismissed with a brief audience. They belong to the class of bores who make long speeches. Having once got the ear of the President, they resolve to keep it. They hang on like a dog to a root. There is no shaking them off until they have had their say; and so hour after hour of the precious time of the head of the nation is thus frittered away.[68]

Stoddard concluded that Lincoln "showed his good judgment of men when he put Mr. Nicolay just where he is, with a kind and amount of authority which it is not easy to describe."[69] Stoddard acknowledged that Nicolay "was much better qualified" for the secretary's job than he himself was: Nicolay "was older, more experienced, harder, had a worse temper, and was decidedly German in his manner of telling men what he thought of them. I was more reticent."[70]

Like John Hay, Nicolay did not get along with the First Lady, who resented the young secretaries for resisting her schemes to defraud the government.[71] In December 1864, Nicolay told his fiancée: "About three days of the week have been taken up with a row with my particular feminine friend here [Mary Todd Lincoln]."[72] As the Civil War drew to a close, Mary Lincoln conspired with her husband's old friend Anson G. Henry to have Noah Brooks replace Nicolay. "I have been working . . . with Mrs. Lincoln to get Nickolay out as private Secretary and Mr. Brooks in his place," Henry reported in March 1865.[73] (Brooks had defended the First Lady vigorously in the press.)[74] Three weeks later, Charles H. Philbrick, who assisted Nicolay and Hay in the White House, confided to a friend that "I dont know who will be in George's [Nicolay's] place; hope some good man for otherwise I wont stay. Mrs L will try to put in her favorite, Mr. Brooks, a newspaper man. What the President may think has not yet transpired."[75] Nicolay evidently resisted the proposal that he go abroad, but on 12 March it was announced that he and John Hay were assigned to diplomatic posts in Paris; soon thereafter, Lincoln invited Noah Brooks to replace them.[76] The assassination scotched those plans.

When that calamitous event occurred, Nicolay was out of Washington; his frail health had prompted him to take a vacation in early 1865. A journalist who interviewed him many years later reported that "the labors of the private secretary were enormous," causing Nicolay "to feel the effects of short sleep and unremitting toil." The president, who "noticed it almost before he [Nicolay] did himself," took matters in hand and "planned a vacation for his young helper. The assistant secretary of state had been intrusted with certain business of importance which necessitated a trip to Havana, Cuba, and was to make the trip in a government vessel. Lincoln called Nicolay in one day and told him of this, saying that he could readily arrange to take the trip, and expressing the belief that without something of the sort his health would give way from overwork." Nicolay resisted at first, but Lincoln eventually prevailed on him to go.[77] Thus, when the president was assassinated, Nicolay was aboard a ship bound from Cuba to Washington.

Nicolay served as consul in Paris from 1865 to 1869, when he returned to the United States to resume his career in journalism. In 1872, with the help of Robert Todd Lincoln, he was appointed marshal of the U.S. Supreme Court, a post he held for the next seventeen years.[78] He spent much of his time in the 1870s and 1880s working with John Hay on a multivolume life of Lincoln that appeared in 1890. Eleven years later, he died in Washington at the age of sixty-nine.

In 1898, looking back on his days as Lincoln's secretary, Nicolay called the president "one of the kindest, most humane and best men that ever lived. He was always gentle and never severe, always eager to reward and sorry to punish. Throughout the long and difficult years of his administration and the fluctuating vicissitudes of the war, through disappointment as well as success, through defeat as well as victory, dealing day by day with some of the most momentous acts of American history, wielding a power greater than that of European monarchs, he continued always to be the same plain, kind, unassuming, good man as when he lived in his father's cabin or sat in the quiet of his Springfield law office."[79] Nicolay derived his greatest satisfaction "from having enjoyed the privilege and honor of being Mr Lincoln's intimate and official private secretary, and of earning his cordial friendship and perfect trust."[80]

Editorial Method

Words that could not be deciphered with certainty have been placed in square brackets followed by a question mark [like this?]. When words were added above the line, with or without a caret, they have simply been inserted into the text. Contractions have been retained. Raised letters have been reproduced as if they were not raised. When words were illegible, brackets have been supplied enclosing a blank space like this [ ]. When words were inadvertently repeated, the second occurrence of the word has been silently omitted. When a period was used where a comma was called for, the comma has silently replaced the period. Otherwise, Nicolay's punctuation is unchanged. Misspellings have been retained without the cumbersome use of *[sic]*. Familiar foreign terms have not been translated; less well known expressions in foreign languages have been translated in notes. Words supplied by the editor to clarify the text have been enclosed within square brackets and italicized *[like this]*.

Persons mentioned in the documents have been identified in notes, if information on them has been found. No annotation has been made for those about whom nothing could be discovered. Sources for annotations derived from manuscript collections, newspapers, and specialized monographs and biographies have been identified, but not those taken from easily available published sources.

*With Lincoln
in the White House*

1860

To William E. Norris, Springfield, 26 May 1860[1]

Mr. Lincoln has been so much occupied with men who have called to see him, that I couldn't get a chance at him, since the receipt of your letter until this morning. I herewith enclose you his autograph.

To Lyman Trumbull, Springfield, 5 June 1860[2]

We have intimations here that the Philadelphia News and Philadelphia Inquirer should receive some attention. Will you please direct the attention of General Cameron and other Pennsylvanians to this.[3]

To Therena Bates, Springfield, 7 June 1860[4]

. . . Mr. Lincoln has engaged me to act as his private secretary during the campaign, and pays me at the rate of $75.00 per month for the service. Of course that will keep me here until the next November election. He has a room here in the State House, and so I go right along without any change of quarters or arrangements of any kind other than that indicated.

To George M. Harrison, Springfield, 9 June 1860[5]

Your letter of May 29th, addressed to Hon. A. Lincoln, congratulating him on his nomination, and recalling many incidents of your early acquaintance, has been received by him, for which, as well as the kind expressions of regard it contains, he desires to thank you.

To Lyman Trumbull, Springfield, 11 June 1860[6]

I have frequent inquiries from friends here as to what are the best documents to send for and use in our coming Illinois campaign. Will you please ask the Secretary of the Rep*[ublican]* Association at Washington to send me a copy *[of]* each of the documents published, that I may examine them and be able to speak advisedly?

Mr. Lincoln is well, and has good reports from all quarters.

To Messrs. Follett & Foster, Springfield, 15 June 1860[7]

I was certainly very much surprised on seeing that in the "slip" advertisements you enclosed me, you announced that your biography of Mr. Lincoln was "<u>authorized</u>"; and certainly astonished beyond degree that in a late card you say that "Finally the thread of our narrative is furnished by Mr. Lincoln's private Secretary, from Mr. Lincoln's own recollections, and our biography is authorized <u>by Mr. Lincoln. He</u> had authorized no other." Also that you write me under date of the 12th, that "Mr. Howard thinks there can be no question as to our full and complete <u>authority to announce</u> that ours is fully authorized."[8]

As I telegraphed you to-day, in all these assertions you are very wrong. Neither Mr. Lincoln nor myself ever said or did anything, which could give Mr. Howard or yourselves any reason to suppose you had such "authority;" on the contrary, Mr. Lincoln told Mr. Howard, in my presence, that there must be no word or intimation, that any of the facts or matter furnished, came from him or by authority. In addition to this, Mr. Howard <u>knew</u> that I should give to at least three other gentlemen precisely the same facts and material, that I gave to him, and that consequently he could not possibly have the exclusive authority claimed in your card.[9]

If Mr. Lincoln could have foreseen this wrangle over an "authority" which he never gave, he certainly would have left <u>all</u> biographers to their own resources, and spared himself the labor and annoyance he incurred, to say nothing of the mortification of thus finding his <u>express</u> wish and direction disregarded, and a sought confidence violated. He certainly never dreamed of thus seeing himself and his private secretary paraded as parties to a seeming favoritism, which his whole effort has been to avoid.[10]

Please therefore to recall your announcements that your biography is in any way authorized by himself or his private secretary, or that either has furnished you "material." As I telegraphed you, Mr. Lincoln neither <u>authorizes</u> yours or any other biography of himself.[11]

To James Q. Howard, Springfield, 19 June 1860[12]

Yours of the 15th reached me last night, and I proceed at once to a brief reply. In addition to what I have already telegraphed and written to Follett & Foster, I will only quote two extracts from your own letter, which fully answer the other portions of the same, viz:

"I never understood that Mr. Lincoln was in any manner to <u>father</u> or be responsible for, this life, or anything that it contained."

That is true; but don't you see that Follett & Foster's advertisements and cards do make Mr. L. "father," and "responsible for" this life?

And again you say:

"Mr. L. told me that the materials he furnished us, should not be so used in the biography so as to indicate that they came from him."

By what kind of reasoning then could you suppose that he was willing to have the source of these "materials" indicated outside of the biography, as in cards and advertisements, for instance? Mr. Lincoln was even more explicit; in my presence he told you "that there must be no word or intimation that this (material) came from him." And yet in spite of this express direction of his, and which you substantially acknowledge, it is boldly announced in a card that "the thread of the narrative is furnished by Mr. Lincoln's private Secretary, from Mr. Lincoln's own recollections, and the biography is authorized by Mr. Lincoln, and that he had authorized no other."

A word as to the delay of which you complain. The time and manner of the publication was entirely at the option of Follett & Foster, free entirely from any control or influence on the part of Mr. L.—he having never given any advice, suggestion or direction in regard to it, and being therefore neither directly or impliedly responsible for any such delay.

Neither can I undertake to determine whether you or Follett & Foster have done wrong; I only know that their announcements are at variance with the instructions you received—I cannot undertake to decide who is in the fault.

I hope that a sober second thought has convinced both yourself and Follett & Foster that Mr. L. cannot act otherwise in this matter than he has done. He cannot "authorize" "endorse" or "be responsible for" the book as a whole, because he does not know what it contains; nor can he authorize any particular fact or facts without distinctly specifying them, and thus in effect, writing an autobiography—a thing which you certainly cannot ask him to do. How could you disclaim his responsibility for the book when at the same time you claim his authority for the "facts, incidents, and narrative?" Are not these the "contents" of the book?

If the style and appearance of the book—the reputation of the author—the character of the publishers, and their connection with the Lincoln-Douglas debates—the fact of their sending an agent here to gather materials and information—the announcement that such men as Yates,[13] Stuart,[14] Butler,[15] & others, the early friends and companions of Mr. L. were the sources of his history, and that he had access to the public files and records at Mr. L's city, be not enough to give your book character and preference over the

Rudd & Carlton and other flash editions of his life then I do not know how it can be adequately endorsed.[16]

For myself I am extremely sorry this misunderstanding has arisen; and particularly so, that it should have grown out of the consent of Mr. L. to oblige Messrs. Follett & Foster, as far as he could, and in spite of his extra precautions to prevent it.

Mr. L. entertains the highest regard and kindest feelings both for yourself and Messrs. Follet*[t]* & Foster; but you must not refuse to see that he being the Republican Nominee for President, and being responsible to his Party for the utmost discretion and care about every word and act of his own, it would be an act of inexcusable folly to lend his express or implied authority to the whole or part of a book of whose contents he knows nothing. He will not consent to do so for himself, and his friends would not permit it, were he willing.

Please show this to Messrs Follett & Foster, as it answers both your letter and theirs to me, as I have not time to copy it.

To Therena Bates, Springfield, 16 July 1860[17]

. . . The only thing really that I have to write to-day, is that I am going to start for Terre Haute, Indiana, to-night, to be gone two or three days.[18] . . .

To Jesse W. Fell, Springfield, 19 July 1860[19]

Yours of the 16th addressed to Hon. A. Lincoln, was duly received and read by him. Enclosed he returns you Mr. Lewis' letter,[20] according to request.

To Miss or Mrs. Ives, Springfield, 27 July 1860[21]

Enclosed please find Mr. Lincoln's autograph which you request

To Therena Bates, Springfield, 9 August 1860[22]

We had an immense meeting here yesterday—too large to count.[23] I was up until two or three oclock both last night, and night before and as a consequence am *[al]*most too tired and sleepy to write a letter. . . .

To Therena Bates, Springfield, 26 August 1860[24]

. . . Did you ever see a real, pretty miniature? I do not mean either an ambrotype, daguerreotype or photograph but a regular <u>miniature painted</u> on ivory. Well a Philadelphia artist (Brown, his name is) has just been painting one of Mr. Lincoln, which is both very pretty and very truthful—decidedly the best picture of him that I have seen.[25] It is about twice as large as a common quarter size daguerreotype or ambrotype, but so well executed, that when magnified to life size one cannot discover any defects or brush marks on it at all. I wish you could see it. It gives one something of an idea of what a painter—I mean a real artist—can do. It has been painted for Judge Read of Philadelphia,[26] who has become so disgusted with the horrible carricatures of Mr. Lincoln which he had seen, that he went to the expense of sending this artist all the way out here to paint him this picture, and which will probably cost him some $300—the price of the painting alone being $175. I had a long talk with *[the]* artist to-day. He says the impression prevails East that Mr. Lincoln is very ugly—an impression which the published pictures of him of course all confirm. Read however had an idea that it could hardly be so—but was bound to have a good-looking picture, and therefore instructed the artist to make it good-looking whether the original would justify it or not. The artist says he came out with a good deal of foreboding that he would have difficulty in making a picture under these conditions. He says he was very happy when on seeing him he found that he was not at all such a man as had been represented, and that instead of making a picture he would only have to make a portrait to satisfy Judge Read. He will go back home as agreeably disappointed in Mr. Lincoln's manners, refinement and general characteristics, as in his personal appearance.[27] . . .

To John M. Read, Springfield, 27 August 1860[28]

The miniature portrait of Hon. A. Lincoln, just painted by Mr. J. H. Brown, is strikingly faithful and correct. It is, in my opinion, as perfect a likeness of him as could be made.

To Robert A. Hall, Springfield, 15 September 1860[29]

Your letter of the 10th addressed to Hon. A. Lincoln, was duly received. He returns you his thanks for the very kind invitation you send him to be present at your State Fair, and regrets that it will be impossible for him to be there.

To William Oland Bourne, Springfield, 18 September 1860[30]

Your letter of the 12th to Hon. A. Lincoln, together with its enclosures, was duly received.

He will hand the slips to the Editor of our paper here.

To Rufus L. Miller, Springfield, 24 September 1860[31]

Your letter of the 16th addressed to Hon. A. Lincoln, came duly to hand. He thanks you for the favor, and is pleased to hear that political affairs look so cheering in your county, and State. He remembers Robert Rutledge very well indeed and sends him his regards.[32]

To John M. Read, Springfield, 5 October 1860[33]

Your letters of Sept. 15th and Oct 1st, addressed to Mr. Lincoln, both came duly to hand. The first, asking a notice of the engraving of Mr. Brown's miniature in our Springfield paper, would have been answered sooner but for the fact that I thought it would be better to wait until we should receive the engraving itself—feeling assured that a positive endorsement of its correctness would be of much more value to Messrs. Brown and Sartain, than a mere editorial opinion that the original would be correctly engraved.

The ten impressions of the picture also came this morning. We are all delighted with their beauty and fidelity to the original.

The "State Journal" of to-morrow morning will contain a good notice of the picture, and I will forward Mr. Brown two dozen copies of the paper, by mail, which he can mark and send to such papers as he may wish to have copy the notice.

I am highly gratified that Mr. Lincoln's friends will at length be enabled to obtain a good likeness of him. Command me at any time for anything I can do to assist Messrs. Brown and Sartain in their sale and circulation.

P.S. I beg to acknowledge the receipt of several copies of the "Inquirer," containing your very able articles "To the People of Pennsylvania" which I have read with much pleasure.[34]

Memorandum, 16 October 1860[35]

All sorts of incidents are of course occurring with visitors—

Mr. Lincoln was coming to his room this morning *[and]* was accosted by a stranger inquiring the way to the same place. Mr. Lincoln offered, of course, to show him the way, and arriving there very much electrified the stranger by turning round and saying to him "I am Lincoln." He had no idea he was being ciceroned by the famous Rail Splitter.

—Among the many things said in a general way to Mr. Lincoln by his visitors, there is nearly always an expressed hope that he will not be so unfortunate as were Harrison & Taylor, to be killed off by the cares of the Presidency—or as is sometimes hinted by foul means.[36] It is astonishing how the popular sympathy for Mr. Lincoln draws fearful forebodings from these two examples, which may after all have been only a natural coincidence. Not only do visitors mention the matter, but a great many letters have been written to Mr. Lincoln on the subject.[37]

Memorandum, Springfield, 25 October 1860[38]

—This morning Gen. Welch of N.Y. called on Mr. L.[39] The conversation having turned on Gov Chase,[40] [and] the fact of his being in the Senate instead of the Presidency, Mr L said—

"And I declare to you this morning General—that for personal considerations I would rather have a full term in the Senate—a place in which I would feel more consciously able to discharge the duties required, and where there was more chance to make [a] reputation, and less danger of losing it—than four years in the Presidency."

—This declaration—made eleven days before election[—] shows that Mr. Lincoln fully appreciated the responsibility of the place, which it seemed his destiny to occupy.

Memorandum, Springfield, 5 November 1860[41]

Sanford Called to see—if the alarms of many persons might not by some means be relieved[42]—the alarms from the South are seriously affecting our work—am myself largely interested—get no orders from the South—

—reassure the men honestly alarmed

—Lincoln—"There are no such men." have thought much about it—it is the trick by which the South breaks down every Northern man—I would go to Washington without the support of the men who supported me and were my friends before [the] election. I would be as powerless as a block of buckeye wood—

(The man still insisted[.)]

L.—The honest man (you are talking of honest men) will look at our platform and what I have said—there they will find everything I could now say or which they would ask me to say.—all I could say would be but repetition. Having told them all these things ten times already would they believe the eleventh declaration[?]

Let us be practical—there are many general terms afloat such as 'conservatism'—'enforcement of the irrepressible conflict at the point of the bayonet'—'hostility to the South &c'—all of which mean nothing without definition. What they [then] could I say to allay their fears, if they will not define what particular act or acts they fear from me or my friends?

(gentleman hands him letters)

"recognize them as a sett of liars and knaves who signed that statement about Seward last year."[43]

(gentleman insists there are other names on the list.) (Mr. L. although he had talked quite good-naturedly before evidently betrayed a little feeling at this part of the conversation.)

(after reading the letter) "Well after reading it, it is about what I expected to find it. (laughing)

"it annoyed me a little to hear that gang of men called respectable. their conduct a year ago was a disgrace to any civilized man."

(the gentleman suggested that the south were making armed preparations, &c.)

L. The North does not fear invasion from the Sl*[ave]* S*[tates]*— and we of the North certainly have no desire and never had to invade the South.

I am rather pleased at the idea that the South is making some 'preparation.' They have talked about a Black Republican Victory until the ———

Gen. Have we backed this time?

L. "That is what I am pressed to do now."

"If I shall begin to yield to these threats—If I begin dallying with them, the men who have elected me, if I shall be elected, would give me up before my inauguration—and the South seeing it, would deliberately kick me out."—

If (my friends) should desire me to repeat anything I have before said, I should have no objection to do so. If they required me to say something I had not yet said, I should either do so <u>or get out of the way</u>.

If I should be elected the first duty to the Country would be to stand by the men who elected me.

Memorandum, 6 November 1860[44]

It is Election day—and Hon. A Lincoln has just been over to vote. The Court House steps, (in which building the polls were held,) were thronged with People, who welcomed him with immense cheering, and followed him in dense numbers along the hall and up stairs into the Court room, which was also crowded. Here the applause became absolutely deafening, and from the time he entered the room and until he cast his vote and again left it, there was wild huzzaing, waving of hats, and all sorts of demonstrations of applause,—rendering all other noises insignificant & futile.

To Therena Bates, Springfield, 8 November 1860[45]

. . . We had a pretty lively time on election day. At night we lighted up the Representatives' Hall, and it was filled nearly all night by a crowd shouting yelling, singing dancing, and indulging in all sorts *[of]* demonstrations of happiness as the news came in. Across the street, in an ice cream saloon kept by a Republican, were a large number of Republican ladies, who had a table spread with coffee, sandwiches, cake oysters and other refreshments for their husbands and friends*[.]* It was "happy times," there also.[46] . . .

Memorandum, 10 November 1860[47]

Mr. Lincoln to-day received from Lieut. Gen. Winfield Scott a document. . . . "Views suggested by the imminent danger (Oct 29 1860) of a disruption of the Union by the Secession of one or more Southern States."[48] . . . Mr. Lincoln replied in a very brief note warmly thanking the General for this renewed manifestation of patriotism as a citizen & soldier.[49]

To Therena Bates, Springfield, 11 November 1860[50]

I supposed I should get quieted down by this time so as to be able to write you a long letter to-day, but when I came to the room this morning (I got up late) I found half a dozen politicians here, talking, and of course such a thing as writing a letter while matters of State were being canvassed, was out of the question; and so the day has slipped by, and I am at this, 5 1/2 P.M. just beginning what had ought to have been in the Post office by this time.

The smoke of the battle has partially cleared away and the Republicans find they have gained a very complete and substantial victory. They have elected Mr. Lincoln, elected their State ticket in this State, and elected a majority in both branches of the Legislature, which will re-elect Judge Trumbull to the Senate, and pass such legislation as the Republicans desire, i.e. make a new apportionment for the Legislature and for Congress and pass a Registry Law. Of course the Republicans are hugely gratified, and the Democrats correspondingly chagrined at the result. I can myself hardly realize that after having fought this Slavery question for six years past and suffered so many defeats, I am at last rejoicing at a triumph which two years ago only we hardly dared dream about. I remember very distinctly, how in 1854, soon after I had bought the Free Press Office, I went to Perry, with others, and heard Mr. Atkinson, (the preacher) make the first anti-Nebraska speech which was made in Pike County in that campaign. Though I was fighting as something more than a private then, I should have thought it a wild dream to imagine that in six years after I should find the victory so near the Commander in Chief.

The contest has been so long and so exhaustive, that this town almost immediately settled down into its usual quietness. Seeing the city, and noticing the people on Friday and Saturday, one would not imagine there had been a Presidential election for a year. People look and act as if they were almost too tired to feel at all interested in getting up a grand hurrah over the victory and I believe they would not do it at all were it not that it is a formality which in this case cannot well be omitted. I suppose we will get up a good celebration some time this week and do our best to show how happy we are. . . .

To Therena Bates, Springfield, 14 November 1860[51]

. . . As I expected, since the election, my work has increased on my hands very considerably. For three days past, Mr. Lincoln has received about fifty letters and present indications still promise a further increase. As a consequence I am kept pretty busy when I have nothing else to look after, and when, as has been the case to-day, I have several other things claiming my attention, I find myself somewhat behind at the end of the day. . . .

Memorandum, Springfield, 15 November 1860[52]

Two gentlemen were in to-day, and the conversation turning upon the existing troubles at the South—threats of secession &c—Mr. Lincoln said to them:

My own impression is, at present, (leaving myself room to modify the opinion, if upon a further investigation I should see fit to do so,) that this government possesses both the authority and the power to maintain its own integrity[.]

"That however is not the ugly point of this matter. The ugly point is the necessity of keeping the government together by force, as ours should be a government of fraternity."

Memorandum, 16 November 1860[53]

Judge Breck of Ky. quite an old man a relative of Mrs. L., and who is on a visit here had a long conversation with Mr. Lincoln this morning.[54] He strongly urged upon him the duty of saving the country by making up his cabinet of "Conservative" men—one or more of them from the South, and who should not be Republicans, saying that by such a course Kentucky could stay in the Union. But that if obnoxious men like Seward, Cassius M.

Clay,[55] &c were put in the Cabinet, and a sectional administration organized, the people of Ky. would feel themselves driven to go with S*[outh]*
C*[arolina]*. Judge B., while he disclaimed any desire to have Mr. L. abate
any principles, yet made a very strong appeal to him to make his administration conservative in the way he pointed out

Mr. L listened to him attentively and only replied, briefly. He asked the
Judge to tell him in what speech Mr. Seward had ever spoken menacingly
of the South?—and said that so far as he knew not one single prominent
public Republican had justly made himself obnoxious to the South by anything he had said or done, and that they had only become so because the
Southern politicians had so persistently bespotted and bespattered every
northern man by their misrepresentations to rob them of what strength they
might otherwise have*[.]*

He told the Judge that the substance of his plan was that the Republicans should now again surrender the Government into the hands of the men
they had just conquered, and that the cause should take to its bosom the
enemy who had always fought it and who would still continue to fight and
oppose it.

He told him he should however give his views a serious and respectful
consideration.

To Therena Bates, Springfield, 18 November 1860[56]

. . . When I went down to dinner, I found a note from an Iowa politician,
whose acquaintance I had made <u>by letter</u>, saying he had been looking for
me. So after dinner, I went over to the American house and talked an hour
with him.[57] Coming back to Mr. Lincoln's room I found him and two or
three others engaged in conversation. I sat down, and from listening five
minutes, listened ten—fifteen—an hour or more—until the clock admon-
ished me that if I would finish a letter before tea I must go to work. So
here I am trying to write away with a running conversation all around me. I
would go and write in my room, but writing materials are not so convenient there.

The letters still keep rushing along to Mr. Lincoln—the last two days
have brought an installment of about seventy each. Fortunately they do not
need much answering. They fall very naturally into two classes—those
merely congratulatory, and those asking for office, neither of which I answer. The majority of the letters I have sent off for a week past have been
those containing Mr. Lincoln's autographs.

While engaged in writing this (5 P.M.) a dispatch has just come in from
San Francisco, indicating that the Republicans have carried California. . . .

Just think of my probably having to read 80 and perhaps 100 letters a day for the next three months! . . .

To Therena Bates, Springfield, 25 November 1860[58]

I wrote you some time ago that one of Frank Leslie's artists was here making sketches for the "Illustrated." I send you by this mail a paper which contains one—that of our room here in the State House.[59] Aside from the fact that it makes the room look entirely too large (the actual measurement being only about 15 by 25 feet) the view is a tolerably correct *[one]*. You will also be struck with the marvellous truthfulness of the representations of Mr. Lincoln, and his elegant and accomplished private secretary who sits writing at the desk. . . .

Mr. Lincoln is still absent at Chicago and will not be home until to-morrow evening. Of course his absence has made it rather quiet here in the room—to me a very welcome state of things as it enabled me to catch up with some of my work which was behind. Letters are falling off a little—only about 50 a day have come for two days past.

I neglected going to church this morning—as usual. It has been so cold out that I have been glad to stay about the warm rooms in the State House—this morning reading the new "Atlantic" and talking with John Hay,[60] who came in, and this afternoon helping about footing up some columns of election returns, that have to be counted to-day.

I shall be very glad when we finally get all the old election matters "fixed up" (what a convenient phrase that is!) and off our hands, and get fairly at the new work to be done. From this *[day]* on, the "Inauguration" will be the next important event which will interest and occupy the expectation of all who are in close relations with Mr. Lincoln. I can see plenty of work ahead for myself. Still there is also the prospect of continual excitement as the new Administration takes shape and proportion, and which will lighten the labor somewhat. In my position I am necessarily among the first who see the new developments as they occur. . . .

To Therena Bates, Springfield, 2 December 1860[61]

I have written you two letters since I received yours, asking me "What about secession?" without in my replies even referring to it—until I fear you are beginning to think I am going to ignore the question altogether. I should have said something about it before, but both letters were written in too much of a hurry to go into political abstractions, and even now I shall not have more than time to briefly tell you what I think about the matter.

First, then, I am as yet not a bit scared about the matter (excuse the tautology, I was writing too rapidly to notice it.) I do not yet think that disunion will result from the present condition of affairs. There is undoubtedly a very considerable excitement in the extreme south.—In South Carolina, the people are no doubt determined on secession, and the Convention which has been called there will in all present probability declare that State out of the Union, on the 17th or 18th of this month. In Georgia there is also great excitement; a convention has also been called there; two or three prominent politicians there, however, have started a strong opposition movement, which leaves the action of the convention in doubt.[62] There is also some secession feeling in Alabama, Mississippi, Louisiana, Texas, Florida and North Carolina, but not enough as yet to make it at all probable that they will want to cut loose from the Confederacy. In Virginia, Kentucky, Tennessee Arkansas, Missouri Delaware and Maryland, all the manifestations thus far have shown a decided disposition to remain in the Union.

Now all their excitement and anger is very foolish, and very unreasonable. There is no single reason why they should secede now, more than there was four years ago when Buchanan was chosen *[president]*. True the Republican party have succeeded in electing their president. But neither Lincoln nor the party have ever avowed any purpose to interfere with, or deprive them of any recognized right, and as both Houses of Congress have a Democratic majority they could not do so if they wanted to. They cannot, for two years at least, even restore the prohibition of slavery in the territories, much less attack it in the States. All the grievances now complained of such as personal liberty bills, the "irrepressible conflict" doctrine &c. existed before the election, and should have been cause for dissolution then as well as now. The truth is that the State of South Carolina is a nest of traitors—disunionists per se who make Lincoln's election the mere pretext not the cause of dissolution.

But suppose dissolution occurs. It is easy enough for a State or States to resolve themselves out of the Union. But a State or nation cannot do without government. So if they leave ours they must establish another. Now to maintain an independent government requires a lot of Executive officers, which must be paid—an army, which must be paid—a navy, which must be paid—ambassadors at foreign courts, which must be paid—a postal service, which must be paid—and a thousand other things which cost money. Where is the money to come from? Why the South now does not even pay her own postage. While she would gain something from the Free trade which she proposes to establish, she would not gain enough to equal her present dividends from the National Treasury.

Again: the South, in addition to her own independence and free trade proposes also to re-establish the African Slave trade. Now the great European powers are much more anti-slavery than we people of the north. This being the case, is she likely to obtain from them, with ease, a national recognition—loans of money, and favorable treaties?

The South has been for at least twenty years past engaged in the effort to establish a line of steamers, and bring about direct trade between Europe and some one of the Southern ports. To effect this she has held many conventions, and passed many wordy resolutions, but the steamers still continue to run to New York—and I very much doubt whether her future re-solves will be any more successful in securing her all the great essentials of a national and independent government. Let South Carolina try the experiment—it will be the most laughable governmental farce of the age.

If such extreme and rash counsels are to prevail—if the union is to be dissolved—if this grand American Experiment of free government is to be a failure—it will be quite as well we should know it now as at any future time. If the caprice of one or half a dozen States is to be stronger than our Constitution, then in God's name the sooner we make the discovery the better. With either result I shall be content—for we can cut off the traitor-breeding Cotton States, and still have the most magnificent and powerful Empire on the globe. . . .

To Therena Bates, Springfield, 5 December 1860[63]

I have no news to write to-day except that this being the day appointed by act of Congress (first Wednesday in December) for the Electors to cast the vote of the States for President and Vice President, the duty so far as this State is concerned was duly performed. . . .

I got your letter on Monday morning. The chain in the corner of the picture *[in* Frank Leslie's Illustrated Newspaper*]* which you inquire about has no special significance. It is whittled out of wood, and is a very perfect model of a common log-chain. It was sent to Mr. Lincoln by some man in Wisconsin who wrote that being a cripple and unable to leave his bed, he had a rail brought in from the fence, and amused himself by whittling it out. . . .

To Therena Bates, Springfield, 9 December 1860[64]

. . . I have no news of importance since my last letter. But *[by]* that I mean, of course, news that interests you and which I am at liberty to communicate. In my position, I necessarily hear something new almost every day, that would be of infinite interest sometimes to one and sometimes to another, but about which my duty is to say nothing. I am gratified to be able to tell you that I have renewed evidence that Mr. Lincoln reposes entire confidence in me, which I deem a sufficient guaranty that my present confidential relation to him will be continued, though not a word has been said about the matter by either of us since the election.

In political matters there is no important change since my last letter. The secessionists are still rampant. . . . The people of the Free States and their Representatives in Congress are all a unit in their determination not to budge an inch from the position they have occupied during the whole campaign. . . . Mr. Lincoln, while he is not unmindful of the troubles which are on hand, and while he sincerely wishes they were not existing, is nevertheless not in the least intimidated or frightened by them. . . .

Memorandum, 11 December 1860[65]

Meredith,[66] and Judge Otto,[67] both of Indiana, came to-day, and pressed the claims of Caleb B. Smith to a seat in the Cabinet, if a man were taken from Ind. at all.[68] They intimated that Hon. S. Colfax was a man of detail and too inexperienced—that his reputation and claims were manufactured by newspaper scribblers.[69] On being inquired of about the coming Senatorial election in Ind. they replied that when Lane took the nomination for Governor, last Spring, there was an implied promise that, in case of success he should be made Senator—and he now claimed a redemption of the promise.[70] In consequence of this Smiths friends had withdrawn him from the contest.

Mr. Lincoln replied that being determined to act with caution—and not embarrass himself with promises—he could only say that he saw no insuperable objections to Indiana's having a man, nor to Smith being the man.

Memorandum, Springfield, 11 December 1860[71]

Mr. Lincoln to-day received a letter from Hon Wm Kellogg, M.C.[72]—the Member from Ill. who has been placed on the Committee of 33, raised by Botelers motion to consider the secession portion of the President's Message—asking advice as to his action in the Committee.[73]

Mr. L. answered, advising him to entertain no proposition for a compromise in regard to the extension of slavery—that if this were done, the work achieved by the late election would all have to be done over again. That Douglas would again try to resuscitate his "Pop*[ular]* Sov*[ereignty]*". That the issue had better be met now than later*[.]*

Mr L. also intimated that he Kellogg knew that he believed the Fugitive Slave clause of the Constitution ought to be enforced.[74]

To Benjamin Turner, Springfield, 12 December 1860[75]

Your letter of the 4th inst. addressed to Hon. A. Lincoln, was duly received.

There must certainly be some mistake about the matter upon which you write. Mr. Lincoln does not remember any such conversation as that you mention.

Memorandum, Springfield, 12 December 1860[76]

Hon. F. P. Blair, Jr to-day had an interview with the President elect.[77] He came in the main to get his views of the duty of the Gen. government in case of attempted secession. Blair does not believe in the right of secession and represents also that Mr. Bates does not for a moment entertain any right or possibility to break up the government under any pretext.[78] He says Mr. Bates scouts the very idea. Blair represents the Republicans of St Louis as being very much incensed at the course of the N.Y. Tribune in advising that the South be permitted to go out.[79] He says this course is demoralizing the Union sentiment in the Border Slave States. They cannot maintain a party for the Union if the North is willing that it shall be destroyed or dissolved.

Blair went away very much pleased with the Presidents views, which are decidedly against the assumed right to secede.

Memorandum, 12 December 1860[80]

Mr. L. to-day ascertained by telegraph that Mr. Bates was at home at St. Louis, upon which he told Mr. Blair that he would pay him a visit on next Saturday.

Memorandum, Springfield, 13 December 1860[81]

Mr. L to-day received a dispatch from Mr. Blair who returned home last night, saying that if Mr. L. preferred Mr. Bates would wait upon him here next Saturday.[82] I telegraphed back that Mr. L. would be glad to see him here on that day.

Memorandum, Springfield, 13 December 1860[83]

From conversations and expressions at different times during the last three weeks I think the following are substantially his opinions about secession:

The very existence and organization of a general and national government implies both the legal (power), right and duty of maintaining its own integrity. This if not expressed is at least implied in the Constitution.

The right of a state to secede is not an open or debatable question. It was fully discussed in *[President]* Jackson's time, and denied not only by him, but also by a vote of [   ] to [   ] in Congress.

It is the duty of a President to execute the laws, and maintain the existing government. He cannot entertain any proposition for dissolution or dismemberment. He was not elected for any such purpose.

As a matter of theoretical speculation it is probably true that if the people, (with whom the whole question rests) should become tired of the present government they may change it in the manner prescribed by the Constitution.

Memorandum, Springfield, 15 December 1860[84]

When I went to breakfast this morning I found the name of Mr. Bates on the hotel Register. He soon after came into the dining room and seated himself at *[the]* head of the table near which I was sitting, and where I had ample opportunity of studying his appearance. He is not of impressive exterior; his hair is grey, and his beard quite white, and his face shows all the marks of age quite strongly.

He came to Mr. L's room at about nine A.M.—entering with very profuse civilities and apologies for having come before Mr. L's hour (he had not yet come from home.) He said that when Mr. Blair informed him that Mr. L. designed visiting him, he had at once replied that he could not think of permitting that to be done; but that it was his duty to wait upon the President elect, &c &c. (His flow of words in conversation is very genial and easy—seeming at first to verge upon extreme politeness, but soon becoming very attractive. Afterwards, in serious conversation with Mr. L. Mr. B. became quite earnest and spoke his thoughts in clear, concise language, indicating a very comprehensive and definite intellectual grasp of ideas, and a great facility in their expression.) Leaving him in the room, with the morning paper to look over, I went to notify Mr. L. of his presence, who soon returned with me.

Their meeting (they had an acquaintanceship of eight years standing) was very cordial; and the ordinary salutations being over, Mr. L. entered at once upon the important subject matter of the interview.

Without further prelude Mr. L. went on to tell him that he had desired this interview to say to him, that since the day of the Chicago nomination it had been his purpose, in case of success, unless something should meantime occur . . . which would make it necessary to change his decision, to tender him (B.) one of the places in his cabinet. Nothing having occurred to make a change of purpose necessary, (he had waited thus long to be enabled to act with caution, and in view of all the circumstances of the case) he now offered him the appointment.

He said in doing this, he did not desire to burden him with one of the drudgery offices. Some of his (B's) friends had asked for him the State Department. He could not now offer him this, which was usually considered the first place in the Cabinet for the reason that he should offer that place to Mr. Seward—in view of his ability, his integrity, and his commanding influence, and fitness for the place. He did this as a matter of duty to the party, and to Mr. Sewards many and strong friends, while at the same time it accorded perfectly with his own personal inclinations—notwithstanding some opposition on the part of sincere and warm friends. He had not yet communicated with Mr. Seward, and did not know whether he would accept the appointment—as there had been some doubts expressed about his doing so. He would probably know in a few days. He therefore could not now offer him (B.) the State Department, but would offer him, what he supposed would be most congenial, and for which he was certainly in every way qualified, viz: the Attorney Generalship.

Mr. Bates replied by saying that until a very few days ago, he had received no word or hint even that any of his friends had made any such application in his behalf. He expressed himself highly gratified at the confidence which Mr. L. manifested in him by the offer just made. He alluded to the fact that [   ] years ago he had declined a similar offer made by Mr. Fillmore.[85] Were the country in the same condition in which it was then,— were things going along in quiet and smoothness, no inducement would tempt him to assume the duties of such a position. But the case was different. The country was in trouble and danger, and he felt it his duty to sacrifice his personal inclinations, and if he could, to contribute his labor and influence to the restoration of peace in, and the preservation of his country.

Mr. Lincoln expressed himself highly gratified at his determination. By way of preparing himself for the questions which the new administration were likely to encounter, he desired him between this time and the inauguration, to examine very thoroughly, and make himself familiar with the constitution and the laws relating to the question of secession, so as to be prepared to give a definite opinion upon the various aspects of the question.

On one other point he desired him also to make some examination. Under the present administration the mails in the South had been violated with impunity, and with the sanction of the Government. Under the new government, he feared some trouble from this question. It was well understood by intelligent men, that the perfect and unrestrained freedom of speech and the press which exists at the North, was practically incompatible with the existing institutions at the South, and he feared that Radical Republicans at the North might claim at the hands of the new Administration the enforcement of the right, and endeavor to make the mail the means of thrusting upon the South matter which even their conservative and well-meaning men might deem inimical and dangerous.

Mr. Bates said he would carefully look into both these questions. On the latter, he had without special investigation always easily arrived at the opinion that the U.S. mails ought of right to be sacred and inviolable. Certainly the present practice, which permitted petty postmasters to examine and burn everything they pleased, would not be tolerated or countenanced by the most despotic governments. At the same time he foresaw the practical difficulty of enforcing the law at every cross-road.

Much further conversation was had both during the morning, and in the afternoon when Mr. L. called on him again at the Hotel. Their views were very frankly and fully exchanged.

Mr. Bates conversation shows him to be inflexibly opposed to secession, and strongly in favor of maintaining the government by force if necessary. He forcibly illustrates his temper by saying that he is a man of peace, and will defer fighting as long as possible; but that if forced to do so against his will, he has made it a rule <u>never to fire blank cartridges</u>.[86]

During the afternoon interview Mr. L. showed Mr. B. a private letter he had just written to Hon. John A. Gilmer of N. C. (an M. C.) who had through Mr. Corwin solicited his opinions upon a number of questions.[87]

Mr. L's letter said that he was averse to writing such a letter as Mr. G. desired, and only wrote <u>in private</u> as he did, to avoid having his silence misconstrued. He could not shift or change the ground upon which he was elected. A new letter or declaration was sought that his enemies might represent him as repenting of and apologizing for being elected. His old record would serve every patriotic purpose in showing the south he was not dangerous. He had no thought of recommending the abolition of slavery in the D*[istrict of]* C*[olumbia]* or the abolition of the inter-state slave trade— even were he to make the recommendation Congress would not follow it. He felt precisely the same about the employment of slaves in Arsenals dock-yards &c. In using the patronage in slave states where there were few or no Republicans, he should not enquire of the politics of the appointees, or whether they owned slaves or not. He would accommodate the people of the several localities if they would permit it. On the territorial question he was inflexible. If any state laws conflict with the Constitution he would be glad to have them repealed. But as a citizen of Ill. or Prest. of the U.S. he could not recommend the repeal of a Vermont or South Carolina statute &c.[88]

To Therena Bates, Springfield, 19 December 1860[89]

. . . Within an hour past, there has been among the visitors to Mr. Lincoln, in the room here, a regular genuine secessionist, with a blue cockade on his hat. He came in quietly with a couple *[of]* other Southerners, one from Kentucky, and the other from I did not learn where. The "cockade" man wore a high-crowned felt hat with the cockade (being simply a blue rosette with a gilt button in the centre) fastened on the side of the crown. He sat down on the sofa, looking rather foolish, and saying nothing, and turning his hat over and over in his hands, as if he didn't exactly know whether it would seem cowardly to appear to be trying to hide the cockade, or whether it would seem to be impudent to be appearing to try to display it. He was a rather ordinary looking man, evidently not at all intelligent. He sat very meekly, say for half an hour, during the latter part of which time Mr. Lincoln engaged him in conversation, about various subjects—not noticing or alluding to his cockade however. On the other side of the room sat a young stout-looking farmer, a yankee, judging him by his talk, who was evidently "riled" by seeing the blue cockade man here, and who kept poking sharp remarks at him all the time, plainly indicating that he would as soon get into a quarrel with him as not. The Mississippian was saying that his State was certainly going out of the Union.[90] "Aint that all gaas naow?" retorted yankee. Upon the suggestion of some one in the room, Mr. Lincoln made him a present of a volume of the "Joint Debates," and it being remarked that perhaps he might be afraid to take it with him to the South, he replied rather indignantly that he dared take it wherever he went. As he was going out of the door, Mr. Lincoln was exchanging some pleasantries with him about "being afraid" &c when yankee again fired after him as a parting salute, "Barking dogs never bite."

Since he has gone out some one says that at the St Nicholas Hotel today,[91] some one offered to bet him that he was nothing but "poor white trash*["]*—that he never had owned a nigger, and that he didn't now own either a nigger or a foot of land anywhere in the South. He didn't take the bet. . . .

Memorandum, Springfield, 22 December 1860[92]

When Mr. Lincoln came to the office this morning, after the usual salutations, he asked me what the news was. I asked him if he had seen the morning dispatches. He replied "no." "Then," said I, "there is an important rumor you have not seen. The Times correspondent telegraphs that Buchanan has sent instructions to Maj. Anderson to surrender Fort Moultrie if it is attacked."[93]

"If that is true they ought to hang him!" said he with warmth*[.]*

After some further conversation he remarked—

"Among the letters you saw me mail yesterday was one to Washburne, (of Ill.) who had written me that he had just had a long conversation with Gen. Scott, and that the General felt considerably outraged that the President would not act as he wished him to in reinforcing the forts &c. I wrote to Washburne to tell Gen. Scott confidentially, that I wished him to be prepared, immediately after my inauguration to make arrangements at once to hold the forts, or if they have been taken, to take them back again."[94]

Afterwards he repeated the substance of the above in another conversation with Wm H Herndon;[95] adding at the close with much emphasis: "There can be no doubt that in any event that is good ground to live and to die by."

To Therena Bates, Springfield, 30 December 1860[96]

. . . Mr. Lincoln and I moved out of our room at the State House yesterday. He went down to his own house where he will stay most of the time to receive visitors, and I have come to a room in what is called Johnson's Building, just across the street from the Chenery House.[97] It is quite a good room, about twenty feet square, newly painted papered and carpeted, and pretty well furnished. This I shall occupy both as a bedroom and office. I shall be here all the time at work, and Mr. Lincoln will come here occasionally, when I need his advice or he my immediate assistance. It is a very comfortable place if I can keep the crowd out during the session *[of the legislature]*. . . .

To George W. Julian, Springfield, 31 December 1860[98]

Yours of the 26th inst addressed to Hon. A. Lincoln has been duly received.

He desires me to reply that he will be pleased to see you at any time it may be convenient for yourself to make the contemplated visit.

Form letter, Springfield, 1860[99]

Your letter to Mr. Lincoln of [   ] and by which you seek his assistance in getting up a biographical sketch of him, is received. Applications of this class are so numerous that it is simply impossible for him to attend to them.

Form letter, Springfield, 1860[100]

Your letter to Mr. Lincoln of [   ] and by which you seek to obtain his opinions on certain political points, has been received by him. He has received others of a similar character; but he also has a greater number of the exactly opposite character. The latter class beseech him to write nothing whatever upon any point of political doctrine. They say his positions were well known when he was nominated, and that he must not now embarrass the canvass by undertaking to shift or modify them. He regrets that he can not oblige all, but you perceive it is impossible for him to do so.

1861

To Therena Bates, Springfield, 6 January 1861[1]

It has turned out to be a sort of muddy, dull, and gloomy Sunday after-noon. . . . [T]he prospect of getting away is not particularly encouraging. Mr. Lincoln brought in seventy-five letters yesterday—an increase that doesn't specially gratify me as I am yet some two days behind hand, since I moved down here.

The Legislature meets to-morrow. There have been quite a number of strangers, members and others, here for several days past. The Chenery House which is a sort of political (Republican) headquarters has been so thronged that dinner is getting to be worth scrambling for. The expecta-tion, among the regular boarders, that the landlord was going somehow to manage to reserve seats for us, has proved entirely illusory, and we find it necessary to take our chances with the rabble.

Politics still remain feverish and uncertain. Within a week past Buchanan has manifested a little more disposition to prevent the government from completely falling into the hands of the traitors. Many of our friends in the East fear the disunionists may make the attempt to inflame a rebellion in Maryland and Virginia so as to afford them the pretext and opportunity to take possession of the Federal Capitol and Government archives. I scarcely think the fear is well founded, as yet. . . .

To Therena Bates, Springfield, 9 January 1861[2]

. . . So far, this week has not brought us much excitement. The Legislature met on Monday—that is to say the Republicans met—the Democrats stay-ing out, I suppose more for a scare than anything else. I think they had an idea that there were some shaky members among the Republicans who might not want to vote for Trumbull *[for U.S. senator]*, and if there were any discontent they would give it time to grow and develop. But as they found themselves mistaken in this, they came in yesterday, helped to orga-nize the House, and to-day at 2 oclock Mr. Trumbull was re-elected for six years.

On yesterday in the House of Representatives the Democrats offered a Resolution eulogizing Gen. Jackson and proposing to adjourn in honor of the "8th".[3] The Republicans quickly added an amendment, of special praise for his resistance of Nullification and Secession in 1832. This was rather more than the Democrats intended when they began; but they concluded it would never do to vote against anything Gen. Jackson had done, and so the resolution was made to endorse his famous Nullification "Proclamation," in which shape the whole House voted for it.[4] It was an [ele.?] *[a page of the letter is missing here]* thing for the Republicans, as they desire no stronger pledge than this from the Democracy to support what they expect Mr. Lincoln to do in the premises. And they are particularly pleased with it, just at this time, as an indication to the whole Union of what the whole people of Illinois feel and mean, about the Secession question. . . .

To Therena Bates, Springfield, 13 January 1861[5]

. . . [D]uring this week, Mississippi, Alabama and Florida have passed secession ordinances, and now consider themselves out of the Union.[6] The merchant steam-ship "Star of the West," which was sent by the President to Charleston to bring re-inforcements to Maj. Anderson in Fort Sumpter, was, when attempting to enter the harbor fired upon by a battery which the secessionists have erected on Morris Island which lies some distance to the seaward from the fort, and compelled to return to New York without landing the men.[7] A number of forts and arsenals in the Southern States have been seized by the secessionists. Last night's dispatches even state that the Governor of Miss. had ordered a battery of artillery to Vicksburg with orders to hail every steamboat which passed.[8]

In the meantime, President Buchanan has listened to the wiser counsels of Gen. Scott;—the traitors in the Cabinet have pretty much all resigned, and had their places filled up with Union men;[9] the Administration thus reconstructed has determined to enforce the laws; the President has announced this determination to Congress in a special message;[10] Gen Scott is organizing the militia in the District of Columbia, and ordering troops into the neighborhood, to secure the peaceful inauguration of Mr. Lincoln, and is also reinforcing some of the important fortresses down south. So you see the whole matter is becoming complicated from day to day, and beginning to wear a war-like aspect. The North is beginning to fire up, and the Legislatures of New York and Ohio have tendered the whole power and resources of these States to sustain the President and maintain the existing government. Events are crowding so thickly upon us that it is impossible to calculate their present or future importance. It is beginning to look very much as if a fight somewhere was almost inevitable. . . .

To Therena Bates, Springfield, 16 January 1861[11]

. . . The weather has been so rainy and foggy for two or three days past that the telegraph wouldn't work well, and we have had very little news of what is going on elsewhere in the world. We scarcely know therefore whether Springfield is in the Union yet or out of it, or what the secessionists are doing. . . .

To Therena Bates, Springfield, 20 January 1861[12]

. . . I have little or no news to tell you. The labor of the week has been of the usual treadmill sort. . . .

To Edwin C. Wilson, Springfield, 23 January 1861[13]

Private Your official communication of the 31st ult. addressed to Hon. A. Lincoln, was duly received.

Mr. Lincoln desires me to answer, that while he does not now deem it necessary to avail himself of the services you so kindly offer him, he is nevertheless gratified to have this assurance from yourself that the Militia of the State of Pennsylvania is loyal to the Constitution and the Union, and stands ready to rally to their support and maintainance, in the event of trouble or danger.[14]

To Therena Bates, Springfield, 27 January 1861[15]

Mr. Lincoln yesterday determined definitely to start from here on his way to Washington, on the 11th of February. He will go through Indianapolis, Columbus, probably Pittsburgh and Cleveland, Albany, New York, Philadelphia, Harrisburgh and Baltimore—occupying perhaps some twelve or fifteen days with the trip. . . .

To Edward Bates, Springfield, 28 January 1861[16]

Hon. A. Lincoln desires me to write to you that he has determined on starting from here for Washington City on the 11th of February. He will go through Indianapolis, Columbus, Pittsburg, Albany, New York, Philadelphia, Harrisburg and Baltimore.

Albany, New York and Philadelphia are not finally decided upon, though it is probable that he will also take them in his route. The journey will occupy twelve or fifteen days.

To J. W. Tillman, Springfield, 28 January 1861[17]

Your letter of the 24th inst addressed to Hon. A. Lincoln, inviting him, on behalf of the State Central Committee of Michigan to pass through that State on his journey to Washington, has been received.[18]

He desires me to reply, with profound thanks for the honor thus cordially tendered him, that having accepted similar invitations to pass through the Capitols of the States of Indiana and Ohio, he regrets that it will be out of his power to accept the courtesies and hospitalities of the people of Michigan so kindly proffered him through yourself and the Committee.

To Elmer E. Ellsworth, Springfield, 30 January 1861[19]

Enclosed I send you the measures taken by the tailor this morning, which I suppose the Chicago one will perhaps understand. Let him exercise his judgment as to the necessary "variations."

If the tailor feels pretty confident of being able to fit me from these "figures" you may order pants and vest in addition *[to]* the coat. I wish you would select what you think a good and rather fine shirt, and bring me one as a sample, when you come.

To Edwin D. Morgan, Springfield, 1 February 1861[20]

Your letter of the 19th ult. addressed to Hon. A. Lincoln was duly received, in which you invite him to visit Albany on his route to Washington, and tender him the hospitalities of the State and your home.

In accordance with the answer just sent to the telegraphic message received from yourself a few minutes since, Mr. Lincoln desires me to write that it has for some little time been his purpose to pass through Albany, and that he would have answered you to that effect before this, but for the fact that as the Legislatures of Indiana, Ohio, New Jersey and Pennsylvania had by resolution invited him to visit them, he thought it probable that a similar resolution would be adopted by the Legislature of New York, and he had therefore waited to reply to both invitations together.

He will cheerfully accede to any arrangements yourself and the citizens of Albany may make for his stay, provided only no formal ceremonies wasting any great amount of time be adopted.

To Edward Bates, Springfield, 5 February 1861[21]

Hon. A. Lincoln directs me to say to you that in case you intend going to Washington about the time he proposes to start (the 11th inst.) he would be pleased to have you accompany him on the trip he contemplates.

He does not desire to have you do this, however, at the cost of any inconvenience to yourself, or the derangement of any plans you may have already formed.

P.S. Mr. Lincoln intended to have said this to you himself when you were here, but in his hurry it escaped his attention.

To Therena Bates, Indianapolis, 11 February 1861[22]

It is now 8 oclock at night, and we have been one day on the journey to Washington. We had a rather pleasant ride over the Railroad from Springfield here; saw crowds of people at every station, found the streets of this city full on our arrival (if it were during a campaign it would be called fifty thousand at least) through which with difficulty we made our way to the "Bates House" (don't I feel at home?) where I am writing this. The House is perfectly jammed full of people. Three or four ladies and as many gentlemen, have even invaded the room assigned to Mr. Lincoln, while outside the door I hear the crowd pushing and grumbling and shouting in almost frantic endeavors to get to another parlor in the door of which Mr. Lincoln stands shaking hands with the multitude. It is a severe ordeal for us, and increased about tenfold for him. . . .

To Therena Bates, Pittsburgh, 15 February 1861[23]

. . . Mr. Lincoln has received an immense reception at every place yet visited—so large that it has been a serious task for us of his escort, to prevent his being killed with kindness*[.]* The expression may be anomalous, but it is nevertheless literally true.

So far we have got along reasonably well. We arrived late at Pittsburg last night, on account of a train being off the track. It had also gone to raining, and was altogether so disagreeable a night that we hardly expected to find a soul at the depot. It was a vain illusion. The depot and grounds were literally jammed full of people. We finally got Mr. Lincoln into a carriage; but having accomplished that, it looked for a while as if we would never get the carriage out of the crowd that was pushing and pulling and yelling all around us. I hope we shall not get into another such.

Today, here at Cleveland, the arrangements have been good (better than we have found anywhere else*[)]* and almost perfect order has been kept. I am longing anxiously for our arrival at Buffalo to-morrow evening, after which we shall have a whole day of rest and quiet. . . .

To Therena Bates, Buffalo, N.Y., 8:30 P.M.,
17 February 1861[24]

. . . Leaving Pittsburg we reached Cleveland in pretty good time but in a snow-storm. Here for the first time we found the crowd tolerably well controlled by the police and military, and got through without any jam, though there was again a great crowd at the hotel. Still, we were assigned to comfortable quarters, treated to a good dinner, and altogether about as well taken care of as was possible under the circumstances. The whole party has very pleasant recollections of Cleveland.

We found a disagreeable contrast here. The usual thousands were awaiting our arrival. A little path had been kept open through the crowd, through which we got Mr. Lincoln. The crowd closed up immediately after his passage, and the rest of the party only got through by dint of the most strenuous and persevering elbowing. Major Hunter had his arm so badly sprained that it is doubtful tonight whether he can continue his journey.[25] Arrived at the hotel all was confusion—the committee not only did nothing but didn't know and didn't seem to care what to do. We took the matter into our own hands and finally arranged pretty much everything. I don't know when I have done so much work as yesterday, and I am feeling the effect of it to-day. . . .

To Therena Bates, Washington, 24 February 1861[26]

We all arrived here safely last evening at about 5 oclock—Mr. Lincoln himself having preceded us the night before. I assure you it was a real pleasure to get to our journey's end—with a prospect of a little rest now and then. During the last week of our trip, in the great whirlpools of New York and Philadelphia, not a moment was our own. My failure to write you my usual mid-week letter was not because of forgetfulness. One of the papers I sent you from New York, I went to the printing office and bought, and had wrapped after two oclock A.M. last Thursday morning.

Of course I need not try to detail the incidents of the trip. These you have no doubt sufficiently gathered from the newspapers.

For the present we are quartered at Willard's Hotel.[27] The original programme was to go to a private house which had been rented for the purpose. This plan having been changed, and no rooms having been reserved, all the party except Mr. & Mrs. Lincoln have but sorry accommodations.[28] Well, next week we hope to be in the White House, where perhaps it may be better.

You need have no present fears about our entire safety here. There is not the least apprehension about trouble at the inauguration or at any other time. That cloud has blown over. . . .

I have not yet been here long enough, nor am I yet sufficiently rested, to write much, or think much, or have many impressions of any kind. I found some two or three hundred letters to be attended here, on my arrival, which though, thank the stars, *[is]* less than I expected, have yet been enough to keep me busy enough to-day Sunday as it is. From what I know so far I can form very little idea of what I may have to do in the future. . . .

To Ozias M. Hatch, Philadelphia, 25 February 1861[29]

Forward the box of letters at once to me by express to Washington.

To the editor of the *Washington Star*, *[Washington, 4 March 1861]*[30]

Please publish the within notice and oblige
    Yours truly

To Therena Bates, Washington, 5 March 1861[31]

As you see from the heading of my letter, I am fairly installed in the "White House." We had a gratifying and glorious inauguration yesterday—a fine day, and a fine display and everything went off as nicely as it could have possibly been devised.

To Therena Bates, Washington, 7 March 1861[32]

. . . Mr. Lincoln is inaugurated, and has got the government started. For the present, as I wrote to you, you need have no apprehensions of danger to him or those about him. I consider myself quite as safe here as I used to be in the Free Press Office years ago.

Since I commenced writing this I have again been called away to appease visitors who are importuning to see Mr. Lincoln so don't be surprised if I break off anywhere and fold it up and mail it to you—for I am going to send you something to-night if it is only an empty envelope.

The first official act of Mr. Lincoln—after the inauguration*[—]*was to sign my appointment as Private Sec'y, and I have been busy enough since (as in fact I had been before) I assure you. As the work is now, it will be a very severe tax on both my physical and mental energies, although so far I have borne it remarkably well. By and by in two or three months, when the appointments have been all made I think the labor will be more sufferable. John Hay and I are both staying here in the White House. We have very pleasant offices, and a nice large bed room, though all of them sadly need new furniture and carpets. That too we expect to have remedied after a while.

We all stayed at Willard's Hotel the week before *[the]* inauguration. There was of course a great crowd there, and so many ladies in the parlors as to make it seem like having a party every night. Since my arrival I have been to one party—one wedding—and the inauguration ball which by the way was really a very successful and brilliant affair. Today the <u>Corps Diplomatique</u> made their formal call upon the President, and tomorrow night the first public reception takes place. . . .

To Ozias M. Hatch, Washington, 12 P.M., 7 March 1861[33]

Don't get impatient that I have written no letters back. If you had passed through what we all have during the four weeks past, you would not want to see or write another for years. We have scarcely had time to eat sleep or even breathe.

The inauguration went off very finely and everything starts off as well as we could have possibly hoped, but the labor which has had to be undergone has been terrible, and God knows how we shall get through that of the three months to come. Illinois is here in perfect hordes. You may look out for a tremendous crop of soreheads.[34] But I must stop writing and try to get a little sleep.

[P.S.] Mr Lincoln and all the folks are well.

To Winfield Scott, Washington, 9 March 1861[35]

I am directed by the President to say he desires you to exercise all possible vigilance for the maintenance of all the places within the military department of the United States; and to promptly call upon all the departments of the government for the means necessary to that end.

To Therena Bates, Washington, 10 March 1861[36]

. . . Although it is Sunday to-day, and I have not of course been pretending to work, yet to read a letter here, to make a memorandum there, and answer a question somewhere else has taken up the entire day, so that at nine o'clock at night I for the first time find an opportunity (and not a very good one at that) to begin a letter to you.

We have had no particular excitement here since I wrote you except the "Reception" on Friday night, which was voted by all the "oldest inhabitants" to have been the most successful one ever known here. For over two hours the crowd poured in as rapidly as the door would admit them, and many climbed in at the windows. It was withal more "ton"-ish than such things usually are. Of course in such a crowd crinoline suffered, and at least fifty men have been swearing worse than "our army in Flanders," ever since they went home that evening, over the loss of new hats and valuable over-coats. But for particulars I must refer you to the "Star" I mailed you this morning.

I cannot yet form much of an idea how I shall like it here. For two or three months the work will of course be pretty laborious. After that I expect to find some time for both recreation and study. As the existing laws do not provide for an Assistant for me, I have had John Hay appointed to a Clerkship in the Department of the Interior, and detailed for special service here at the White House, so that he gives me the benefit of his whole time.[37]
. . .

To Therena Bates, Washington, 14 March 1861[38]

. . . I sit down in the hurry and confusion of my morning work, having a few minutes to spare just now, to merely say that I am still well, and getting through the almost overwhelming pressure of work which is upon me, with, I think a wonderful degree of good temper. . . .

To Therena Bates, Washington, 20 March 1861[39]

. . . Excepting the fact that the two little boys *[Willie and Tad Lincoln]* have the measles, every body about the White House is in good health, notwith-standing the fact that some of us have work and annoyance enough to make almost anybody sick. There is consolation in the fact however that this rush cannot last many weeks longer and that then we will enjoy our leisure all the better. . . .

To Therena Bates, Washington, 24 March 1861[40]

. . . So far the extra labor and fatigue to which I am subjected seems to have no immediate bad effects. The intense pressure does not seem to abate as yet but I think it cannot last more than two or three weeks longer. I am looking forward with a good deal of eagerness to when I shall have time to at least read and write my letters in peace and without being haunted con-tinually by some one who "wants to see the President for only five min-utes." At present this request meets me from almost every man woman and child I meet—whether it be by day or night—in the house or on the street. . . .

To Therena Bates, Washington, 29 March 1861[41]

. . . The Senate adjourned on yesterday and of course the rush of business culminated in a pressure that was almost impossible to get through. Hereafter I hope it may not be quite so bad as it has been. . . .

To Ozias M. Hatch, Washington, 31 March 1861[42]

<u>Private</u> The mail is about ready to go, and I am only writing a few words now to suggest to you the propriety of ending the Post Office squabble in Springfield by having our boys take up Mrs. Lizzie Grimsley (who is here) as their candidate, and with her beating the whole pile of the other contestants?[43] Wouldn't the other aspirants there be more easily reconciled to be beaten by a woman than by one of themselves? I think the President would be pleased to have the riddle solved in that way.

If this reaches you before the election is held, and you think it expedient, suggest the matter to prudent friends—without letting it be known however that the plan originates here*[.]*

To Therena Bates, Washington, 31 March 1861[44]

. . . To-day we have been pretty quiet here, and I am in hope that we have seen the worst of the rush. Last night I got the President (it still seems queer to speak of Mr. Lincoln in that way although I am becoming used to it) to agree to let me have his business hours limited to from 10 in the morning to 3 in the afternoon. This will be a very great improvement, as he has heretofore worked, on an average full twelve hours a day. And it will relieve not him alone but all the rest of us, from a burden of labor which it would be impossible to sustain for a great length of time.

John Hay and I took quite a stroll this afternoon, and I feel much rested and refreshed by it. So far we have been out very little, but we shall not neglect the opportunities we <u>expect</u> to have by and by. I have not yet spent a single hour in sight-seeing although there is much about the city that is well worth seeing. Well, I suppose I need not hurry as I have a prospect of ample time and leisure to study the city in detail. . . .

To Therena Bates, Washington, 2 April 1861[45]

. . . We still have plenty of hard work to do, although we are somewhat relieved from the "outside pressure" by the President's having limited his reception hours from 10 to 1 o'clock. Under this arrangement we do get the bulk of the crowd shut out in the afternoon at least. . . .

To Therena Bates, Washington, 7 April 1861[46]

. . . The President having limited his hours for seeing people on business, has relieved us very much, and given us time at least to eat and sleep, which is a considerable gain. The crowd however hangs on with a wonderful perseverance, and although it is five weeks since the inauguration, I cannot yet begin to estimate when we shall be free from them.

All the excitement we have here now is over the prospect of a war with the South which the newspapers and the gossiping public insist is near at hand. I myself do not see the prospect in so gloomy a light. That there may be a little brush at Charleston or Pensacola is quite possible but that any general hostilities will result from it I have not the least fear. I do not think that either the authorities or any considerable number of the people of either section want a civil war, and I think they will very soon get heartily sick and tired of the little fighting that is barely possible at the points named, instead of being inflamed into a prolonged contest as many fear. . . .

To Therena Bates, Washington, 11 April 1861[47]

. . . For the past week the crowd about the house here has rather increased than abated and I cannot therefore very well calculate how it will continue.

Don't get alarmed at the "rumors of wars" which you hear from this direction. There is some idle gossip about danger of a demonstration being made by the secessionists against this capitol but I do not regard it being at *[all]* probable. The Southerners will I think need all their forces in their own country and will scarcely make an attempt so foolhardy as that of attacking this city. Besides, the government is determined not to be surprised here. On yesterday and to-day a Regiment (1000 men) of the Volunteer Militia are being mustered into active service of the U.S. in the District and another Regiment will be added if it is needed. Guards are nightly set about the public buildings. John Hay and I were challenged by a sentinel last night as we were returning from down town to the White House. . . .

To Therena Bates, Washington, 14 April 1861[48]

I sat down this morning at my desk thinking I should have plenty of time to write my letter to you, and also to overhaul and answer a whole pocketfull of letters which had accumulated during the week. Very soon however the members of the Cabinet came in (although it was Sunday, I suppose in revolutionary times like the present it may be excused.) The result was that instead of writing my letters as I had intended doing, I was soon engaged in copying the Presidents proclamation, which you will have seen before you receive this. Political and patriotic labors like this occupied me until noon or rather dinner-time (2 o'clock.) After dinner the President expressed a wish to go out riding; so I had the carriage got up, and he and I and the little boys took a ride. The ride lasted till near supper-time, and since supper one thing after another has diverted me from my writing, until it has got to be 12 oclock at night.

As it has reached so late an hour I shall not write much. The news you will of course have read before you could possibly see it in this letter—that Fort Sumpter has been taken by the Southern rebels—that the President has called out 75,000 men to put down the rebellion, and that Congress is to be convened in July.[49] All these things will make stirring times, and I hardly realize that they are so, even as I write them. . . .

Memorandum, ca. 18 April 1861[50]

Mails suspended. The telegraph cut. Lane's improvised Frontier Guards perform squad drill in the East Room and bivouac on the velvet carpet among stacks of new muskets and freshly opened ammunition boxes.[51]

Memorandum of events, 19 April 1861[52]

Friday April 19th 1861 is likely to become historic in the nation's annals. The 6th Regiment Mass Volunteer Militia in passing through the city of Baltimore, was assaulted by a mob, and finally in self-defence fired upon the mob in return. At about 2 P.M. the P[resident] received a dispatch from Gov. Hicks and Mayor Brown, that a collision had occurred between the troops and the citizens and that several were killed. The dispatch closed with the request "send no troops here," &c.[53] About an hour and a half later a special messenger on a special train arrived bringing P[resident] a verbatim copy of the dispatch in writing.

About 1 A.M. that night, a committee arrived from Balt. desiring an interview with P[resident]. The messenger waked me and instead of waking P[resident] I went to the War Dept. where the Sec War was staying, to be prepared for emergencies. The mission of the committee was if possible to induce the govt. to send no more troops through Baltimore. I woke the Sec. War, who was not disposed to listen to such a proposition, and went to sleep again. I learned however from the Chief Clerk that there were no troops (to their knowledge[)] on the way which would reach Balt. before 8 next morning when they could see P[resident] with their proposal.[54] This satisfied them for the time being, and they went away.

Next morning by 8 they were with P[resident] or rather met him at the foot of the stairs as he was going down to speak to Gen. S[cott] who was in his carriage at the door.[55] They mentioned their errand to both, and Gen. S. promptly suggested, "Send the troops round Baltimore.[*"]* The P[*resident*] agreed to the suggestion, "if in a military point of view" it were practicable, and gave the committee a note saying that was his wish, in order to avoid further present difficulty. With this they went home apparently satisfied.

To Therena Bates, Washington, 10 P.M., 19 April 1861[56]

. . . [W]e are having rather stirring times here. The Presidents proclamation has been responded to unanimously by the people of the North; and their enthusiasm has stirred the secession feeling and fanaticism of Virginia, and fanned its rebellion into flames. Yesterday and last night demonstrations were made both against Harper's Ferry Arsenal, and the Norfolk Navy Yard, by the Virginia rebels. The officer in command at Harper's Ferry finding he could not hold the works against the force attacking him withdrew his men and burned down the works and arms to prevent their falling into the rebels hands.[57] From Norfolk we have no reliable news, except that some small vessels had been sunk in the channel to prevent our getting out our ships of war which lie at anchor there. A war vessel the "Pawnee" has started from here to-night to go to their relief or to destroy them.[58] At Baltimore to-day a collision occurred between the troops (a Massachusetts Regiment) coming here to defend this city, and the secessionists, in which several were killed on both sides.[59] It is I believe the first bloodshed in this civil war, and singularly enough is the anniversary of the first bloodshed in the Revolution. We are expecting more troops here by way of Baltimore, but are also fearful that the secessionists may at any hour cut the telegraph wires, tear up the railroad track, or burn the bridges, and thus prevent their reaching us, and cut off all communication. We have rumors that 1500 men are gathered and under arms at Alexandria (seven miles below here) supposed to have hostile [*designs*][60] against this City, and an additional report that a vessel was late this evening seen landing men on the Maryland side of the river. All these things indicate that if we are to be attacked at all soon it will happen to-night. On the other hand, we have some four to five thousand men under arms in the city, and a very vigilant watch out in all the probable directions of approach. All the public buildings are strongly guarded, the Secretary of War will remain all night in his Department, and Gen. Scott is within convenient reach. I do not think any force could be brought against the city to-night, which our men could not easily repel, and therefore do not feel seriously alarmed, although the apprehensions of danger are pretty general. Unless they are obstructed somewhere on the way we think there will be enough troops here by to-morrow evening to render the city very safe. . . .

(At this point Col. Lamon is just in from the War Department and tells me that all is quiet so far, but that a "brush" is expected by the Secretary of War tonight.)[61] Well, there is nothing to be done but to wait and see what the night brings forth.

The organization of the Militia, and the late arrivals of troops have been making things seem quite warlike for a few days past; but we have been much more impressed with the conditions surrounding us by the arrival this evening of Miss Dix, who came to offer herself and an army of nurses to the government gratuitously, for hospital service.[62]

———— Saturday Morning *[20 April]*. The City and its surroundings are all still quiet. We hear however of additional troubles between here and Philadelphia—burning of bridges &c and a determination to stop all troops coming here by rail. This will in all probability very soon result in stopping all communication and transit except the slow process of marching large armed forces. We expect two additional Regiments here by a different route, to-night or tomorrow, with which it is thought we can easily maintain ourselves. . . .

Memorandum of events, 20 April 1861[63]

Saturday April 20th the P*[resident]* telegraphed Gov. Hicks and Mayor Brown to come to Washington for consultation about affairs.[64] At about midnight a dispatch came from Mayor Brown saying Gov. H. had gone to Annapolis, and asking if he should come alone. I dispatched for the P*[resident]* "Come."

Memorandum of events, ca. 20 April 1861[65]

Pinkerton was first man to get through the rebel lines during first blockade of Washington—came up to the White House and into the Cabinet room—took off his coat and ripping open the lining of his vest took about a dozen or more letters which he had thus brought to the President from the north.[66]

Speed Butler was second man to get through.[67] He brought a requisition from Gov Yates for arms from Jeff*[erson]* Barracks.[68] Order was endorsed by Capt Lyons.[69] N*[icolay?]* went to Gen Scott with Butler who promptly endorsed on same half sheet of paper an order for the delivery of the arms to Gov Yates, after which Butler hurried back &c.

Memorandum of events, 21 April 1861[70]

Sunday morning the 21st he *[Mayor Brown]* came with several other gentle-men, one of them *[being]* one of the Committee which had come the night before. The first committee had asked only that troops might not be per-mitted to come through Baltimore, and had gone home seemingly perfectly satisfied with having them come around the city. But a day had made a won-derful transformation. The day before the President had said to them half playfully, "if I grant you this, you will come to-morrow demanding that no troops shall pass around."[71] His words were literally verified. This second Committee assumed as a fact that the people of Baltimore and Md. were highly incensed at what they believed to be preparations for the invasion and subjugation of the South and were up in arms and were resolved to the sacrifice of their lives to permit no more troops to come through their State. The P*[resident]* replied that the Capitol being in the center of Md. and be-ing in danger, the troops must come to defend it and must of necessity come through Md.—there being no other route. He referred again to Gen Scotts suggestion to bring troops round by the Relay House.

Memorandum of events, 19–30 April 1861[72]

[19 April] Attempt of Mass troops to pass through Balt.
Dispatch of Gov Hicks at 2 1/2 oclock about collision
Special train & messenger "Send no Troops"—
Com. arrived at one oclock at night. (went to Cameron.)
Com had interview with Prest in the morning.
Prest. & Gen Scott promised to try & send troops around Balt.
[20 April] Saturday Prest telegraphed to Gov Hicks & Mayor Brown to come
Gov. Hicks had gone to Annapolis—could not*[—]*Mayor asked by dis-patch whether he should come alone I woke up the Prest at 1 P.M. *[A.M.]* Saturday night, and by his direction telegraphed "come".
Interview—Complaint of Mayor—Prest shows dispatch in justification.
They start home—receive dispatch—
Return post haste to Prest—
Have another interview with Prest
He orders troops back from Cockeysville
Gen Scott & Sec War dissent.[73]

———

[20–21 April] Harpers Ferry Armory evacuated & burned.
Gosport Navy Yard & vessels destroyed.[74]

———

[21 April] A dreary and anxious Sunday—
Committee of "Christians."
[22 April] Monday—Resignations[75]
Rumors of demonstrations against Capitol
Intercepted Dispatches. No communication—
Seward writes letter to Gov Hicks.[76]
[23 April] Tuesday—Great public anxiety.
Talk of proclaiming martial law.
Suspension of business—
[24 April] Wednesday d*[itt]*o—Return of "Pawnee" with marines from
Gosport—
Insecurity of City—Navy Yard—Conversation with Capt. Dahlgren—Militia of Dist*[rict]* unreliable.
[25 April] Thursday—Arrival of 7th *[N.Y.]* Regt
Great public Relief—
Gov. Hicks convenes Leg*[islature in Frederick]*—Proposition to disperse or arrest. Prest vs. Writes to Scott giving his reasons—but empowering him &c.[77]
Change of feeling in Balt. Officers take their offices—Offers to permit the reestablishment of travel & communication
[27 April] Saturday—Dispatch from Md Leg that Com Pub Safety Bill had passed to second reading in the Senate, &c
Com. from Leg.—Bob McLean[78]—Speech—submissive
[28 April] Sunday—Sewards letters about negroes.
[30 April] Tuesday—Com from Govs. of Pa. O. Ind Ill Mich. Wis.

To Gideon Welles, Washington, 22 April 1861[79]

The President desires a meeting of the Cabinet at 3 P.M. to-day.

To Ozias M. Hatch, Washington, 26 April 1861[80]

<u>Private</u> I enclose you Tuck's letter of the 20th, and which would have been here sooner had we not been entirely without a mail or communication of any sort from the North and East from Saturday night last *[20 April]*, until last night. It seems to indicate that McNeil *[McNeal]* will be appointed.[81]

The New York "7th" Regiment reached here yesterday morning, and terminated a very anxious suspense we had been in, ever since last Sunday. We had during all that time but about 2000 men in the City that we could really <u>count on</u>. True we had some 3000 of the District Militia under arms; but nobody depended upon them. We *[had]* no positive assurance but that in the very crisis of any contest which might come upon us they would turn their guns against us. While we never felt any apprehension that the City could be taken from us, we were in a condition to be most seriously annoyed and harassed by an assault from without, or a panic or riot among the citizens. You may therefore be sure that we were glad to have another so good a Regiment as the "7th" actually on the ground here and a further knowledge that six or seven more were at Annapolis, and on their way. From this time we shall have no trouble either to keep a communication open, or to get a sufficient number of men here to place the safety of the Capitol beyond a doubt.

Do not get impatient at apparent delays. Baltimore and other nests of treason will be attended to in due time.

In getting up the Illinois troops look to <u>efficiency</u>—to perfection in drill, equipment &c. Have them ready for <u>work</u> and not for show.

To Therena Bates, Washington, 26 April 1861[82]

The mail to-day *[was]* (the first we have had since last Saturday) . . .

I wrote you a letter last Saturday. . . . If you did not get it . . . you may charge it all to the Baltimore secessionists who interrupted not only the mails, but <u>all</u> communications with the sensible, civilized northern world. And I have not written since for the reason that I knew the letter would only go as far as the Post office in this city, or at farthest only into the hands of the Baltimore barbarians, and therefore not in the least relieve the suspense I knew you would be in about the condition of things here.

We too had our burden of suspense here. As I have already told you, our intercourse with the outside world was cut off. We heard frequently from Baltimore and different parts of Maryland, but the news had little of encouragement in it. Uniformly the report was that all heretofore Union men had at once turned secessionists, and were armed and determined to the death to prevent a single additional northern soldier's crossing the soil of Maryland. Here we were in this city, in charge of all the public buildings, property and archives, with only about 2000 <u>reliable</u> men to defend it. True we had some 3000 men in addition, of the District Militia under arms. But with the city perfectly demoralized with secession feeling, no man could <u>know</u> whom of the residents to trust. We were not certain but that at the first moment when fate would seem to preponderate against us, we would have to look down the muzzles of our own guns. The feeling was not the most comfortable in the world, I assure you. We were not only surrounded by the enemy, but in the midst of traitors.

Not that we were at any time in extreme danger. With the reliable force at our disposal we could have held the city against largely superior numbers. But had the rebels suddenly precipitated five or six thousand men upon us, and which it seemed possible for them to do, it would have given us an infinite deal of trouble. Then there was another danger. As Sunday, Monday and Tuesday successively passed by without bringing the expected reinforcements the suspense and uncertainty among our city population grew to such a pitch that a very small untoward circumstance or accident would have stirred up a riot or a panic. Fortunately everything went on quietly and smoothly until the arrival of the Seventh Regiment from New York, adding a third to our defensive force, and also bringing us the certain information that several additional Regiments were at and this side of Annapolis. This at once put an end to the suspense. It made the city safe in every contingency, and men went to talking laughing, trading and working as before; and since yesterday morning at ten o'clock you could not discover from anything except the everywhere-ness of uniforms and muskets, that we are in the midst of revolution and civil war, the end of which will be a serious matter to the side that has to "go to the wall.". . .

To Therena Bates, Washington, 27 April 1861[83]

. . . [O]nly for a few days did we feel ourselves at all likely to have any trouble, and then only through some marauding assault from our kind Virginia neighbors or a riotous uprising among our city population. Either would have been very troublesome and annoying, but in the end not really dangerous. That is all past now. We have to-day 10,000 efficient and reliable northern troops in the city, and plenty more coming every day, capable not only of defending it against any assault, but also of keeping the whole surrounding country clear of assailants. I shall be quite as safe here, and sleep quite as soundly as if I were in New York or Springfield. . . .

To Therena Bates, Washington, 1 May 1861[84]

. . . [E]verything is still perfectly quiet and safe here. We have plenty of troops here for all possible contingencies, and about a Regiment arriving every day. In addition forces are being raised and organized all over the Northern States more rapidly than they can be put to use.

I am perfectly well, and you can rest entirely easy about my safety and welfare in every relation.

The mail arrangements have been put in some sort of order again, and I think we shall have no further interruption of them. . . .

To George W. Caldwell, Washington, 1 May 1861[85]

Private Your letter of the 25th ult. addressed to the President was duly received, and considered.[86] Will you please to write to me, where and how soon, (and let the day be an early one) the leading and responsible men engaged in your movement can meet together, to receive and consult with such gentlemen as the Government may send to represent its views about the matter.[87]

Memorandum, 7 May 1861[88]

Going into the P[resident]'s room this morning found Hay with him. The conversation turning on the subject of the existing contest he remarked that the real question involved in it, (as he had about made up his mind, though he should still think further about it, while writing his message *[to be delivered to Congress on 4 July]*) was whether a free and representative government had the right and power to protect and maintain itself. Admit the right of a minority to secede at will, and the occasion for such secession would almost as likely be any other as the slavery question.[89]

During the forenoon, a committee of gentlemen representing a Convention of the Governors of Pa O Ind Ill Wis & Mich. lately held at Cleveland came to say to him that these Governors and States renewed the pledge of all their resources, and any number of men which might be required, to sustain the Govt. and assist in crushing out the rebellion.[90] They only demanded that a positive and vigorous policy should be pursued and pushed by the Administration.

They did not excuse or justify the impatience existing in some quarters at the course pursued, but their States did desire some assurance that the Govt was in earnest and would go forward earnestly without parleyings or compromises.

A question had arisen as to how these states should protect their borders. If for instance Ky should secede, as was feared, Cincinnati would be insecure without the possession of Covington Heights across the river. Yet if they took them, the whole State would be in arms at the pretended invasion. The Gen. Gov[ernmen]t had not indicated what it would do in this case. P[resident] desired to know, whether in such case local or federal authority should act.

To Therena Bates, Washington, 10 May 1861[91]

We (I mean the President and four of five others of us from the White House) spent a very agreeable afternoon from about 3 to 6 o'clock P.M. yesterday. The 71st Regiment New York Volunteers are quartered at the Navy Yard, and having several good musicians in the ranks, and a fine regimental band, by way of pastime improvised a regular concert . . . in one of the large store-rooms in the Navy Yard, which they occupy as barracks. They had an elegant audience of some two or three hundred invited guests, and made the enterprise a great success.

The concert being over we went down and on board one of the ships, and witnessed a little cannon-practice; several shots were fired for our edification from a large Dahlgren gun mounted on shore for trial. The target, perhaps 25 or 30 feet square is out in the river some 1300 yards, just the distance at which the nearest battery was built to Fort Sumpter. We would hear the explosion and as quick as thought afterwards see the ball (a shell 11 inches in diameter) flying through the air at about two-thirds the distance to the target—could follow it distinctly with the eye until it struck, then see its <u>ricochet</u> cast up the spray—one, two, three, four, five six, seven or eight times. I had not thought before that the flight of a cannon-ball could be seen so distinctly.[92]

Leaving the ship we next saw the 71st Regiment on "dress parade," and then went home

At night we had a reception, here of the military officers in the city. For once, the few ladies present, (as it was purely a military reception, and as most of the officers here are strangers of course there could be but few ladies to come with them or belonging to their families) had every and ample opportunity to gratify their <u>penchant</u> for admiring "brass buttons.". . .

To Therena Bates, Washington, 12 May 1861[93]

. . . The secession war remains about in the same condition it was in a week ago except that the preparations of arms, men and munitions in the North everywhere is going steadily forward, and is being put into an available shape. The South is also pushing forward her preparations, but of course cannot vie with the North in extent or rapidity. Three or four weeks more will see 100,000 of the Northern men under arms, and in tolerable drill while the Southern effective force cannot certainly reach half that number.

There will probably be some important army movements before a great while, though I cannot now give you definite information about them*[.]*

My everyday life is about the same. I still have plenty to occupy me during the most of the day, but remain quite well.

To Therena Bates, Washington, 23 May 1861[94]

. . . I had a visit yesterday from Mrs. Davis (formerly McCook) who came to ask me to help her get an interview with the President, so that she might get her brother appointed into the army.[95] . . . I could not get her the desired interview, and it would not have helped her in the least if I had. I advised her to have the application made to the Secretary of War, where she will be as likely to accomplish the object, as by seeing the President. . . .

To Therena Bates, Washington, 25 May 1861[96]

I had supposed myself to have grown quite indifferent, and callous, and hard-hearted, until I heard of the sad fate of Col. Ellsworth, who, as you will already have read, was assassinated at the taking of Alexandria by our troops, on last Friday morning; but since that time I have been quite unable to keep the tears out of my eyes whenever I thought, or heard, or read, about it, until I have almost concluded that I am quite a weak and womanish sort of creature. I had known and seen him almost daily for more than six months past, and although our intimacy was never in any wise confidential as to personal matters, I had learned to value him very highly. He was very young—only 24 I think—very talented and ambitious, and very poor—a combination of the qualities upon which sadness and misfortune seem ever to prey. He had by constant exertion already made himself famous, and that against obstacles, that would have been insurmountable to any other. Since my acquaintance with him, my position has enabled me to assist him in his plans and aspirations, until I felt almost a direct personal pride and interest in his success. Knowing his ability and his determined energy, I knew that he would win a brilliant success if life were spared him. So that to me his death seems almost a fatality, and though I know the whole nation will mourn for him, yet I am grieved also to feel that they do not half appreciate his worth or their loss. . . .

To Therena Bates, Washington, 31 May 1861[97]

In company with John Hay and Bob Lincoln who is here on a short visit from College, I took, on yesterday afternoon my second horseback ride since I have been here. . . .

To Therena Bates, Washington, 2 June 1861[98]

. . . We have music here in the Presidents grounds every Wednesday and Saturday evening, when the grounds are opened to everybody. Yesterday at about half after five, there was quite a large crowd here promenading in the grounds, when all at once a very brisk firing of musketry became heard on the other side of the river. There was almost an instantaneous excitement in the crowd and everybody rushed down to the edge of the grounds where they could see across the river. Several of us went on top of the house, and with a spy-glass could see that it was no battle, but only a detachment from one of the Regiments over there engaged in practice at loading and firing "<u>at will</u>." They kept it up for about half an hour, and we had a chance to hear what a small battle or skirmish would probably sound like, at a distance.[99]

To Therena Bates, Washington, 24 June 1861[100]

. . . Nous n'avons pas beaucoup de "nouvelles du jour" ici à present. La guerre reste comme avant; et tout le monde attend l'assemblage du Congres. Mais nos soldats à l'autre cote de la riviere sont près du celles de l'ennemi et il ne serait pas étrange d'entendre des nouvelles d'un bataille à quelque heure.[101] . . .

To Charles H. Spafford, Washington, 25 June 1861[102]

I should have answered your letter of May 27th much sooner, but in a few days after I received it I made a trip out west, on which I was gone some two weeks, and then when I returned here I found a considerable accumulation of work on my hands which has so far kept me quite busy.

When Col. Ellsworth went from here to New York to recruit his Regiment, he left but very few of his papers with us here, and those were mere memoranda; and after his return here he was so constantly busy with his men that we saw comparatively little of him. I think that if the two letters which you mention were not mailed by him, they must have been put into his trunk, which was taken home to his fathers with his remains. He left no correspondence whatever here.

Of the immediate circumstances attending his death, I know scarcely anything more than has already been published. On Wednesday night of that week he was here, and I gave him a letter from your daughter, which she had enclosed to my care. He was as usual very self possessed and cheerful. This was the last time I saw him alive.

Capt. Dahlgren, of the Navy Yard, who command*[ed]* the vessels (3 in number) which conveyed the Col. and his men across the river, from his camp to the town of Alexandria, described to me the occurrences of the trip.[103]

"I landed at his camp at midnight" said the Captain, "and reported myself to the Col. who promptly responded that he was ready. I pointed out to him the difficulty of getting the men embarked which he at once readily comprehended, and at which he rendered me marked assistance both in advice and direct help. His men obeyed him perfectly, and here as well as during the whole trip (and there was danger in the very voyage itself with so many men crowded into a small vessel) behaved with all the confidence and steadiness of veterans. The same thing was apparent again at the landing at Alexandria. I was" repeated the Captain "remarkably impressed with the Col's. promptness, his constant good judgment and discretion, the perfect command which he had of his men, and of his coolness and bravery. He acted with the apparent experience of a trained officer of the regular service, and his men kept perfect silence and composure and executed with alacrity every order and direction he gave them."

The Captain shook hands with the Colonel and bade him God speed, on their way down the river; what he had seen of him would have made him his friend forever: but it proved their last meeting.

I think I never experienced a greater shock than when I heard he was dead. I had been with him daily—almost hourly for the six months past; I had talked over with him his plans, hopes and aspirations, and had learned to know so well his great talents as well as his great goodness, that I felt a direct personal interest in everything he did. That the brilliant career which awaited him should be so early ended, and that the fruitful promise of his usefulness to his country should be so suddenly blasted, will with me never cease to be a source of deep regret. His death was to me more than a brother's loss.

To Therena Bates, Washington, 30 June 1861[104]

. . . On Tuesday night I attended a little party at Mrs. Eames'.[105] Mr. Eames was formerly connected as editor with the Washington Union, for many years the organ of the Democratic Administrations here, though now like many other things passed away. Afterwards he went as Minister to Venezuela.[106] Both he and his wife are very intelligent amiable and hospitable, and by reason of their position and long residence here as well as abroad, know almost everybody, and constantly draw around them the most interesting class of people that visit Washington. Although they have but a small house, and live in very moderate style, their parlor is really a sort of focal point in Washington society, where one meets the best people that come here. By the "best" I do not mean mere fashionable "society people," but rather the brains of society—politicians, diplomats, authors and artists, and occasionally too, persons whose social and political positions merely, and not their brains entitle them to consideration, such as titled foreigners, pretty women,

&c. Politically it *[is]* a sort of neutral ground, where men of all shades of opinion—Republicans, Democrats, Fossil Whigs, with even an occasional spice of a secessionist*[—]*come together quietly and socially. Usually, we go there on Sunday evenings—say from 8 to 11—without any formality whatever, merely "drop in"—coming and going entirely at pleasure, and talking to whom and about what every one pleases. A variety of people of course bring with them a variety of languages and so while the key-note is always the English, the conversation runs into variations in French, German, and Spanish—Mr. & Mrs. Eames speak all of them but the German. . . .

To Therena Bates, Washington, 3 July 1861[107]

. . . Since my return from Illinois *[18 June]* the President has been engaged almost constantly in writing his message *[to Congress]*, and his *[has]* refused to receive any calls whatever, either of friendship or business, except from members of the Cabinet, or high officials. This has relieved me very much, both of annoyance and labor, but I expect that from to-morrow and during the session of Congress, I shall again have my hands full. . . .

After the session, which I hope may not continue more than two or three weeks, the work will, I think, be reasonably light again, although we shall certainly not lack for something to do during the whole summer. There is much more probability that my situation here will have the tendency to make me lose my temper than my health.

On the subject of the war I cannot tell you much. This place will not under even any remote chances be attacked. We have now I should think between 75,000 and 100,000 men here and on the other side of the Potomac. The whole "Confederate" army would not dare to make an attack. I think there is likely to be some activity in army movements soon. Gen Patterson is moving down into Northern Virginia, and has had a little fight.[108] . . . Gen. McClellan is in Western Virginia, where I am expecting to hear every hour of his making that part of the country very hot for the rebels,[109] while I think the large accumulation of troops in this City, betokens some forward movement on the other side of the river. . . .

Memorandum, 3 July 1861[110]

This evening the President in conversation with Mr Browning to whom he had just read his message[111]—not yet completed—said:

"Browning, of all the trials I have had since I came here, none begin to compare with those I had between the inauguration and the fall of Fort Sumpter. They were so great that could I have anticipated them, I would not have believed it possible to survive them."

"The first thing that was handed to me after I entered this room, when I came from the inauguration was the letter from Maj. Anderson saying that their provisions would be exhausted before an expedition could be sent to their relief.[*"]*[112]

To Therena Bates, Washington, 7 July 1861[113]

The interest of the week just past of course centres around the "Fourth," and the special session *[of Congress]* which began on that day. . . . On the morning of the "fourth" there was a rather fine review by the President and others of 23 Regiments of New York Volunteers, which as you may imagine formed a procession of considerable length. One very pretty incident varied the monotony of the marching by of the troops.

Among the Regiments is one called the "Garibaldi Guards" made up entirely *[of]* foreigners, many of whom have served in European wars. There are, let me say, by way of somewhat describing the Regiment, men of six or eight different nationalities in it, which speak as many different languages. It is said, I know not with how much truth, that the Colonel gives his commands in French, that being the universal language, and understood by all the captains of the companies, who repeat them respectively in German, Spanish, Italian, French, Hungarian, &c &c. to their men. In preparing for the review, each man had stuck a small bouquet of flowers, or a sprig of box or evergreen into his hat, and as the successive ranks passed the platform on which stood the President and other officers, they took them out and threw them towards him, so that while the Regiment was passing, a perfect shower of leaves and flowers was falling on the platform and the street, which latter was almost covered with them. It was unexpected and therefore strikingly novel and poetical. Day before yesterday the "Garibaldians" were sent across the river, and having an idea that there was a fight ahead, they went over the long bridge with their loaves of bread stuck on the points of their bayonets and singing the "Marseillaise."[114] . . .

To Therena Bates, Washington, 10 July 1861[115]

. . . Congress being in session, Mrs. Lincoln had a reception last night. Although it rained in the evening there was still a very good crowd in attendance.[116] Of course collars and gloves suffered.

The war remains about the same. We are in almost hourly expectation of news of a battle from Gen. McClellans division in Western Virginia. Preparations are being made by Gen. McDowell,[117] I think for a forward movement from opposite here towards Manassas Junction. . . . When the movement is made we do not expect defeat. . . .

Memorandum, 13 July 1861[118]

The President, Gov. Seward and Mr. Browning were together, and had considerable conversation about the case of Mr. Harvey.[119] The Republican Senators this morning held a caucus over the matter many of them fierce for having the Senate demand his recall, and there being considerable difficulty in even procuring a postponement of action. A committee consisting of Foote[120]—Sumner[121] and [Doolittle][122] was appointed to wait upon the President to obtain his explanation, which they accordingly did. I was not present at the interview but from what the President said this evening I suppose he stated the case as I have often heard it, asking them to report to those who had sent them, and then report back to the President their opinions and actions.

Mr. Browning came this evening more particularly to tell the President that he was satisfied that even if the Senate caucus should vote to take no action, that he had heard individual Senators declare their purpose to take the responsibility, and themselves introduce such resolutions as would cause an overhauling and public investigation of the whole matter.

During the conversation the case was again re-stated to Mr Browning, substantially as follows by Gov. S*[eward]* and the President.

Harvey was appointed to gratify the "Old Whig" interest—represented by such papers as the National Intelligencer and Phil. North American. Although H. had been one of my bitterest enemies said Gov. S. even up to the day of the Chicago Convention I thought I could afford to be magnanimous and forget it and recommended his appointment*[.]*

He had been for many years said the President one of those newsmongers, connected with newspapers, whose constant passion is to obtain "items" and as such was still here. He was a South Carolinian had been a classmate and intimate friend of Judge McGrath, who had been corresponding with him to keep himself posted about the probable action of the government.[123] H. being of the "compromising and conciliating" class of politicians had constantly hoped for a peaceable arrangement, and had frequently advised McGrath.

The "Commissioners" had come here, and though they never presented themselves either in person or by letter to me (the Prest.) yet they had informally left, so that it fell in Mr. Sewards hands a paper setting for*[th]* their mission &c. He in reply had informally written an answer (without signature) which was permitted again to fall into their hands, and which informed them substantially that they could not be received &c. Justice Campbell of the Sup. Court was also here and exerting himself constantly, to effect some understanding or agreement.[124] In this way he became a sort of medium of communication between Gov. S. and the Comrs. talking frequently with each.

During the time when we were all, continued the Prest. debating what was to be done with fort Sumpter, it seemed that all our secrets got out, and the impression gradually gained ground outside that it was to be evacuated. Though that was never determined, some members of the Cabinet being for it and others against it, yet the idea got out and gained credence until even the Comrs and Judge Campbell believed it. I think that perhaps during the time I told Mr Seward he might say to Judge C. that I should not attempt to provision the fort without giving them notice. That was after I had duly weighed the matter and come to the deliberate conclusion that that would be the best policy. If there was nothing before to bind us in honor to give such notice I felt so bound after this word was out, and accordingly the notice was given. Harvey who was laboring in the same way, had been writing to McGrath that he believed the fort would be evacuated, and when he accidentally discovered the expedition was going to provision it, he believed his honor involved and felt it his duty to give McGrath notice which he did.[125]

We had a spy over the telegraph said Gov. S. who brought us a copy of the dispatch the same afternoon that he sent it. I at once said to the President that we must take away his commission. As our notice to Governor Pickens was an official document of which as keeper of the seal I had charge,[126] and as the paper was sent by a messenger from my Department I felt the more annoyed because the affair subjected me to the suspicion at least of having afforded the means of divulging the secret. It was thought afterwards that the matter leaked out through one of the clerks in the war Department. So when I got the dispatch I called H. to me and said to him, what have you done? You have ruined yourself, ruined me and the Administration by this act. To my surprise, instead of showing any penitence he began to charge me with having deceived him, &c.

I at once told him I could hear no such talk as that—to go home—think of the matter coolly for an hour and a half and come back and then tell me his conclusions. He did so and at the end of that time came back and acknowledged his error, and thanked me for having shown it to him.

Thinking it over coolly I concluded it wrong to punish a man for being a stupid fool, when really he had committed no crime.[127]

To Therena Bates, Washington, 14 July 1861[128]

We are all in a high state of gratification here at the continued good news which Gen. McClellan sends concerning his battle with the rebels at and near Beverly, Virginia.[129] Day before yesterday he transmitted despatches of a pretty sharp engagement and of his driving out a rebel force of about 2,000 under command of Col. Pegram from their entrenched position at Rich Mountain, capturing their guns and camp equipage;[130] yesterday he sends additional *[news]* that he had pushed on to Beverly, and forced Garnett's command, 10,000 strong to retreat in great confusion, leaving all their works and camp equipage even to their cups;[131] and this morning he telegraphs again that the remainder of Pegram's force (about 600) had surrendered to him, and that he should have about 1000 prisoners, six pieces of cannon several hundred wagons and tents &c. as the trophies of his three days' work. That the loss of the enemy was about 150 killed, while our loss was eleven killed and about thirty wounded. He reports that those who surrendered are very penitent and promise never again to take up arms against the government. There are one or two other detachments of the rebels yet in his region of country which he also hopes to bag, and which will completely clear out the insurrectionists from Western Virginia. So far he has been remarkably successful in planning and executing his movements, for in his previous dispatches to General Scott he confidently promised the results which *[he]* has now the satisfaction of reporting as fully achieved.[132]
. . .

To Therena Bates, Washington, 16 July 1861[133]

Where the enemy will stop and give battle, or whether they will do so at all we do not of course know, and are therefore anxiously awaiting news every moment.

To Therena Bates, Washington, 18 July 1861[134]

. . . As you will probably already have read in the telegraphic dispatches the "grand army" under Gen. McDowell, on the other side of the Potomac, 35,000 strong yesterday moved forward towards the rebels at Manassas Junction. Our troops proceeded as far as Fairfax Court House, from which about 6000 of the enemy retreated most precipitately, leaving a variety of things behind them. They went in such haste that one of their officers had to abandon on his table, the breakfast which he had just prepared for his delectation. Where the enemy will stop and give battle, or whether they will do so at all, we do not of course know, and are therefore anxiously awaiting news every moment. . . .

To Therena Bates, Washington, 20 July 1861[135]

. . . Our army is very near the enemy at Manassas Junction, but our news from there is that there was no fighting yesterday. It may of course begin at any moment. . . .

To Therena Bates, Washington, 12 M., 21 July 1861[136]

<u>Private</u> . . . We still have no news of any decisive battle at Manassas Junction, though it is thought probable that there will be skirmishing all day, and perhaps a small fight. I think Gen. McDowell's object is to get to the rear of the enemy's position before he will offer a general battle. Actions are however almost always controlled more or less by accidents which cannot be foreseen, so that we cannot know his plan of operations. Even while I write this, dispatches come which indicate that a considerable part of the forces are engaged, so that we may know by night whether we are to be successful in this fight or not. We shall therefore have to discontentedly content ourselves with being impatiently patient until we get reliable news of either success or defeat.

Of course everybody is in great suspense. General Scott talked confidently this morning of success, and very calmly and quietly went to church at eleven o'clock.

_____

3 1/2 P.M. —— Since I wrote the foregoing—during say two hours, the President has been receiving dispatches at intervals of 15 minutes from Fairfax station, in which the operator reports the fluctuations of the firing, as he hears it, at the distance of three or four miles from the scene of action. For half an hour the President has been somewhat uneasy as these reports seemed to indicate that our forces were retiring. After getting his dinner he went over to see Gen. Scott, whom he found asleep. He woke the General and presented his view of the case to him, but the Gen. told him these reports were worth nothing as indications either way—that the changes in the currents of wind—the echoes &c &c. made it impossible for a distant listener to determine the course of a battle. The General still expressed his confidence in a successful result, and composed himself for another nap when the President left.

—From about 4 to 6 dispatches continued to come in saying the battle had extended along nearly the whole line—that there had been considerable loss on both sides but that the secession lines had been driven back two or three miles (some of the dispatches said to the Junction.) One of Gen. Scott's aids came in and reported substantially, that the General was satisfied of the truth of this report and that McDowell would immediately attack and capture the Junction perhaps yet to-night but certainly by to-morrow noon.

—At six o'clock, the President having in the meanwhile gone out to ride, Mr. Seward came into the Presidents room, with a terribly frightened and excited look, and said to John *[Hay]* and I who were sitting there

"Where is the President?"

"Gone to ride," we replied.

"Have you any late news?" said he.

I began reading Hanscom's dispatch to him.[137]

Said he, "Tell no one. That is not so. The battle is lost. The telegraph says that McDowell is in full retreat, and calls on General Scott to save the Capitol" &c. Find the President and tell him to come immediately to Gen. Scotts.

In about half an hour the President came in. We told him, and he started off immediately.[138] John and I continued to sit at the windows, and could now distinctly hear heavy cannonading on the other side of the river. It is now 8 o'clock, but the President has not yet returned, and we have heard nothing further.

Monday Morning, July 22d. Thus go the fortunes of battle. Our worst fears are confirmed. The victory which seemed in our grasp at four o'clock yesterday afternoon, is changed to an overwhelming defeat—a total and dis-graceful rout of our men. The whole army is in retreat, and will come back as far as the lines of fortifications on the other side of the river. These have all the time been kept properly garrisoned and are strong enough to make the city perfectly secure. . . .

To Therena Bates, Washington, 23 July 1861[139]

. . . [T]he result*[s]* of the late battle near here are not any more disastrous than I reported yesterday. Our forces retreated as I wrote you, but so far we have not heard that they were pursued even an inch by the enemy. I have no doubt that we had fairly won the battle, and that had the stampede not occurred among our troops, the enemy and not we, would have retreated. But the fat is all in the fire now and we shall have to crow small until we can retrieve the disgrace somehow. The preparations for the war will be con-tinued with increased vigor by the Government.

To James Lesley, Jr., Washington, 24 July 1861[140]

Please issue an order or authority, that if Captain G. A. Seidel of New York shall within twenty one days from *[this]* date have ready an organized Regi-ment, (Maximum 1046 men—or Minimum 866) it will be accepted and mustered into the service of the United States. And further, that if at that time less than ten and more than five companies be organized they shall be mustered into the service upon the condition that they agree to permit themselves to be attached to some other incomplete Regiment. Of course add your other conditions.

To Therena Bates, Washington, 26 July 1861[141]

. . . Things remain here about as they were—there has been no further fighting, and the gloom and oppression of the late disaster is somewhat wearing off. Quite a number of the Regiments which enlisted for three months, and whose time has expired have gone home within a day or two past, and others have come to take their places. We hear of no particular movements on the part of the enemy in this neighborhood. . . .

To Therena Bates, Washington, 28 July 1861[142]

. . . The city is still very quiet. There were one or two sensation rumors on the street yesterday but they didn't prove to be of any significance whatever. Just at nightfall the city was on the qui vive at hearing some cannon firing apparently across the river somewhere, and timid nerves were startled with the impression that the city was being attacked. It turned out that one of our steamers which had gone on a pleasure excursion down the river, returned and was firing salutes on her way to the landing. Of course there are constantly plenty of incidents, on which to found rumors, and plenty of disturbed and lively imaginations to give them shape and utterance. . . .

One of the most affecting incidents of the late battle at Bull's Run, is connected with the McCook family, Mattie's brothers. One of them—the youngest, I think, was killed while engaged in some duty about one of the hospitals, in one of the many such inhuman assaults the enemy made upon the sick and wounded. As he was being carried away after he fell, his brother who is a Colonel of one of the Ohio regiments, went to him and kissed him, and said "Good bye, Charley, die like a man," and went to the head of his regiment which had that moment received marching orders, and led them bravely and gallantly to the fight.[143] I think that almost the perfection of heroism.

To Alexander D. Bache, Washington, 31 July 1861[144]

The President finds it difficult, among the multitude of calls upon him from civil and military officers of the government, to make a certain and definite appointment for an interview; but will endeavor if possible to see yourself and Dr Bellows at 9 o'clock this evening.[145]

To Therena Bates, Washington, 2 August 1861[146]

. . . Congress being yet in session I am kept pretty busy. I am in hopes now that they will adjourn on Monday or Tuesday next, as they have pretty nearly finished up the business for which they were convened. . . .

Prince Napoleon who is now in New York is coming to Washington, and dines with us here at the Executive Mansion on Saturday (to-morrow) at 7 o'clock.[147] Princess Clothilde is not coming to dinner, preferring for the present to avoid the profanation of vulgar eyes.[148]

To Therena Bates, Washington, 7 August 1861[149]

. . . The Extra Session of Congress was finally adjourned on yesterday, and of course everything has since Sunday been rushing along in double-quick time.

I have made up my mind to try to get away from here on to-morrow or next day to go to Newport, R.I. to take a breathing-spell of a week or two. . . .

To John Hay, Newport, R.I., 21 August 1861[150]

Governor Andrew very earnestly desires that Capt Thomas J. C. Armory of the seventh Regiment Infantry now on recruiting service in Boston which could be just as well discharged by one of less experience be permitted to become Colonel of the 19th Mass Volunteers.[151] I have just seen the Gov'r & think it important that he be gratified. See the president & get if possible a favorable answer to me at once

To Therena Bates, Washington, 31 August 1861[152]

. . . I reached home again this morning all safe and sound, and very considerably improved in general health; at least I feel so now. If I could have stayed six weeks longer I think I should have felt better than I have done for several years.

But I could not take the time to stay. John Hay met me in New York. He himself had also been sick and was compelled to leave. He is going to Illinois to stay three or four weeks. . . . From present appearances it will keep John and I both pretty busy to keep one well Secretary here all the time. . . .

To Benjamin F. Butler, Washington, 1 September 1861[153]

If the copy of your Report concerning our late victory at Fort Hatteras is finished,[154] please give it to the bearer, Mr. Gobright, Agent of the Associated Press,[155] who will have it telegraphed to the Associated Press. If the copy is not already made, I will be gratified if you will permit him to use the original, so that he may telegraph the same.

Both the President and the Cabinet concluded this morning that the Report might at once with propriety be published, and I will vouch that Mr. Gobright will faithfully use and return the original

To Therena Bates, Washington, 2 September 1861[156]

I supposed I would have time yesterday to write to you, but in the morning Gen. Butler came up here to read to the President and the Cabinet his official report of the capture of Forts Hatteras and Clark, and that was of so much interest as to absorb everybodys attention during the whole of the morning. In the afternoon a tempting offer to ride out to one of the camps with the President, Mr. Seward and the latter's family again carried me off, and on our return the day was finished up by my stopping to dinner at Mr. Sewards.

To Therena Bates, Washington, 8 September 1861[157]

. . . This being here where I can overlook the whole war and never be in it—always threatened with danger and never meeting it—constantly worked to death, and yet doing (accomplishing) nothing, I assure you grows exceedingly irksome, and I sometimes think even my philosophy won't save me. It is a feeling of duty and not one of inclination that keeps me here. . . .

To Joseph Holt, Washington, 11 September 1861[158]

Permit me to acknowledge for the President the receipt and consideration of your favor of the 3rd inst.

To Therena Bates, Washington, 11 September 1861[159]

. . . Everything remains quiet as yet on the other side of the river except the ordinary picket skirmishing, which is a sort of necessary result, I guess, for it is constantly occurring notwithstanding the Generals efforts to keep it down. The enemy is showing no signs of any disposition to attack us, and if they did, we should not be much put out about it as our positions seem impregnable with the forces we have on hand. Whether we shall attack them is a subject upon which I have no light, though I do not expect any advance of our forces at present. So we stand here waiting for something to turn up, which in its own good time will no doubt come.

The condition of the West, and particularly of Missouri is attracting considerable attention, and it is somewhat difficult to understand how it happens that with more and better organized forces in Missouri than at any former time, the State is still in more danger both of being converted and coerced into secession than ever before.

Perhaps upon that subject too we shall have some light before long.

September 12, 1861

I got as far as the above yesterday when I was compelled again to lay it aside.

During the afternoon we heard a great deal of firing across the river, and rumors of an attack on our lines were rife on the street. It turns out however to have been a "reconnaissance in force" by our troops, which was successfully accomplished not without some loss however. . . .

To Therena Bates, Washington, 15 September 1861[160]

. . . On Friday evening our men on the other side of the river thought they had discovered some signs that the enemy intended to advance to the attack, but Saturday proved to be as quiet a day as any we have had, and we have as yet no further evidence that the rebels intend to move forward. . . .

There is a sort of sameness in everything that surrounds us here—that makes it almost impossible to get one's self interested in anything but that which somehow pertains to the war, or the troubles of the country; the subject is one of intense interest but when one is situated as I am, where they themselves cannot do anything whatever either to advance or retard it, the continued contemplation of it grows irksome at times. . . .

Memorandum, 17 September 1861[161]

One of the most troublesome affairs which the Govt has yet had upon its hands is the difficulty which has lately grown up in the West with Gen. *[Frémont.]*[162] High hopes had been entertained of him by the Admin and the country, particularly the people of the West when he assumed his command there. All went on well for awhile. The first trouble experienced were symptoms of recklessness in expenditures which were first felt by the Q*[uarter]* M*[aster]* Genl. Dept. It was found that orders were given and contracts were made in very loose and irregular manner, and entirely independent of the central office, and that supplies were purchased at exorbitant rates. This was not however so much wondered at, as his improvidence has been proverbial.

But the case soon assumed a different shape. It is now about in the third week since the *[Blair]* family who were mainly instrumental in urging his appointment upon the Prest., came to him and with many professions of humility and disappointment said they were compelled by the indisputable evidence of experience to confess that in regard to his capabilities for the important duties to which he had been assigned, he had to their perfect satisfaction proven himself a complete failure, and that they now urged his immediate removal, as strenuously as they had formerly urged his apptmt. Their testimony was supported by Gov. G*[amble]* of Mo. who came on purpose to Washington to inform the President, that he had gone to St L*[ouis]* to confer with the Genl. about the defence of the State, and that after waiting patiently for two days, he was utterly unable to obtain an interview with or admittance to him, and that this necessity had compelled him to come here.[163] A Mr. Broadhead, State Senator of Mo also traveled all the way here with a similar complaint.[164] Letters were also received from other parties making similar statements, particularly one from S*[amuel]* T. G*[lover]* Esq an eminent lawyer & citizen of St L.[165] The substance of the various statements seemed to be that the Genl had placed upon his staff and surrounded himself with a sett of men who had been with him in California and elsewhere and who made it entirely impossible for any one except his pets to gain access to him &c &c.

Meanwhile the Genl. had, without the least notice to or consultation with the Admn issued his proclamation of Aug. 31st, declaring all slaves of rebels free. This at once troubled the Prest and Gen. Scott exceedingly, as they both saw that it would have an exceedingly discouraging effect upon the efforts of the Union men of Ky. who had been pretty successfully coaxed along by the Admn to keep their State loyal. So upon consultation the Prest wrote a private letter to Gen. *[Frémont]* saying that as a matter not of censure but of caution he desired him to modify his proclamation to conform to the act of Congress, and not to have any rebels shot until he should himself first be advised of the case.

The Genl. wrote back, discussing the matter somewhat, pleading necessity and urgency as a reason for not consulting with the Govt. and saying that he would rather the Prest would make an open order directing him to modify his proclamation as it would seem like a letting down for him to do it himself.

So the Prest wrote his letter of Sept 11th.[166]

This matter of the Proclamation, however, while it involved important principles and results did not enter into the trouble with the Gen. His alleged general mismanagement and incapacity formed the subject of a long session of the Cab*[ine]*t and the next day, one week ago, the P*[ost]* M*[aster]* Genl. and Q*[uarter]* M*[aster]* Gen*[eral Montgomery Meigs]* went to St L. to look into the affair somewhat.[167]

Day before yesterday the P.M.G. sent a dispatch to the Prest. asking him immediately to appoint M. C. M*[eigs]* by telegraph to supercede the Genl.[168]

On the same day the Prest held another Cabt. Council, where he announced his purpose in which he was sustained by all the members, not to act precipitately, but to await the return of the P.M.G. & Q.M.G. and hear their story. On the same evening I for him sent a dispatch to both these Gentlemen saying the Prest desired their immediate return.

Yesterday Gen*[eral Frémont]* sent a dispatch to Gen. Scott reporting regularly to him that he had ordered Col F*[rank]* P. B*[lair]* Jr under arrest.

To Therena Bates, Washington, 20 September 1861[169]

. . . Just now we have for our "lion" a sprig of French royalty, the Prince de Joinville, a son of Louis Phillippe, and the best claimant to the French throne, should the Bourbons again get into power.[170] I went to call on him, and his two sons (who accompany him) on night before last,[171] soon after his arrival, and last night met him (them) again at a little party given him by Mr. *[Miguel de]* Lisboa, the Brazilian Minister. I have no particular comment to make on them except to say that the Royal blood in their veins does not prevent their being very intelligent, amiable and courteous gentlemen, who impress very favorably every one that meets them.

To Therena Bates, Washington, 23 September 1861[172]

. . . It begins to feel a little more as if civilized people could live here—a proposition which seemed to me very doubtful during the summer months.

——— Having got this far, I am overwhelmed with a detachment of office-seekers, who have invaded my office, and to whose tax upon my attention I must sacrifice my duty of finishing this letter.

To Therena Bates, Washington, 2 October 1861[173]

. . . I am really a good deal oppressed with the quantity of bad and discouraging news which comes from the West. Pretty much everything appears to be going wrong there, if we may credit all the reports we get. And it seems to be in such a confusion that we are not exactly able to tell at this distance where the fault lies.

John Hay has not yet returned, though I am looking for him every train.

Memorandum, 2 October 1861[174]

A Private Paper, Conversation with the President

<u>Political</u>

Fremont ready to rebel

Chase despairing.

Cameron utterly ignorant and regardless of the course of things, and the probable result.

Cameron

    Selfish and openly discourteous to the President.

    Obnoxious to the Country

    Incapable either of organizing details or conceiving and advising general plans.

<u>Financial</u>

Credit gone at St Louis

    "   Cincinnati

    "   Springfield

Over-draft to-day Oct 2, 1861. = 12,000,000.

Chase says the new loan will be exhausted in 11 days.

Immense claims left for Congress to audit.

<u>Military</u>

Kentucky successfully invaded

Missouri virtually seized

October here, and instead of having a force ready to descend the Mississippi, the probability is that the army of the West will be compelled to defend St. Louis.

Testimony of Chase

    Bates

    The Blairs

    Meigs

    Glover

    Gurley[175]

    Browning

Thomas,[176] that everything in the West, military & financial is in hopeless confusion.

To Therena Bates, Springfield, 15 October 1861[177]

. . . I shall be detained here for several days—perhaps a week. . . .

To President Lincoln, Springfield, 17 October 1861[178]

I have just conversed with Speed Butler who is here, having left Otterville Mo., where Pope's Division[179] is stationed, on Tuesday morning. Speed says that Fremont, with his army (of which Popes Division forms a part) at and near Tipton[180] (Pope is 13 miles west)—that they have no transportation and that they cannot possibly follow Price, who has had full time to reach the Arkansas line.[181] Speed represents everything in the worst possible condition, with no hope for reform. Neither Pope nor Hunter have any faith that Fremont will or can accomplish anything whatever on the contrary are quite convinced that he will not. This I learn from other and reliable sources. Speed says there is nothing but carelessness, confusion and dissatisfaction in the army, and that the Illinois troops in particular are utterly and completely disgusted.

On the day before Cameron reached the General, Fremont issued orders to the army to prepare to march, as soon as possible, detailing plans of movements &c. In about an hour afterwards the order was countermanded, and so remained up to the time Speed left.

P.S. Please keep this confidential, as it renders all these officers liable to a reprimand, if it is ascertained that they communicate with you in any other way than through their superiors[.]

To President Lincoln, Springfield, 21 October 1861[182]

I have taken some pains to learn the feeling here as to Fremont. The universal opinion is that he has entirely failed, <u>and that he ought to be removed</u>—that any change will be for the better. I am told that since the surrender of Mulligan no one has ventured to even defend him except Gov. Koerner, who was here for a day or two.[183] So far as Illinois is concerned, there will not be the least risk or danger in his unconditional removal at this time.

To President Lincoln, Springfield, 21 October 1861[184]

N. W. Edwards Esq, by virture of his appointment as Brigade Commissary, has somehow obtained the superintendence of contracting for all the

Commisary supplies in the State, and our men say that Gov. Matteson has contracts under him, <u>and is personally engaged in delivering the supplies at the various camps.</u>

Mr. Edwards starts for Washington to-night to obtain further authority to make <u>all contracts</u> of all kinds for the State, and our friends say that the whole business of furnishing the State troops, will thus fall into Gov. Mattesons hands, and that this necessarily brings the Gov. into business relations with all our friends in the State, who will thus be bound to recognize and deal with him.[185]

To John Hay, Springfield, 21 October 1861[186]

Enclosed I send you a check on Riggs & Co for One Hundred Dollars; also two unsigned receipts, a duplicate and original.

If, on the first of the month, Major Watt comes to you,[187] and says that he <u>must</u> have Mrs. Watt's salary for this month, then take this check to the bank, get the money, and pay it to Mrs. Watt, <u>after</u> she has signed these two receipts.[188] . . .

Before doing all this, ask the Major if he cannot get along without the money until I return; if he can, then delay the matter until that time. . . .

P.S. Fremont is "played out." The d——d fool has completely frittered away the fairest opportunity a man of small experience ever had to make his name immortal.

To Therena Bates, Springfield, 7 November 1861[189]

I reached here last night at about eleven o'clock after a safe and not particularly disagreeable trip. Coming back into this denser and more rapid current, I already have a premonition of my Washington life, by meeting grumblers on every hand, that even now disgust me with a harassing prospect of vexatious official duty. . . .

To Therena Bates, Springfield, 10 November 1861[190]

I shall start for Washington tonight. . . . I think the trip has sufficiently recruited my health so that I shall be able at least to get through the winter at Washington without any further trouble. . . .

Memorandum, 20 November 1861[191]

Went out to-day to see the grand review at Munson's Hill—President and others in his carriage—Hay and I in coupé. Clear track and good road going out. Received by McClellan and by McDowell who was in immediate command of review. Fifty thousand men in line. At about 12 M. the President mounted a horse as also did Cameron—Seward I think remained in his carriage. The President then with McClellan on his right and McDowell on his left rode several horses' lengths ahead while a cavalcade of perhaps a hundred officers (myself among them) followed at a swift hard gallop. The President rode erect and firm in his saddle as a practical trooper—he is more graceful in his saddle than anywhere else I have seen him.

The troops in line covered an immense extent of ground. We were fully two hours first along the front and then the rear of each regiment. Cameron gave out and dismounted before we were half done, while the President went through the whole without the least symptom of fatigue. When we had finished the circuit, the President and officers took position while the troops were put in motion and filed past. Hay and I started home near sundown and the columns had not yet finished passing.[192]

To Therena Bates, Washington, 21 November 1861[193]

The incident of the week has been the great review of 50,000 men, which took place near Munson's hill on yesterday. It must be some six or eight miles out there. John and I started in our carriage at about nine oclock in the morning and got out there with tolerable facility though the road was already pretty full of teams horsemen and a very large number of people who walked the whole distance on foot.

Arrived there, we were on an open plot of ground comprising perhaps four or five hundred acres; and being on a sort of "rise" in about the centre (there were considerable undulations in all directions,) we could see pretty well. The masses of troops were grouped about in all directions, drawn up in lines so that the reviewing officers could pass before them. The "crowd" was of course kept off at one side of the field—only the President and dignitaries being in the centre where we were.

Gen. McClellan and staff, and his Brigadier Generals and their aids-de-camp, in all about a hundred officers soon came on. The usual salutes were fired by the artillery; then several horses were brought, and the President, Secretary of State, and Secretary of War, Col. Scott the Assistant Sec. of War,[194] and myself mounted and joined the cavalcade. Off we dashed over the field at a round gallop, helter-skelter. It was not particularly consoling that one of the officers said to me, "There is more danger in a ride like this than going into battle; look out for kicking horses where so many are for the first time brought together." But there was no time for a lecture on horse-training; Gen. McClellan and the President led, and the rest of us followed, without stopping to inquire whether the road had been "worked" or not. It was a pretty long ride too; it must have been an hour and a half before we got back to where we started.

Having returned, the General, and his staff and the President and Secretaries of War and State took their position, while the troops took up their march and passed by and off the field to their several camps. Regiment, Brigade, Division, one after another came on and it seemed as if the line was endless. Like other things it too came to an end, and we were home again by six in the evening, safe, sound, and well. I had tired myself out, lost my dinner, spoiled my pantaloons, and having got tangled in the road among a troop of cavalry had come pretty near getting our carriage broken to pieces—but I had seen the largest and most magnificent military review ever held on this continent.

To Therena Bates, Washington, 24 November 1861[195]

. . . Since the review, we have had nothing new except "Hermann" the "Prestidigitateur." . . . I went to see him at the theatre on Thursday night, and last night, after his performance was over there, he came up here to the Executive Mansion and showed a few of his tricks to a few friends whom Mrs. Lincoln had invited here. His skill at "leger-de-main" is really marvellous.[196] . . .

To Hamilton R. Gamble, Washington, 11 December 1861[197]

There is no intention whatever to order Gen. Schofield away from his command in Missouri[198]

To Therena Bates, Washington, 16 December 1861[199]

. . . The only excitement of the day is the late news from England which looks a little squally, and is therefore making all the weak knees that are in the country shake.

So far, however I do not see anything that is sufficient cause for alarm. England has, throughout our whole trouble acted in a contemptibly mean and selfish spirit, and we need therefore not wonder in the least if we hear her bluster over even a suppositious error on our part.

This is purely a question of international law, to be settled by diplomacy, and I think when they come to hear our argument they will begin to draw less hasty conclusions than now. A pretty full examination, establishes the clear legality of the act of Commodore Wilkes.[200] . . .

To Therena Bates, Washington, 22 December 1861[201]

. . . Our English difficulties have assumed a tolerably serious shape; still I do not think the prospect of a war with Great Britain at all imminent. There is, in my opinion still ample time in which to arrive at an understanding by means of calm talk. War would be quite a serious thing for England as well as for us, and the advantages she might hope to gain by one, are after all very temporary. She might break our blockade, and obtain cotton for her manufactories; she might cripple our navy, and render us a less dangerous rival on the seas; she might possibly burn or destroy some of our seaport towns. All these would be serious injuries for us, but we could recover from them, and could retaliate by similar injuries on Canada. The worst phase of such a contest would be that it would retard the solution of our war with the South. The final result would still be inevitable, viz, that the people of the free northern States are to be the substantial masters—the dominating power—within the present limits of the Union, perhaps of the continent.

Brought to the actual test, the latent resources of this country will be found very great. The nation's strength in the matter of <u>intelligence</u>—I mean its diffusion—and in <u>improvement</u> will be found to play a very important part, should a really great struggle be upon us. We have during our fifty years of peace learned to <u>learn</u> everything rapidly. See for example the result of seven months study in war. In this time we have learned more about it than we had done before in the whole fifty years. If necessity compels us to study it for five or ten years longer, I feel confident we shall not stand at the foot of the class.

In all the material resources we are quite strong. Financial ruin would come: but that would not lessen the number of bushels of corn, the number of horses or fighting men.

Such a probability or even a possibility is of course not an agreeable anticipation; but should it come, I for one will accept the fact and still have faith that our national strength is equal to the task. . . .

To Therena Bates, Washington, 25 December 1861[202]

. . . John and I are moping the day away here in our offices like a couple of great owls in their holes, and expect in an hour or two to go down to Willards and get our "daily bread" just as we do on each of the other three hundred and sixty four days of the year. . . .

1862

To Therena Bates, Washington, 3 January 1862[1]

. . . The reception at the Executive mansion began at 11 A.M. at which time the Cabinet and their families and the Diplomatic Corps in all their stars and crosses and gold lace appeared and were presented to the President. At 11:25 came the Judges of the Supreme Court; at 11:30 the officers of the army and navy in uniform and at 12 M. the public. This lasted until 2 P.M. when the doors were closed. Of course there was a great jam. . . .

To Therena Bates, Washington, 5 January 1862[2]

. . . Tomorrow Congress meets, and regular hard work will begin again.
    . . . Life here at this time—even in its best phase—is a sort of treadmill which promises little else than weariness and disgust at the end of each day's task. I am not at all sure that it is any better any where else, and so am trying to bear it without too much complaint.
    We have no news here. We are all hoping that active army operations will begin soon but do not know.

To David Davis, Washington, 5 January 1862[3]

Among a lot of letters which the President took from his table a few days ago, and gave to his Secretaries to dispose of, was a note from yourself to Mr. Dole,[4] under date of Nov. 11th, 1861, in which among other things you say,
    "I am afraid letters addressed to Mr. Lincoln through his Secretaries don't reach him. That opinion is, I find, quite prevalent."
    Literally considered, this is true. A moment's reflection will convince you that the President has not the time to read all the letters he receives; and also, that say of a hundred miscellaneous letters, there will be a large proportion, which are obviously of no interest or importance. These the President would not read if he could.
    Your implied charge, however, that his Secretaries suppress the impor-

tant letters addressed to the President, is as erroneous as it is unjust. Of this class of communications they bring to him daily, many more than he can possibly get time to read. So far as I know your own letters have always received a special attention not only from the Secretaries, but from the President himself.

If, as you intimate, any other persons have similar just and definite grievances to lay at the door of the President's Secretaries, it is due alike to me, to the President, and to the public service that you communicate them at once to me or to the President.

I write this because yours is the first complaint of this character which has come from any man of standing and prominence, and because I feel sure you do not desire to wrong any one by the utterance or repetition of a mere unfounded suspicion. I have shown this letter to the President, and have his permission to send it.

To Charles Sumner, *[Washington, 12 January 1862]*[5]

The President would like to read your speech on the Trent question. I have mislaid my copy—can you send me one?

To Therena Bates, Washington, 14 January 1862[6]

. . . The President made an item of news yesterday for the country by appointing Edwin M. Stanton of P*[ennsylvani]*a Secretary of War in place of Simon Cameron whom he sends as Minister to Russia.[7] Cassius M Clay of Kentucky, now holding that place will come home and take a generalship in the army. Quite a little shuffle all round.

So far as the Secretaryship of War is concerned I think the change a very important and much needed one. I don't know Mr. Stanton personally but he is represented as being an able and efficient man, and I shall certainly look for very great reforms in the War Department. So far the Department has substantially taken care of itself. . . .

To Therena Bates, Washington, 15 January 1862[8]

We had another public reception here at the Executive Mansion last night, at which there was a very considerable crowd notwithstanding it was a cold and disagreeable night. I think that during the last ten days more visitors have come to the city than during any four weeks before. . . . I suppose they *[White House receptions]* are both novel and pleasant to the hundreds of mere passers-by who linger a day or two to "<u>do</u>" Washington; but for us who have to suffer the infliction once a week they get to be intolerable bores.

To Therena Bates, Washington, 19 January 1862[9]

I sent you yesterday a "Harper's Weekly" containing a wood cut of the reception here on New Year's Day, in which you will discover accurate and elaborate portraits of John and myself. . . .

We have still no news from Burnside's expedition, although we are in constant expectation of it.[10] . . .

To Therena Bates, Washington, 26 January 1862[11]

. . . We still have no news from the Burnside expedition although expecting something every day. Meanwhile the victory at Mill Springs Kentucky is no insignificant affair, and serves to keep us quiet till we can hear something better.[12]

To Nathaniel P. Banks, Washington, 27 January 1862[13]

If you can leave your post long enough without danger or detriment to the service, the president desires you to come here and see him at once

To Therena Bates, Washington, 30 January 1862[14]

. . . At last we have heard from the Burnside fleet, but the news is not cheering. A great storm encountered, a fleet dispersed, a vessel wrecked, and a Colonel drowned, the result doesn't sum up well at all. However they are off again on their mission—better success go with them this time! . . .

To Therena Bates, Washington, 2 February 1862[15]

Mrs. Lincoln has determined to make an innovation in the social customs of the White House, and accordingly has issued tickets for a party of six or seven hundred guests on Wednesday evening next. For years past dinners and receptions have been the only "Executive" social diversions or entertainments. But from what I can learn "La Reine" has determined to abrogate dinners and institute parties in their stead. How it will work remains yet to be seen. Half the city is jubilant at being invited, while the other half is furious at being left out in the cold.[16] . . .

We have still no news of the Burnside expedition. Yesterday one of our returned prisoners of war was here who came directly from Col. Corcoran, having been with him in his prison at Columbia, South Carolina only last

Sunday.[17] About three hundred of our prisoners are confined there he says, and up to within a short time past had been very destitute of all the comforts of life.

Jack Grimshaw[18] has been here a week or ten days trying to ascertain and straighten out the troubles Reuben Hatch has somehow got himself into over his Quartermaster's affairs.[19] . . .

To Therena Bates, Washington, 6 February 1862[20]

The grand party came off last night according to programme, and was altogether a very respectable if not a brilliant success. Many of the invited guests did not come, so that the rooms were not at all over-crowded. Of course the ladies were all beautifully dressed having no doubt brought all their skill and resources to a culmination for this event. A lamentable spirit of flunkeyism pervades all the higher classes of society; they worship power and position with a most abject devotion, and cringe in most pitiable slavishness to all social honors and recognitions. Those who were here, therefore, (some of them having sought, and almost begged their invitations,) will be forever happy in the recollection of the favor enjoyed, because their vanity has been tickled with the thought that they have attained something which others have not.

I will not attempt the labor of a detailed description of the affair. . . . Suffice it to say that the East room filled with well-dressed guests looked very beautiful—that the supper was magnificent, and that when all else was over, by way of an interesting <u>finale</u> the servants (a couple of them) much moved by wrath and wine had a jolly little knock-down in the kitchen damaging in its effects to sundry heads and champagne bottles.[21] . . .

To Carl Schurz, Washington, 9 February 1862[22]

I brought the subject of our conversation to the notice of the President and Secretary of War last night. The latter promised to write this morning to Gen. Halleck,[23] and urge the utmost prudence and caution.

At the President's request I enclose you Gov. Koerner's report to the President, together with copies of the correspondence, which will enable you to understand the exact condition of things.

Assure the editor of the Anzeiger of the President's entire confidence in and high esteem of Gen. Sigel. Please preserve and return to me the enclosed papers.[24]

To Therena Bates, Washington, 11 February 1862[25]

. . . I enclose you one or two newspaper slips describing the great party of last week. Since then one of the President's little boys has been so sick, as to have absorbed pretty much all his attention, and the next—the youngest is now threatened with a similar sickness.[26] . . .

We have intelligence this morning through rebel sources (which I hope may prove true) that the Burnside Expedition has taken Roanoke Island.

To Therena Bates, Washington, 14 February 1862[27]

. . . We are much gratified this morning to have the news of Burnside's success confirmed, and also to learn that it was attended with a comparatively small loss of life, which makes the victory the more pleasing. We are anxiously awaiting news from Fort Donelson Tennessee, where a battle was probably fought yesterday or to-day, and in which many of our Illinois troops will be engaged.[28]

To Benjamin F. Wade, Washington, 15 February 1862[29]

The President will be pleased to see yourself and other members of the Committee *[on the Conduct of the War]* at 8 o'clock this evening, agreeably to the request contained in your note of yesterday.

Journal entry, 17 February 1862[30]

The long suspense about the conflict at Fort Donelson, Tenn. was to-day relieved by the welcome news that the garrison (about 15,000 including three generals) surrendered to our forces *[under]* Gen. Grant yesterday (Sunday) morning at [ ] oclock.[31] The President yesterday sent a long telegram to Gen. Halleck suggesting several important points of military strategy not to be lost sight of.[32]

To-night, the Secretary of War brought over a nomination of Gen. U. S. Grant to be Major Gen. of Vols, which the Prest signed at once. Talking over the surrender, and the gallant behavior of the Ills. troops, the Prest said: "I cannot speak so confidently about the fighting qualities of the Eastern men, or what are called Yankees—not knowing myself particularly to whom the appellation belongs—but this I do know—if the Southerners think that man for man they are better than our Illinois men, or western men generally, they will discover themselves in a grievous mistake."

——— "What a great pity that Floyd escaped," some one suggested.[33]

"I am sorry he got away" said Stanton. "I want to catch and hang him." Continuing he said: "The last I saw of Floyd was in this room, lying on the sofa which then stood between the windows yonder. I remember it well—it was on the night of the 19th of last December *[1860]*—we had had high words, and almost come to blows in our discussion over Fort Sumpter. Thompson was here—Thompson was a plausible talker,[34] and as a last resort, having been driven from every other argument, advocated the evacuation of the Fort on the plea of generosity. South Carolina was but a small state with a sparse white population—we were a great and powerful people, and strong vigorous government—we could afford to say to S.C.— 'See we will withdraw our garrison as an evidence that we mean you no harm.' I said to him, 'Mr. President, (Buchanan) the proposal to be generous, implies that the government is strong, and that we as the public servants, have the confidence of the people. I think that is a mistake. No administration has ever suffered the loss of public confidence and support as this has done. Only the other day it was announced that a million of dollars had been stolen from Mr. Thompson's department. The bonds were found to have been taken from the vault where they should have been kept, and the notes of Mr. Floyd were substituted for them. Now all I have to say is that no administration, much less this one, can afford to lose a million of money and a fort in the same week.' Floyd lay there and never opened his mouth. The next morning he sent in his resignation and never came into the room again."

To Therena Bates, Washington, 17 February 1862[35]

We have been waiting here in the greatest anxiety for two or three days to hear the result of the battle at Fort Donelson, but are still nearly as much in the dark as ever. Yesterday morning we received despatches, detailing how Com. Foote with his six gunboats attacked the Fort on Friday, but also how his boats were disabled, and he forced to withdraw just when victory was in his grasp.[36] Last night we had accounts of some of Saturday's fighting, and a dispatch that our forces had taken the "upper fort;" but not knowing its location, we cannot estimate the value of the capture, nor its relation to the work which may yet remain to be done.

We have never feared here but that we would get the Fort, unless aid arrives for the rebels from the outside; but we have been very uneasy lest all the rebel forces from Bowling Green should suddenly be thrown upon us at Fort Donelson, before we might have time to bring up adequate reinforcements. I hope we may hear to-day that our army has been enabled to compel the capitulation of the rebel fort and forces.

The military operations of the past two weeks have been lively enough, and I anticipate a very stirring activity for some time to come. I do not think the rebels will anywhere be able to repel our advances, when at all prudently made. Unless some great calamity befal*[l]*s us, we shall conquer them, at least so as to destroy the military strength and preparation*[.]*

One of the most gratifying things is the unexpected development of Union sentiment in all parts of Tennessee. From present indications, we shall be almost enabled to hold that state by merely liberating public opinion from the thrall of terrorism, in which it has been suppressed. From Tennessee we can easily reach every one of the Cotton States, and they cannot withstand a simultaneous land and sea attack of our forces.

Journal entry, 18 February 1862[37]

Willie continues to sink and grow weaker and the President evidently despairs of his recovery.

Journal entry, 20 February 1862[38]

The same routine to-day—the President very much worn and exhausted.

At about 5 o'clock this afternoon, I was lying half asleep on the sofa in my office, when his entrance aroused me. "Well, Nicolay," said he choking with emotion, "my boy is gone—he is actually gone!" and bursting into tears, turned and went into his own office.

———— Browning came in soon after, bringing some enrolled bills from the Senate, to whom I told the news of Willie's death. He went and saw Mrs. L and promised at once to bring up Mrs. B.

Later I went to see the Prest. who had lain down to quiet T*[ad]* and asked him if I should charge Browning with the direction of the funeral. "Consult with Browning" said he.[39]

To Therena Bates, Washington, 21 February 1862[40]

The Executive Mansion is in mourning in consequence of the death of the President's second son "Willie," a bright little boy of about twelve years, which happened yesterday afternoon. He had been very low for a number of days so that his death was not altogether unexpected. He is to be buried on Monday next. . . .

Journal entry, 25 February 1862[41]

An order was issued today by the Sec of War and telegraphed all over the Union, forbidding the publication of intelligence concerning military operations, whether received by telegraph or otherwise—papers violating *[the]* order to be debarred from use of the telegraph entirely.

Journal entry, 27 February 1862[42]

It is understood that Gen. McC. has been gone a day or two, to superintend a movement from Banks division on Winchester which has been agreed on, for the purpose of permanently opening the Balt*[imore]* & O*[hio]* R.R. This evening, 7 P.M. the Sec of War came in and after locking the door read the President two dispatches from the Gen.[43] The first one stated that the bridge (pontoon, at Harper's Ferry) had been thrown in splendid style by Capt. *[James C. Duane]* & Lieuts *[Orville E. Babcock, Chauncey B. Reese,]* & *[Charles E. Cross]* whom he recommended for brevets. That a portion of the troops had crossed—that although it was raining the troops were in splendid spirits and apparently ready to fight anything. The President seemed highly pleased at this. "The next is not so good" remarked the Sec. War. It ran to the effect that the "lift-lock" had turned out to be too narrow to admit the passage of the canal boats through to the river. That in consequence of this he had changed the plan and had determined merely to protect the building of the bridges and the opening of the road. (Leaving the obvious inference that he proposed to abandon the movement on Winchester. In fact he so stated, the impossibility of building the permanent bridge as he had expected would delay him so that Winchester would be reinforced from Manassas, &c.)

"What does this mean?" asked the President.

"It means" said the Sec. War, that it is a d——d fizzle. It means that he doesn't intend to do anything.

The President was much cast down and dejected at the news of this failure of the enterprise. "Why could he not have known whether his arrangements were practicable" &c.

The Secretary of State came in and the three had a long conference.

Afterwards Gen. Marcy came in for whom the Prest had sent earlier in the evening and the President had a long and sharp talk with him.[44] "Why in the —— nation, Gen. Marcy" said he excitedly, "couldn't the Gen. have known whether a boat would go through that lock, before he spent a million of dollars getting them there? I am no engineer: but it seems to me that if I wished to know whether a boat would go through a hole, or a lock, common sense would teach me to go and measure it. I am almost despairing at these results. Everything seems to fail. The general impression is daily gaining ground that the Gen. does not intend to do anything. By a failure like this we lose all the prestige we gained by the capture of Ft Donelson. I am grievously disappointed—grievously disappointed and almost in despair." &c.

Gen. Marcy endeavored to palliate the failure—said that no doubt the

Gen. would be able to explain the causes—that other operations would go on, &c. and that he was satisfied plenty of activity in movements &c.

"I will not detain you longer now Gen." said the President, and though the Gen. (Marcy) showed a disposition to talk on, the President repeated his dismissal and Gen. M. took up his hat and went away.[45]

About midnight to-night came a dispatch from Halleck stating that Gen. Pope was moving on New Madrid with 10,000 men. The *[That]* he had heard nothing definite from the Tennessee or Cumberland as yet.[46]

Memorandum, 28 February 1862[47]

Additional telegrams received this morning from Gen. McC. indicate that he is occupying Charlestown, and that it will be wise and prudent to continue the policy he has so far adopted: to protect the opening of the road, and establish depots of supplies for further movements.[48]

Journal entry, 9 March 1862[49]

The papers of this morning contain telegram that the rebels have evacuated, and Col. Geary has occupied Leesburg.[50]

————— I went in this morning to read to the President the additional articles in the Tribune and Herald concerning his Emancipation message[51]—both papers continuing to warmly endorse and advocate it. Before this, he had brought me a letter to copy which he wrote and sent to Hon. H. J. Raymond, concerning the Times' opinion of the impracticability of his scheme on account of expense. After thanking him for the favorable notice of it he asked if he had studied the fact that one half-days expense of this war would buy all the slaves in Delaware at $400 per head—and that 87 days expense of the war would buy all in Del. Md. D.C., Mo. & Ky. at the same price? and whether it would not shorten the war more than 87 days and thus make an actual saving of expense? Think of this, said he, and let there be another article in the Times.[52]

While I was still reading to him Mr. Blair came in. "I sent for you, Mr. Blair," said he, "about this: Since I sent in my message, about the usual amount of calling by the Border State Congressmen has taken place; and although they have all been very friendly not one of them has yet said a word to me about it. Garrett Davis has been here three times since; but although he has been very cordial he has never yet opened his mouth on the subject.[53] Now I should like very much, sometime soon, to get them all together here, and have a frank and direct talk with them about it. I desired to ask you whether you were aware of any reason why I should not do so."

Mr. Blair suggested that it might be well to wait until the army did something further.

"That is just the reason why I do not wish to wait said the President. If we should have successes, they may feel and say, the rebellion is crushed and it matters not whether we do anything about this matter. I want them to consider it and interest themselves in it as an auxiliary means for putting down the rebels. I want to tell them that if they will take hold and do this, the war will cease—there will be no further need of keeping standing armies among them, and that they will get rid of all the troubles incident thereto. If they do not the armies must stay in their midst—it is impossible to prevent negroes from coming into our lines; when they do, they press me on the one hand to have them returned, while another class of our friends will on the other press me not to do so." &c &c. Mr. Blair said he would try and see the border state Congressmen during the day and have them all come and see the President at 9 A.M. tomorrow.

———— Today has been eventful. Hardly had Mr Blair been gone when Mr. Watson Asst Sec War,[54] brought in a despatch from Gen. Wool[55] saying the Merrimack[56] was out—had sunk the Cumberland,[57] compelled the Congress to surrender,[58] and that the Minnesota was aground,[59] and about being attacked by the Merrimac, Yorktown & Jamestown.[60] Two other dispatches soon came along one from Captain of a vessel arrived at Baltimore which had left Ft Monroe at 8 P.M. yesterday,[61] and another to the N Y. Tribune giving more details. The Sec of War came in very much excited, and walked up and down the room liked a caged lion. The Sec of Navy, of State, Gen. McClellan—Watson—Meigs—Totten[62]—Com. Smith,[63] and one or two more were sent for. The Presidents carriage being just ready he drove to the Navy Yard and brought up Capt Dahlgren. For a little while there was great flutter and excitement—the President being coolest man of the party. There were all sorts of suggestions—all sorts of expressions of fear. One thought she would go to New York and levy tribute—another to Phila—a third to Baltimore, or Annapolis where a large flotilla of transports has been gathered—another that she would come up and burn Washington. Several concluded it was part of a plan and the beginning towards moving down the Army at Manassas to invest and take Fort Monroe. After much rambling discussion, it was determined and ordered that the restrictions upon the telegraph be suspended and that all news concerning the affair should be permitted to go. Messages were sent to Balt. Phila. N.Y. and all the seaboard cities apprising them of the facts and urging what preparations could be hurriedly made. Messages were sent to the Governors of N.Y. Mass. & Maine, that naval men here thought timber rafts the best temporary defence and obstruction against her. Gen. McC. went to his Head Quarters to give orders to have the transport flotillas at Annapolis moved as far as possible out of danger, up into shoal water; also to prepare a number of vessels to be sent down to the "Kettle bottoms" to be sunk as obstructions in the channel in case of necessity.

Great anxiety was felt to hear further news, when at about 4 P.M. it was announced that a cable had been laid across the bay giving us a telegraphic connection with Ft. Monroe. Soon news came that the Merrimack did not get out to sea. Then a dispatch was received from Capt Fox who went to Old Point yesterday,[64] informing us that the "Monitor" our new iron-clad gunboat had arrived at the Fort at about 10 o'clock last night—had gone up immediately to where the Minnesota was still aground to defend her—that at 7 A M today the Merrimack, and two other steamers and several tugs had come out to attack the Minn. That the Monitor met and engaged them—the wooden boats withdrew at once. The Merrimack and Monitor fought from 8 A M until 12 M. when the Merrimack withdrew, it was thought disabled.

Much other important news has come in today. From Gen. Hooker we learn that the Potomac batteries are reported about to be abandoned.[65] Later dispatches from him confirm this. They have spiked their guns, burned their camps and tents blown up their magazines, and burned the little steamer "Page" which has been blockaded in Aquia Creek all the fall and winter.[66] Reports also come in brought by contrabands that the rebels are retreating from Manassas. Gen McC. went over the river this afternoon to satisfy himself as to their truth.

Tonight he telegraphs that we have Fairfax Court House, and Sangster's station—that he has ordered movements to cut off as far as possible the retreat of the rebels. It seems now certain from the occupation of Leesburg, the abandonment of the Potomac batteries—we have dispatch that the flotilla has actually raised our flag over Cockpit point, and McClellan's dispatches of tonight, that Manassas is being abandoned.[67]

To Therena Bates, Washington, 10 March 1862[68]

. . . Yesterday and today events have crowded upon us so thickly—we have been so much occupied with the excitement and details of the naval fight at Fort Monroe, and with the apparent evacuation of the rebel army from Manassas, that I have only time now to write that I am alive and well and will write soon.

To Therena Bates, Washington, 23 March 1862[69]

. . . We have no news. We have been waiting patiently for two days to hear the result of the attack on Island No. 10,[70] but no decisive result seems to be reached yet. Meanwhile a considerable number of the troops from here have gone down the Potomac to Fortress Monroe. The rebel "Merrimac" has not ventured out from Norfolk since her famous fight with the Monitor. The chances of her reappearance are pretty closely watched.

To Therena Bates, Louisville, Kentucky, 1 April 1862[71]

I left Washington last Friday evening, reached Cincinnati Sunday morning, and this place Sunday night. My primary object was to take a short trip for recreation, but came by this route to attend to some business for the Treasury Department. . . .

To Salmon P. Chase, Nashville, 5 April 1862[72]

I arrived here night before last, and yesterday morning communicated your instructions to Mr. Allen A. Hall, who concurred with the other officers in approving the change made to facilitate commerce.[73]

Mr. Hall informs me that according to information so far received, there are some eight or ten thousand bales of cotton, and some twenty or thirty thousand hogsheads of tobacco within the region of which this is the commercial centre, and which he hopes will before a great while find their way to northern markets.

This city has thus far been very quiet under the Union occupation.[74] The secession sentiment is still strongly predominant, and manifests itself continually in taunts and insults to federal soldiers and officials. The Union men are yet too much intimidated to speak out and act. They still fear and the rebels still hope that our army will have reverses and that the confederate troops will return and occupy and control not only this city, but the State. On the contrary, there appears to be quite a decided impression, that if we win another important battle in the neighborhood of Corinth or Decatur, active secessionism in Tennessee will wilt and die out. I am quite satisfied from my own observation that if our forces meet and vanquish the present rebel armies, Tennessee will return to and remain in the Union without further struggle.

I return to Louisville tomorrow and go at once from there to Cairo and St. Louis.

To Therena Bates, Washington, 4 May 1862[75]

. . . This morning we received news that the rebels have evacuated Yorktown, leaving in our possession their entire line of defensive works, over fifty pieces of cannon, large amounts of ammunition, camp equipage &c.[76] We have no intimation as yet to what point they have gone. The first thought is that they have come north to overwhelm either McDowell or Banks, but as that would leave Richmond exposed it is not so plausible. We shall probably know pretty soon as McClellan is pushing after them. . . .

To Therena Bates, Washington, 9 May 1862[77]

The President has left the City for the first time since his inauguration. On Monday evening last he, the Secretaries of War and the Treasury, and some others got on board the revenue cutter Miami, and went down to Fort Monroe. By telegraph we learn that he has been up to Newport News, and taken a look at the Merrimac which lies in sight. I suppose he will be home in a day or two if the rebels dont catch him.[78]

The progress of our arms still continues to be everywhere most encouraging. The victory at New Orleans will rank among the most brilliant exploits of history.[79] McClellan seems to be making good headway towards Richmond; all the appearances indicate that the repeated retreats and disasters of the rebels must have a most demoralizing effect upon their army. Verily the present is full of hope and promise.

To Therena Bates, Washington, 16 May 1862[80]

I am again two days behind time with my letter to you, on account of pretty constant occupation. Since the President's return *[on 12 May]* from Fortress Monroe of course there has been a great rush to see him, a week's accumulation during his absence being added to the current business. . . .

To Maj. John Fitzgerald Lee, Washington, 19 May 1862[81]

I learn that Capt. R. B. Hatch, Asst Q. M. Vols. who was released and ordered to duty by Gen. Halleck, has been again placed under arrest by Gen. Thomas, of the Western Dept.[82] Will you be so kind as to furnish me a copy of the charges against him for this second arrest?[83]

To Therena Bates, Washington, 19 May 1862[84]

We have settled down here into a sort of belief that our news hereafter will all come on Sundays. For the last three or four weeks, singularly enough it has so happened. While we did not get much yesterday, it was more than we had had for several days before.

Our fleet of gunboats, it seems went up the James River to within some eight miles of Richmond, where they came to a fort (Darling) situated on a high hill or bluff some 200 feet above the water. They could not sufficiently elevate their guns to reach this well, and the river was obstructed by sunken vessels so that they could not run by it. After a four hours' engagement (on Thursday last*)]*, the fleet was compelled to withdraw; the <u>Galena</u> one of our new iron-clad ships, having been struck twenty eight times and pierced eighteen times. The Monitor was struck three times but not hurt. The Stevens (Naugatuck) burst her gun at the first fire.[85]

We are not much surprised at the result with the Galena, good judges having always been of the opinion that she was a failure. The Monitor still proves herself the true gold. She is literally without a rival in the world.

We get news from Halleck this morning that his lines have moved up to within two miles of the enemy's works. It seems to me that a battle must almost necessarily result from such close proximity.[86]

To Therena Bates, Washington, 21 May 1862[87]

. . . Expectation is all on tiptoe again at hearing that McClellan's army moved forward to the Chickahominy yesterday and that a battle is imminent—perhaps already in progress. We shall hear to-day probably. My own apprehension is that the rebels will again fall back, and cause another long and tedious delay. I am beginning very much to fear that we will have to have a new General before we get any decisive results from the Army of the Potomac. . . .

To Therena Bates, Washington, 25 May 1862[88]

Sunday is keeping up its reputation for being our most important news day. We have been "stampeded" all day with news from Gen. Banks' army in the valley of the Shenandoah. The enemy has appeared there in force, and has compelled him to fall back from point to point, until the probability is that he will not be able to stop before he reaches Harper's Ferry, if indeed he is not captured before he gets there. The rumors are that he attacked the enemy in front of Winchester at daylight this morning but was driven back, burned the town and his stores, and is in retreat on Martinsburg and Harper's Ferry.[89]

There are also rumors on the street that there are riots progressing all over the city of Baltimore, and that another rising there is imminent. So that perhaps this letter and the mail which carries it may be captured by the rebels, and not reach you at all.

Of course the authorities here are not idle, but have set counter movements in progress which may perhaps bring down the scale on the other side.

The city is a good deal excited. Only a few minutes ago, a woman came up here from Willards to see me to ascertain if she had not better leave the city as soon as possible. . . .

To Therena Bates, Washington, 30 May 1862[90]

This morning brings us important news from the West. The enemy has evacuated Corinth, and two or three Divisions of our army are today taking possession of the entrenchments and the town. Where they are going, or what will be the effect, military and otherwise of the movement, of course we cannot yet tell.

We are all pretty well recovered from the scare and annoyance about Banks' retreat across the Potomac at Williamsport. Jackson with his rebel forces seem still to be about Martinsburg and Winchester; if this be so, then we have some hopes of retrieving the misfortune by capturing his army, for we have our forces so posted behind and around him as to leave him but little chance to get out except by fighting his way out with superior forces, which it is hardly probable now that he has got. This goes on the assumption that Fremont does not make another such serious blunder as to march in almost the opposite direction from where he was ordered to go.[91] A day or two more will give us a little clearer light on all these points. . . .

To Therena Bates, Washington, 2 June 1862[92]

Our usual budget of Sunday news came along yesterday, viz. that a very considerable battle was progressing before Richmond. Rather, let me say that the first despatch came along at about eleven o'clock on Saturday night, giving only vague rumors it is true, but leaving the inference very evident that we were having the worst of it. We got no more information until near noon yesterday, when we heard that after a severe conflict during the forenoon, we had finally repulsed the enemy at all points. It seems that they attacked us at about one o'clock on Saturday, and whipped us pretty badly until night, but that we recovered our losses during the next morning. We have as yet no particulars of the affair, though one or two dispatches received this morning indicate that it is more of a success for us than we at first supposed.[93]

The latest information from the Shenandoah Valley indicate*[s]* that

Jackson's force has slipped through our fingers there, notwithstanding that he was almost surrounded by our armies.[94]

From Corinth, it appears that the evacuation of the rebels will probably demoralize their armies very much, and will give us absolute control of the entire Mississippi River, though we are yet without sufficient details upon which to build sound conclusions. Altogether the events of the week seem to be favorable and encouraging. I am still quite well—John is recovering from his shakes.

To Maj. John Fitzgerald Lee, Washington, 4 June 1862[95]

The President directs me to say that the rules of law stated in your within letter, are correct, and approved by him, and that he desires them to be followed.[96] The order in Capt. Cothrans case, mentioned in your letter, was evidently an oversight, and is not to be regarded as a precedent.[97]

To Therena Bates, Washington, 5 June 1862[98]

Yesterday's telegraph again brought us a good report from Gen. Pope, showing that he had caught some ten thousand prisoners of the rebel forces on the retreat from Corinth. Besides this, the indication that Beauregard's whole army is much demoralized, is of very considerable importance.[99] I still adhere to my old opinion that if we can somehow scatter or destroy the present armies of the rebels they will never be able to raise new ones. In the West we seem to be in a fair way to accomplish this result. I confess I am not so sanguine as to our eastern operations. McClellan's extreme caution, or tardiness, or something, is utterly exhaustive of all hope and patience, and leaves one in that feverish apprehension that as something <u>may</u> go wrong, something most likely <u>will</u> go wrong. Risks of battle are proverbially uncertain; but I am beginning to feel that the apprehension of defeat is worse than defeat itself. In this view of the case I am getting very nervous at the long delay before Richmond. The battle fought there the other day seems to me to be hardly decisive enough to pay for the very large loss it involved.[100]

To Therena Bates, Washington, 8 June 1862[101]

Our Sunday news, this morning, while it is not so unexpected, nor of so startling a character, is nevertheless valuable and important. The evacuation by the rebels of Forts Wright[102] and Randolph[103] and the city of Memphis,[104] will it seems to me necessarily bring in their train the entire clearing out of the Mississippi River, and the restoration of commerce along its entire length. Although it will not at once resume its full former extent and activity, yet it will help materially to relieve all the western markets which have been so long deprived of this outlet for produce. It must produce too, among the rebels of the Mississippi valley new ideas of our military strength and resources, and of their weakness, as well as of the advantages and disadvantages of war against the old flag. The mass of mankind everywhere are conservatives, that is to say, satisfied with, and against disturbing, the existing order of things, be it good, bad, or indifferent. This amount of dead weight, which for a year past has counted for the rebel cause, will, if we can keep the Mississippi open for three months, again be for us.

——— Since writing the above I have been to Church (Dr Pyne's—Episcopal)[105] and on my return find a dispatch here from the commander of our gunboat fleet, saying that in an engagement at Memphis day before yesterday, he destroyed and captured seven boats of the rebel fleet which he found there, one only escaping, and which is being pursued, and received the surrender of the city of Memphis. This crowning victory I think effectually clears the Mississippi.

To Therena Bates, Washington, 12 June 1862[106]

. . . We have but little news that is pleasant. Fremont and Shields seem both to have had a battle with the forces of Jackson in the Shenandoah Valley, and although it is claimed by them as a sort of draw game, it looks to me very much like a repulse of our men.[107] It is comparatively a small matter either way, but our progress during the Spring operations has been so continually successful, that even a little reverse is painful and irritating.

To Therena Bates, Washington, 15 June 1862[108]

. . . Mrs. Lincoln moved out to the "Soldiers Home," about a mile and a half from the city this past week, so that John and I are left almost alone in the house here.[109] The President comes in every day at ten and goes out again at four. I am very glad of the change for several reasons; particularly that it gives us more time to ourselves, the crowd only coming when they know the President to be about.

To Therena Bates, Washington, 23 June 1862[110]

Yesterday passed away again without our usual Sunday news, although I half way expected we would have some. This morning we get a report by way of the Richmond papers that a battle was fought a week ago today near Charleston S.C., about five thousand being engaged on each side. There seemed to be no decisive result on the night of the battle, although the rebel dispatches indicate that we had gained the advantage and that the fight was expected to be renewed the next day.[111]

Matters seem to be drawing to a crisis before Richmond. I think there must be a fight or an evacuation before long. Meantime we can only wait in quiet patience and hope that we may have a decisive victory.

We are all rejoiced here at the prospect that the New Constitution of Illinois has been defeated.[112] That at least relieves us from the certainty of Democratic, or rather semi-secession rule for the next ten years in our State. I feel the more especially grateful as I expected that through the negligence and discord of our Republican leaders it would certainly be adopted. Thank God that Destiny at least, if not man's wisdom seems to be on the side of the Union and the cause of Liberty.

To Richard Yates, Washington, 27 June 1862[113]

Permit me herewith to introduce to you Mr. Zaklika, now of Galena, Illinois, and formerly a Captain in the Austrian Guards, who will apply to you for an appointment in the new Illinois Regiments to be formed.

I do not know Mr. Zaklika personally, but give him this letter at the request of Count Gurowski, a friend of his in this city, who knows him well, and who recommends him as a gentleman of worth and ability, in view of which I hope you will consider his application and claims as favorably as possible.[114]

To Therena Bates, Washington, 27 June 1862[115]

So far this week has been pretty quiet—excepting of course the President's sudden visit to West Point, which set a thousand rumors to buzzing, as if a beehive had been overturned.[116] There was all sorts of guessing as to what would result—the Cabinet was to break up and be reformed—Generals were to be removed and new war movements were to be organized. You have no idea how rapidly rumors are originated and spread here, nor how *[much]* importance even the coolest and most discriminating of our people attach to them, notwithstanding the fact that they are daily served with the most extraordinary Munchausens.[117] My own impression is that the President merely desired and went to hold a conference with Gen. Scott about military matters, and that no immediate avalanches or earthquakes are to be produced thereby. . . .

To Therena Bates, Washington, 29 June 1862[118]

Before this can reach you, you will probably have heard definite reports of the events of which we even yet have but imperfect and fragmentary reports here. There has been fighting before Richmond for three or four days, and very important strategic movements by the whole army. What it will all result in, we cannot yet even guess, having no very definite despatches upon which to base conclusions. I suppose that nearly all, if not the whole army has been engaged in the battles, (for there have been several) and that the fate of the whole army, and perhaps of the country is to be decided by the result.

We have so far only enough news to lead us to believe that up to the last advices we were even in the game. I am however beginning to look upon great pitched battles as the worst and most hazardous species of gaming, so that to me it is neither a cause of much hope or great fright.

Our army had pressed forward upon Richmond, until it became evident to the rebels that they must either attack and beat us back or slowly but surely give up the city. It seems that they decided to do the former, and accordingly began on Thursday last. Since then, the success appears to have alternated, sometimes for and sometimes against us. There have been changes of lines and positions, apparently made with deliberation and advantage, but of course also attended with new risks and drawbacks. The final result we have not yet heard.[119]

The city here is almost wild with rumors and suspense. The news has been so completely kept from the public that up to this morning no one had a serious suspicion of what was going on. This morning, however several persons reached the city who left Fortress Monroe yesterday, and of course brought with them all the rumors prevailing there. These have been caught up here with great avidity and repeated with their usual additions and embellishments. Some enterprising newsgatherer has collated these, sifted an intelligent report out of them as nearly as he could, and posted it up on the bulletin board at the Hotel. I think it makes the story much better for us than it really is. The bulletin board is surrounded by a crowd about ten deep, all making frantic efforts to read the news. As reliable reports from the war department have been heretofore posted up at the same place, many will go off much deceived as to the value of their intelligence.

Of course this suspense is terrible, but we have to learn to bear it very patiently here.

To Therena Bates, Washington, 4 July 1862[120]

. . . I have been at work at my desk most of the day; fortunately the President has been away at the War Department, so that I have not been so much pestered with a large crowd here.

The news from Richmond comes in slowly; the following is about the substance of it: There were battles on last Thursday, Friday, Monday and Tuesday, in all of which the victory was substantially with us, the enemy's loss exceeding ours. But as it was a sort of running fight, during the movement of the army by which Gen. McClellan changed his position so as to open a communication by the way of the James River and abandon that by way of the York and Pamunkey, we have been constantly getting farther from Richmond, and have therefore <u>appeared</u> to retreat. Our loss is perhaps 15,000 killed and wounded.[121] We have however established our communications with the James River, and secured a new and good base of operations.

Of course everybody here has been terribly blue about it for several days.[122] I do not however see anything very discouraging in this affair taken by itself, although it is to be deplored that we lose the prospect of the early capture of Richmond. But <u>nous verrons</u>.

To Therena Bates, Washington, 6 July 1862[123]

. . . *[O]*ur last advices from the Peninsula state that the Army of the Potomac is for the present where it can according to every appearance maintain itself, and *[is]* therefore reasonably safe. Burnside is also bringing some re-inforcements to it. There still appears to be some danger that the enemy might blockade the James River and thus cut off his supplies, but that fear too is becoming quieted.

In the city here there is no excitement of any kind except the arrival of the wounded from the Peninsula in the late battles who are filling up the hospitals pretty rapidly. When they shall all be full there will be a very large number of patients here, nearly all the churches in the city having been fitted up to receive them. . . .

To Salmon P. Chase, Washington, 7 July 1862[124]

Gov. Curtin has just sent me the following dispatch:[125]
"Jno G. Nicolay
Your dispatch rec'd & Much obliged for your kindness. Will not move in the matter until I rec'd Mr. Chase's letter."

To Therena Bates, Washington, 13 July 1862[126]

. . . Congress has been hurrying up its business so as to enable it to fix next Wednesday for its adjournment, and consequently my office has been overflowing with work, and I am really yet about a day behindhand.

I am right glad that Congress is going, although there are still some measures of importance that should have been passed. Altogether however it has done well, and much more than could reasonably have been expected of it—certainly much more than any former Congress has done.

The news of the day is that Morgan, the rebel partisan leader has stampeded all Kentucky and the adjacent states by either a real or pretended march against Louisville with 1500 or 2000 men.[127] I hear that reinforcements have been hurried there to head him off or capture him. What will finally come of it I cannot yet guess.

The President made a flying visit to McClellan's army on the Peninsula this week, starting on Monday morning last and returning on Thursday evening.[128] I have not yet had much opportunity to talk with him about the result of his observations, but my impression is that he came home in better spirits than he went in, having found the army in better condition and more of it than he expected, after having passed through its long and trying ordeal of battle.

The past has been a very blue week here among all classes of society except the President and his Cabinet. I don't think I have ever heard more croaking since the war began than during the past ten days. I am utterly amazed to find so little real faith and courage under difficulties among public leaders and men of intelligence. The average public mind is becoming alarmingly sensational. A single reverse or piece of accidental ill-luck is enough to throw them all into the horrors of despair. I am getting thoroughly disgusted with average human nature.

To Therena Bates, Washington, 18 July 1862[129]

I couldn't write to you yesterday for the reason that the adjournment of Congress took place, and which kept me on the run all the morning. The President always goes to the Capitol on the day of adjournment in order to be at hand to sign the bills that are hurried through at the end of the session. However as the Congressmen are getting away from the City as fast as possible I shall have a little more leisure in a few days.

I am heartily glad that Congress is at last gone, and am sure I shall enjoy the relief from the constant strain of petty cares and troubles which their presence imposes. They always have a multitude of trivial requirements, which keep me constantly vexed and anxious and constantly busy. . . .

To Therena Bates, Washington, 20 July 1862[130]

My usual trouble in this room, (my office) is from what the world is sometimes pleased to call "<u>big bugs</u>"—(oftener humbugs)—but at this present writing, (ten o'clock P.M. Sunday night) the thing is quite reversed, and <u>little</u> <u>bugs</u> are the pest. The gas lights over my desk are burning brightly and the windows of the room are open, and all bugdom outside seems to have organized a storming party to take the gas light, in numbers which seem to exceed the contending hosts at Richmond. The air is swarming with them, they are on the ceiling, the walls and the furniture in countless numbers, they are buzzing about the room, and butting their heads against the window panes, they are on my clothes, in my hair, and on the sheet I am writing on. They are all here, the plebeian masses, as well as the great and distinguished members of the oldest and largest patrician families—the Millers the Roaches, the Whites, the Blacks, yea even the wary and diplomatic foreigners from the Musquito Kingdom. They hold a high carnival, or rather a perfect Saturnalia. Intoxicated and maddened and blinded by the bright gaslight, they dance, and rush and fly about in wild gyrations, until they are drawn into the dazzling but fatal heat of the gas-flame when they fall to the floor, burned and maimed and mangled to the death, to be swept out into the dust and rubbish by the servant in the morning.

I would go on with a long moral, and discourse with profound wisdom about its being a not altogether inapt miniature picture of the folly and madness and intoxication and fate too of many <u>big bugs</u>, whom even in this room I witness buzzing and gyrating round the great central sun and light and source of power of the government, were it not for the fear I have that if I should continue you might begin to think that I too have learned to hum, and for the still more pressing need of getting all the bugs out of my clothes and hair, and after that the yet more important duty of seeking bed and sleep to gain rest and vigor for the morrow's labor. . . .

To William Henry Seward, Washington, 23 July 1862[131]

I showed your note to the President and he replied, "Tell him I can't say that just now. Ask him to talk to Mr Chase."

To Richard Yates, Washington, 25 July 1862[132]

Your letter received. The rule of the Department requires a Surgeon's certificate of disability. If Col. Morrison sends such certificate showing that he needs the leave, he can have it.[133]

To Ozias M. Hatch, Indianapolis, 29 July 1862[134]

I am here, (detained a few hours by the train) this far on my way to Minnesota where I am going to spend four or five weeks in a trip to Red River. I shall pass through Springfield tonight, stay two or three days in Pike, but will be back in Springfield, I think next Sunday or Monday, and stay a day or two before I proceed to Minnesota.

I received your letter about Mudd,[135] but could not talk with him as he had gone away. I have recommended both him and Grigsby for Assessor of the 9th Dist,[136] but have instructed John Hay to tell the President which of the two is to be the man as soon as I can see you and telegraph to him. I wish you would have your mind finally made up about it when I see you next Sunday or Monday. I don't think the appointments for Illinois will be made before that time. As soon as I find out from you, I will telegraph or write John Hay, and he will lay the final decision before the President. If you think it will become necessary to determine before that time, you may telegraph him the determination.[137]

To Ozias M. Hatch, Pittsfield, Illinois, 31 July 1862[138]

I wrote the enclosed letter two days ago at Indianapolis, when I was so tired and sleepy that I could hardly hold my eyes open, but did not send it because I thought it would be an unintelligible jumble of words. On reading it again here I find that it makes tolerable sense, and so I send it along just as I wrote it.

To John Hay, Springfield, 4 August 1862[139]

I telegraphed you to-day to have Major John J. Mudd appointed Assessor for the Pike (the 9th) District. Attend to the matter and see that it be certainly done, and telegraph the fact to Hatch as soon as it is fixed.

If the papers in the case are yet in your hands, leave out that relating to Grigsby, and file only that concerning Mudd.[140]

I will write again.

To President Lincoln, St. Paul, Minnesota, 28 August 1862[141]

We are in the midst of a most terrible & exciting Indian war thus far the massacre of innocent white settlers has been fearful a wild panic prevails in nearly one half of the state[.] All are rushing to the frontier to defend settlers.[142]

To John Hay, Fort Ripley, Minnesota, 8 September 1862[143]

Enclosed I send several letters which you forwarded to me, with directions marked thereon. That addressed to Dr Pond, you may leave in my desk till I return.

We have been unable to effect any peaceable arrangement with the Chippewas. I fear they too will be in open hostility in a day or two.

We shall probably leave here for St. Paul on Wednesday the 11th inst.

To John Hay, St. Cloud, 12 September 1862[144]

I left Fort Ripley this morning and am this far on my way to St. Paul—My scalp is yet safe, but day before yesterday it was not worth as much as it is tonight. . . .

To Therena Bates, Washington, 9 October 1862[145]

. . . I have of course had my hands full of the deferred and delayed business, and the President having been absent a few days on the upper Potomac, he was perfectly overwhelmed with the crowd on his return.[146] I have as yet had but little chance to talk to him, but think from all I can learn that he found the Army in a better condition than he expected to. . . .

Allan Pinkerton's report to George B. McClellan of a conversation with Nicolay, ca. 12 October 1862[147]

Nicolay intimated that the President was much gratified at his visit to you and had since then repeatedly expressed his confidence in you and his lack of confidence in Halleck, and from what Nicolay said I have no doubt but that after you give the Rebels one more good battle you will be called here to the command of the whole Army.

To Therena Bates, Washington, 13 October 1862[148]

The crowd still continues here as usual, and leaves me but little time for anything but to listen to their importunities and requests, and to invent and plead excuses and explanations for their disappointments. It is very irksome, very.

Nothing of interest has transpired here during the week past. Buells fight in Kentucky is still enveloped in much doubt and anxiety.[149] Stuarts rebel cavalry have made another astonishing dash into Pennsylvania, and made a complete circuit around McClellan's army, escaping again into Virginia unhurt.[150] It is a little thing, accomplishing not much actual harm, and yet infinitely vexatious and mischievous. The President has well-nigh lost his temper over it. I wish he would sometime get angry enough to dismiss about half the officers in the army—I think the remaining half would do more work and do it better by the example. . . .

To Therena Bates, Washington, 16 October 1862[151]

. . . We are all blue here today on account of the election news. We have lost almost everything in Pennsylvania, Ohio and Indiana. We have not yet heard from Iowa, but expect that that too will be swallowed up by the general drift. It never rains but it pours.[152]

We have no further army news. Buell, after turning over and rubbing his eyes a little, week before last, suddenly *[has]* gone to sleep again more soundly than ever. It is rather a good thing to be a Major General and in command of a Department. One can take things so leisurely![153]

Gen. Prentiss and quite a number of officers who were taken prisoner at Shiloh, have reached this city and called on the President today.[154] Prentiss looks well, but reports that he has received very bad treatment at the hands of the rebels. He is very bitterly incensed against them, and says we can hardly have an idea how our Western prisoners have suffered in their captivity.

To Therena Bates, Washington, 20 October 1862[155]

We still have no exciting or startling changes here. Everything goes on in its usual quiet way; the fine dry weather of the autumn is daily passing, and I discover no sign of life in the Army of the Potomac which gives me hope of adequate energy and activity. The President is anxious that it should move and fight, and I still hope that even if McClellan refuses or neglects to take the responsibility, the President himself will give the order to "forward, march!" . . .

To Cassius M. Clay, Washington, 21 October 1862[156]

The President would be pleased to see you immediately.

To Gustavus V. Fox, Washington, 23 October 1862[157]

The bearer Jesse Pratt, whom you enlisted in the Navy is anxious to get on board the "State of Georgia," because he has friends on her. Will you see him and advise him in the premises?[158]

To Therena Bates, Washington, 26 October 1862[159]

. . . The President is subjected to all sorts of annoyances. Going into his room this morning to announce the Secretary of War, I found a little party of Quakers holding a prayer-meeting around him, and he was compelled to bear the infliction until the "spirit" moved them to stop. Isn't it strange that so many and such intelligent people often have so little common sense?[160]

To John Hay, Washington, 26 October 1862[161]

Nothing new of importance. The treadmill goes round as usual. The President keeps poking sharp sticks under little Mac's *[McClellan's]* ribs, and has screwed up his courage to the point of beginning to cross the *[Potomac]* river today. . . .

To William Henry Seward, Washington, 1 November 1862[162]

The President will be pleased to see you immediately.

To Peter H. Watson, Washington, 1 November 1862[163]

Have you any information in your Department, as to whether Wm. F. Switzler, of Springfield, Mo. is the Military Secretary of Hon. J. S. Phelps, Military Governor of Arkansas, or whether said Switzler is in any wise in the employ of the Government?[164]

To Therena Bates, Washington, 3 November 1862[165]

. . . I have but little hope until we can somehow get McClellan out of the command of the army. He wont fight offensively.

To Therena Bates, Washington, 9 November 1862[166]

. . . The President's patience is at last completely exhausted with McClellan's inaction and never-ending excuses, and *[he]* has relieved him from the command of the Army of the Potomac.[167] The President has been exceedingly reluctant to do this. In many respects he thinks McClellan a very superior and efficient officer. This with the high personal regard for him, has led him to indulge him in his whims and complaints and shortcomings as a mother would indulge her baby, but all to no purpose. He is constitutionally <u>too slow</u>, and has fitly been dubbed the great American tortoise. I am sure sensible people everywhere will rejoice that he, and not the army, goes into "winter quarters."

It is barely possible that the secession element of the Democratic party will endeavor to make him a leader of an opposition movement and party; but I think his popularity is too fictitious for that. He has been made a hero by a most vigorous and persistent system of puffing in the newspapers. I do not know that he has instigated this; but he could hardly help knowing that his friends and hangers-on were doing it, and that too always in connection with an attack on somebody else. He should not have permitted this. During his country's peril every man should avoid even the imputation of selfishness. If any man ever had reason to be not only unselfish, but humbly grateful, to the Administration and to the country, it was McClellan; they have given him position, power, confidence and opportunity without stint. He has illy repaid the generosity.

I suppose that either Hooker or Burnside will succeed him, and shall hope for active movements. Defeat could scarcely be worse than the endless suspense to which McClellan has subjected us. . . .

Editorial, 12 November 1862, probably by Nicolay[168]

DEMOCRATIC WAR PLEDGES

In the political discussion of the campaign just closed, the Democratic leaders—with here and there an exception—pledged themselves loudly, and with an apparent earnestness, to a vigorous and unflinching support of the war. While they criticised and condemned the alleged shortcomings and excesses of the Administration and of Congress, and the inaction of the army and navy, they avowed and reiterated the necessity of crushing the rebellion by the strong military arm of the nation. Some were undoubtedly sincere in this expression; many, we regret to believe, used the argument merely as a clever electioneering trick.

Whether the avowal was true or false, the people accepted their war pledges as genuine, and will expect them to redeem them with suitable words and acts. The people are for the war; for earnest, unrelenting war; for war now and war to the bitter end, until our outraged and insulted flag shall have been everywhere triumphantly vindicated and restored. Whether they desire it or not, this public sentiment will compel the Democratic members elect to sustain and carry on the war. To sustain the war, they must sustain the President in his war measures and war policy. He is the constitutional commander-in-chief. He appoints the generals and orders the campaigns. He establishes the policy to be pursued, and directs the means to be employed. Of themselves, the Democratic congressmen can do none of these things; they can only prosecute the war with vigor by carrying out and enforcing the directions of the President. Either they must do this or be false to their pledges to the people.

We take it for granted that, whatever may have been their original purpose, they will respect the popular sentiment of the country, and lend the President their moral and legislative aid to crush the rebellion. To do this, they must sustain and carry out the essential war measures which he has thus far adopted, viz:

1. The raising of an army and navy by volunteers and by the draft.

2. Its organization, equipment, and supply.

3. The tax, to furnish the "sinews" of war.

4. The blockade by sea and on the inland frontier.

5. The proclamation of martial law, and the arrest and imprisonment of domestic traitors.

6. The enforcement of the confiscation law.

7. The proclamation emancipating the slaves in States and parts of States in rebellion on the 1st of January, A.D. 1863.

The Democrats of the next Congress will of course have the right to differ with the President about merely political questions and political legislation; but they must not flinch from giving their voice and their vote for the essential war measures we have named. It is not for them to question their policy, timeliness, or efficacy. When a captain orders his men into battle, it is not for them to question whether they should advance at common time or on the double-quick—whether they should fire at long range or charge bayonets, or to refuse to do either because they may desire to do the other. That would be insubordination, mutiny. The President, the lawful commander-in-chief, must decide when, where, and how the enemy is to be attacked, and the Democratic members elect must redeem their war pledges to the people by executing the President's military orders.

Of course we shall expect nothing from the covert or open traitors that may have seats in the next House. The House owes it to its own purity and dignity to deal promptly with them whenever they shall raise their heads or open their mouths. The ignominy of expulsion, and the pillory of public execration, should be their reward. The people have asked that the Administration shall deal more sternly with rebels; let their representatives also take off their gloves when they have traitors to handle.

To Therena Bates, Washington, 13 November 1862[169]

We have nothing new here since the removal of Gen. McClellan[.] So far there has not been the least excitement about it; he had the prudence and good taste to submit quietly to the President's decision, and to go home without saying anything on the way. Whether he will continue to behave himself properly or not, is of course yet a question, though I think he will. He can't himself help knowing something of how great a failure he has made, and what glorious opportunities he has wasted. . . .

To Samuel F. B. Morse, Washington, 15 November 1862[170]

Your despatch of yesterday was received.[171] On enquiry I learn that the sale of the Beaufort Library was stopped several days ago.

To Therena Bates, Washington, 16 November 1862[172]

Nothing new today, again. If this calm portends another storm soon, I hope it may result propitiously for us. It is time that the fates should be on our side again, if they intend to distribute their favors impartially. Nay, I think there is a considerable balance due us on the past, if we take our whole trouble into account.

I have passed the day rather quietly at home here, up to this time; talked to the President a while this morning—wrote a little—read "Les Miserables" a good deal,—went to dinner, and came back and "loafed" the balance of the day about the office. Being busily occupied so much of my time inclines me to the opposite extreme of listlessness and laziness when I get leisure. A more even distribution of my occupations would be an improvement.

To Andrew Washburn, Washington, 17 November 1862[173]

The President has today made the following endorsement on the opinion of the Judge Advocate General in your case:

"Executive Mansion

Nov. 17, 1862

The Governor of Massachusetts having expressed the desire to reappoint Andrew Washburn, (late Major of the 14th Regt. Mass. Vols., and dismissed by court martial,) is hereby given permission to do so.

(signed) A. Lincoln."

To Lucius E. Chittenden, Washington, 27 November 1862[174]

In answer to your letter of Oct. 9, asking estimates,[175] I beg leave to report that the sum of One Thousand Dollars will be required for the Contingent Expenses of the Executive Office including stationery, for the next fiscal year, it being the same amount that was appropriated for the present fiscal year.

To Therena Bates, Washington, 30 November 1862[176]

. . . Tomorrow Congress begins its session again, and I suppose that for a week or two I shall have my hands full. There is consolation in the fact however that this session is limited to the 4th of March next. We have no special army news. Gen. Burnside was here yesterday in consultation with the President and Gen. Halleck.

To Therena Bates, Washington, 7 December 1862[177]

. . . While I have been writing this a message has come up from Mrs. Lincoln inviting myself Mr. Hay and Mr. Stoddard, to dine with her at five o'clock this evening.[178] This is a startling "change of base" on the part of the lady, and I am at a loss at the moment to explain it. However as etiquette does not permit any one on any excuse to decline an invitation to dine with the President, I shall have to make the reconnaissance, and thereby more fully learn the tactics of the enemy.

To General Henry H. Sibley, Washington, 9 December 1862[179]

The President directs me to call your special attention to the case of Robert Hopkins, <u>alias</u> Chas-Kay-don no. 163 by the record one of the condemned Indians now in your custody, that you may not be led by a similarity of names to confound him with Chaskaydon, or Chaskaystay No 121 by the record, one of those whose sentence of death the President has confirmed.

It appears by numerous representations made to the President from trustworthy sources, that Chaskaydon (No 163) by his own personal exertions saved the lives of the family of Rev. Mr. Williamson[180] and was also instrumental in procuring the release of Mrs Huggins. The President desires to guard against the possibility of his being executed by mistake before his case shall be finally determined.

To Therena Bates, Washington, 11 December 1862[181]

Gen. Burnside has at last let slip his dogs of war. Up to the time at which I write, eleven oclock, P.M., we have dispatches received during the day and evening that at five o'clock this morning our troops began the movement for crossing the Rappahannock, but being resisted in their attempt to throw the pontoon bridges across the stream, the town of Fredericksburg was bombarded, and badly battered. The rebel sharp-shooters stuck to their cover with great tenacity, and a volunteer party was finally sent across in boats which dislodged them with the bayonet, capturing one hundred of them. The last account states that we are in possession of the town, and that everything is quiet, the rebels having retreated to their fortifications, but that a battle is expected tomorrow.

——— So we are perhaps again on the eve of great events. There is so much of chance in war that all speculation based on single movements or battles, is vague and unreliable. Only in great combinations does war become a positive art, or science. I shall however trust in the wisdom of our leaders, in the valor of our troops and the favor of the god of battles, and sleep in the firm faith that the conflict of today and tomorrow will directly or indirectly, vindicate and establish our good cause.

To Therena Bates, Washington, 17 December 1862[182]

I went down to Fredericksburg on last Saturday, and did not return until yesterday evening.[183] . . .

To Therena Bates, Washington, 23 December 1862[184]

We had a Cabinet crisis here last week . . . which again kept me too much occupied to write on Sunday and yesterday.[185]

The trouble is all over for the present. The President determined that he would retain both Mr. Seward and Mr. Chase, meddlesome outsiders to the contrary notwithstanding. I think the Cabinet and the government is much stronger than it was before the shaking up it received. Mr. Seward particularly has achieved a triumph over those who attempted to drive him out, in this renewed assurance of the President's confidence and esteem. . . .

Editorial, 23 December 1862, probably by Nicolay[186]

It is already known to our readers that, owing to the action of a late Republican Senatorial caucus, Secretary Seward, on Wednesday evening last, tendered the President his resignation. On Thursday evening a committee of the caucus waited upon the President and presented him the resolutions which had been adopted. On Friday evening the same committee met and had a conference upon the same subject, with the President and all the members of the Cabinet, except Mr. Seward. On Saturday morning Secretary Chase also sent his resignation to the President.

On Saturday afternoon, after mature deliberation, the President sent a joint note to each of the two Secretaries, to the effect that, in his best judgment, the Government could not dispense with their services, and asking them to resume the duties of their respective Departments.[187] This they have both to-day done, and the Cabinet crisis is over.

We feel sure that the country will heartily concur in the President's decision. In the many days of bitter trial through which the Administration has already passed, he has had every opportunity to judge the qualities and test the merits of these two men. By his action in this instance he assures the country that he has found them faithful, valuable, and patriotic. The task of government is no light or easy one, and it were worse than foolish to throw away the skill and experience of tried public servants. Suppose even they have made a mistake here or there; who shall cast the first stone at them? The country has a right to demand the best efforts of every man in his place; perfect service we fear no one will be able to render.

We cannot better express our comments on the recent Cabinet imbroglio than by publishing our editorial, written for last Saturday morning's Chronicle *[20 December]*, when we only as yet had the rumor about Secretary Seward's resignation:

We do not know whether the thousand and one rumors which are rife on the street be true or false, or what degree of credibility to attach to any or all of them.

But if anything could forcibly demonstrate the extreme folly of wrangling dissensions among the friends of the Administration, it is the confusion and feeling of helplessness which even the mere rumor of a breaking up of the Cabinet has created in the public mind here.

The whole "crisis" is artificial, and has been produced by no tangible or definite cause; but on the contrary by a mere indefinite nervousness of the public sentiment consequent on the late reverse at Fredericksburg.

If it be said that the repulse but furnished the culminating point of suspicions and dissatisfactions heretofore latent, but nevertheless existing in the opinion of the country, then it may be answered that these suspicions and dissatisfactions exist without cause.

There are no more or no weightier reasons why Seward should leave the Cabinet than why Chase, Stanton, Blair, or any other member should do so. There is no single good reason why either or any of them should quit it, but, on the contrary, many good reasons why each and all of them should remain in it.

Should either of them go out of the Cabinet, there would be the same differences of opinion among Republicans as to who should succeed him, as there now is as to his remaining.

The popular impression that the Cabinet is weakened by internal dissensions is essentially and entirely untrue. Upon all important Administration measures, there have been only such differences of sentiment as would be found among any seven gentlemen of high intelligence, of long public experience, and of strong independent thought and judgment. All such differences of opinion, whenever they have occurred, have been cheerfully and promptly yielded to the views of the majority or the decision of the President; and every measure determined on has been ably and heartily sustained and forwarded by each and all of them.

As to the justice and necessity of prosecuting the war to the bitter end, to the complete subjugation of the rebels, and to the restoration and perpetuation of the Federal authority over the whole Union, there has never been in the Cabinet a whispered or even suspected question.

As to the policy of the Government regarding slavery, the President himself has assumed its sole decision and full responsibility.

These two are the great questions of the day; minor matters have been more influenced by time and circumstance, than by Cabinet likes and dislikes.

Republicans of Congress, and of the country! If you presume to sit in judgment upon individuals, every officer of the Government, including yourselves, will be wanting in the wisdom, the faith, and the patience adequate to the crisis! If, on the contrary, you will review the acts of the Administration and of the party, while you may find the fraction to condemn, you will as surely find the great aggregate to praise, and to be proud of.

Patriots, our country is in peril; the foe is without and within, strong, relentless, and confident. Shall we go to battle with a united or a divided front? The good Ship of State is strained by the storm of the rebellion; shall a foolish mutiny abandon her to the elements? The gale may part the loosened strands; it can never rend the twisted rope.

Let us throw away our suspicions and sacrifice our prejudices. Let us not distract and embarrass, but encourage and support the Cabinet, the President, the country, the cause, the hope of humanity!

To Therena Bates, Washington, 28 December 1862[188]

The little things of the war as well as the large ones still continue to go against us. Last night we received word that the rebel cavalry had again attacked Dumfries between here and Fredericksburg, and had captured some guns and several companies of our infantry and cavalry left there.[189] Coincident with this comes the news that the rebel steamer "Alabama," who goes rampaging about on the high seas lately overhauled and detained the "Ariel" one of our California steamers and compelled the captain to give bond in the sum of $228,000 for her ransom before he would let her proceed on her way. This last will of course set all New York howling about the ears of the Administration again.[190]

If you ask me when all this is to cease or be changed, I am really unable to answer. I suppose when Providence interferes to give our generals a little sense or skill. We have plenty of troops, who are well placed and well supplied, but the numbers of adverse accidents, and the scarcity of favorable ones inclines me at last to believe that military genius is not as plenty as blackberries in our armies.

Nevertheless my faith is yet unshaken, and my ardor unquenched. We <u>must</u> and <u>will</u> succeed.

To Ward Hill Lamon, Washington, 29 December 1862[191]

Please notify the Supreme Court that the President will receive them on New Years Day at fifteen minutes past eleven o'clock A.M. precisely.

> Also the
> Court of Claims,
> The Circuit Court, &
> The Criminal Court
> that he will receive them at twenty minutes past eleven o'clock A.M. precisely.

To Horace Greeley, Washington, 31 December 1862[192]

The *[Emancipation]* Proclamation cannot be telegraphed to you until during the day tomorrow.

1863

Editorial, 2 January 1863, probably by Nicolay[1]

THE PROCLAMATION

True to his warning and his promise, President Lincoln has to-day, by vir-
tue of his office as Commander-in-Chief of the Army and Navy of the
United States, proclaimed freedom to all persons of African descent held as
slaves within such States and parts of States as are now in rebellion against
the Government.

Through the mistaken leniency of the authors of our Constitution, the
anomaly of African slavery became fastened upon our system of free representative government, and intrenched itself securely behind the authority
of State law, where it was sheltered from all possibility of interference, or
danger of extinction from any power, except the voluntary action of the
States in which it existed. But prosperity and influence made it bold, and
having succeeded in ruling the national council[s] for many years, it finally
sought to usurp its power, and spread its own sway over the whole land. An
exciting, but peaceful struggle at the ballot-box, extending through an entire decade, ensued, and ended in its being completely baffled and over-
thrown by the public judgment of the land.

In the desperation of its defeat, it resorted to the last means for success;
it organized secession, and instituted war against the Government. For
nearly two years past it has defied law, stolen and destroyed property, abro-
gated liberty, and taken human life.

But in doing this it had to emerge from behind its bulwarks of State protection. A Constitution of a State is not a political letter of marque against
the Constitution of the United States. "They that take up the sword shall
perish by the sword." Slavery caused the war: it is with the sword of his war
power under the Constitution that President Lincoln now destroys the right
arm of the rebellion—African slavery. Let us briefly look at the different aspects of the great event:

First, as to its effect upon the war. During the entire continuance of the rebellion, a population of three millions of blacks have given their labor to sustain the armies of the rebels, and supply them with provisions, transportation, and fortifications. Henceforth, this same population, as rapidly as it can be brought within the Union lines, shall give their labor to furnish the Union armies with provisions, transportation, and fortifications; in addition, they shall swell the Union armies by giving military service to garrison forts and stations, and to man ships and steamers.—Better than either, the enfranchised blacks, drawn to our standard by the promise and protection of liberty, will furnish us detailed and accurate information concerning the numbers, position, and intention of the enemy, which during the war thus far we have been unable to obtain from any other source, and which is as necessary to military success as the possession of men and munitions.

Secondly, its effect upon the nation. From being, at the foundation of our Government, an insignificant and apparently temporary evil, it had grown; until, at the last Presidential election, four millions of blacks, with their estimated chattel value, their immense annual agricultural product, their control of a commercial staple apparently indispensable to the world for a single year, and their overshadowing influence in the national councils by their three-fifths representation in Congress, gave them, through their aristocratic taskmasters, the virtual control of the immense powers of the Government. How this power fired their ambition to found a great slave empire, and how it has enabled them to grapple with the Government in a death-struggle, we need not here recapitulate.

But this was not all. This immense power was only at the beginning, not at the acme of its growth. Reliable statistics show that it had a vitality which would have doubled it every twenty-five years. Thus, in 1885 we should probably have had eight millions, in 1910 sixteen millions, in 1935 thirty-two millions, and in 1960 sixty-four millions of slaves. If, with its present numbers, it has so completely demoralized, and so nearly destroyed the Government, what could it not have done a hundred years hence? Could this terrible engine have been safely placed and kept within the reach of man's selfishness, cupidity, and ambition? This was a political nightmare which has perpetually haunted the otherwise blissful dreams of our most sanguine patriots and sages.

Fortunately we now have the solution of the problem. This temple of our idolatry is cast down—this Baal of our wickedness is destroyed. Instead of growing to double or quadruple its present proportions, slavery is this day practically annihilated. It will yet here and there disturb the nation with the convulsive struggles of its death throes. But ere long the Union, freshly baptized in the blood of her new regeneration, and freed from the dead and effete bulk of the slain monster will grow in a stateliness of strength, and a glory of progress and civilization, which shall shame the beauty and dazzle the splendor of the fairest future we had dreamed for her under her blank incubus of old.

And this result will surely follow whatever may be the final issue of this present war, or whatever may be the fate of our beloved Union, and our venerated Constitution. Whether the nation lives or dies, whether the Government survives or perishes, whether the Union triumphs or disunion succeeds, slavery is equally dead in all possible contingencies. Thus far, our second great revolution has been a struggle of principles as well as a struggle of arms. To-day, the principle of right and justice and liberty has dealt its antagonist the mortal wound from which it can never recover; and there remains but the struggle of arms for the integrity of the Republic, in which the God of battles will as surely give us the victory.

Thirdly, its effect upon mankind. This day is also the initial point of the separation of the black from the white race. The two races cannot live together under the contingencies of future growth and expansion. The white man is the child of the snow, the black man is the child of the sun. One finds his natural and congenial home in the North, the other in the South. The accidents of destiny may confuse and change their abiding place for a time, but the same destiny is in its grander operations always true to nature, and will in due time lead each to his land of promise. We can hardly be mistaken in predicting that the United States are to be the theater of the white man's achievements for some centuries to come; and we may as confidently hope that a great and useful future may be wrought out by the black race in the equatorial regions of Central and South America. That statesman will be both wise and benevolent who begins now to study and solve the problem of an eventual exodus from the United States, and a successful and prosperous colonization within the tropics of this continent of the black nation today liberated by the President's wise and just decree. So separated and so reorganized, what political seer shall foretell the happy influence of both in the great work of enlightening and civilizing and humanizing the whole brotherhood of man by their labors in agriculture, in commerce, in art, and in government?

So much for the material aspect. But is not the moral view also worth a single thought? From Plato to Hugo, those idle dreamers, the philosophers and poets, have exhorted the world to love and adopt Justice and Liberty, and to hate and abandon Wrong and Oppression. As nations have approximated to these ideals, they have become prosperous and happy; as they have discarded them, they have become degraded and miserable. Call them crazy enthusiasts if you will; but do not forget that our eighty years of practical national happiness is the direct fruition of their insane ravings. In view of this, shall not the President's act of to-day become a great moral landmark, a shrine at which future visionaries shall renew their vows, and a pillar of fire which shall yet guide other nations out of the night of their bondage?

And for this New Year's gift, the man who has wrought the work, amid the doubts of friends, the aspersions of foes, the clamors of faction, the cares of Government, the crises of war, the dangers of revolution, and the manifold temptations that beset moral heroism, Abraham Lincoln, the President of the United States, is entitled to the everlasting gratitude of a despised race enfranchised, the plaudits of a distracted country saved, and an inscription of undying fame in the impartial records of history.

To Therena Bates, Washington, 4 January 1863[2]

We are in a state of feverish anxiety here about the final result of the battle which Rosecrans has been fighting near Murfreesboro Tenn. and which has now lasted three or four days.[3] We get no official dispatches from any of the officers, and have to rely solely on the reports that come to the newspapers and which have been so far so evenly balanced in their general tenor that we neither glean victory nor defeat from them. As the telegraph lines are this morning reported to be again in order perhaps we may hear some decisive news soon.

Our famous and favorite "Monitor" has had a short as well as a brilliant career*[.]* We learned yesterday afternoon, so reliably that there seems no room for doubt that she foundered in a gale off Cape Hatteras, taking two officers and twenty eight men down with her.[4] It seems to*[o]* much like losing an old and trusted friend! I shall never forget how we all hailed her as a deliverer when amid our consternation here which the appearance of the Merrimac created, she came so opportunely to relief. . . .

To Therena Bates, Washington, 11 January 1863[5]

. . . We have but little news from the war in addition to the fact that our army did not succeed in its first attempt on Vicksburg.[6] We hope to hear better results soon, as well as good reports from the operations of Gen. Banks from New Orleans upwards.

I think we have great dangers to apprehend from the treasonable attitude which the Democratic party of the North is everywhere preparing to assume. Under the subterfuge of opposing the Emancipation Proclamation they are really organizing to oppose the War. It is a very bold issue for them to make and I do not think they can succeed with it, but they may give us great trouble. So much depends upon the success or failure of our arms that it seems idle to speculate at all about the matter.

To Therena Bates, Washington, 15 January 1863[7]

. . . Our military condition I am sorry to say, does not appear as yet to improve. Little disasters still tread on each others heels. Nevertheless every point is being strained by the government, and we must continue to hope in patience.

To Therena Bates, Washington, 18 January 1863[8]

. . . I hardly know what to write you this morning, as we have no news except the little crumb of comfort of McClernand's success in taking Arkansas Post, with seven thousand rebel prisoners, the report of which he telegraphed us last night over his own signature so that we may take it as a fact.[9] . . .

To Therena Bates, Washington, 23 January 1863[10]

Nothing of interest has transpired here since my letter of last Sunday, except the trial and dismissal of Maj. Gen. Fitz-John Porter. From the great ability with which his legal counsel conducted his defence on the trial, public opinion had settled down into the belief that he would certainly be acquitted. It however turns out otherwise, and of course all his friends are howling with indignation. I have no doubt the court investigated the case fairly and impartially and that the finding was warranted by the testimony.[11] Whatever may be the justice of the sentence, I have no doubt the result of the trial will have a salutary influence on the discipline and morale of the army, teaching the officers that the principle of accountability to the government is not yet obsolete.

The army of the Potomac was to have made another movement a day or two ago, but the late heavy storm has in all probability frustrated the design.[12]

To Therena Bates, Washington, 25 January 1863[13]

I walked up this morning to the Senate Chamber to hear a sermon by M. D. Conway, an Abolitionist, but one of the most eloquent men of the country.[14] I should be willing to go to Church every Sunday, if I could hear a sermon of equal power[.]

We have no further news from the army. General Burnside was here this morning in consultation with the powers that be.[15] I have not learned either the object or result of the conference. . . .

To Therena Bates, Washington, 1 February 1863[16]

. . . We have had nothing new except a severe snow-storm that has given us the severest touch of winter we have yet had. It made our streets almost impassable, and brought with it many other disagreeable consequences, not the least of which is that it for the present leaves the Army of the Potomac hopelessly stuck in the mud. . . .

We have news of a little brush between our troops and the rebels on the Blackwater in which we had the advantage, but as it was comparatively a small fight it will not bring any decisive results.[17]

We hope to hear good news soon from the region of Vicksburg.

To Therena Bates, Washington, 8 February 1863[18]

. . . We have still no news of importance, although beginning to expect some from several different directions—Vicksburg, Port Hudson, Charleston, and several minor points. The army of the Potomac is for the present stuck in the mud, as it has been during nearly its whole existence. We hope however that it may yet do something, by accident at least, if not by design. I think we all doubt its ability to help in the great struggle more because of the sort of fatality which has hitherto attended it, than by any just estimate of its strength and discipline. Whether or not Hooker can manage it is yet an experiment.[19] We hope for the best.

To Simon Cameron, Washington, 10 February 1863[20]

Your note of the 8th has reached and been read by the President. It however mentions a letter from Mr. Gittings which has not come to hand. I write you this thinking that perhaps you forgot to inclose it as you may have intended.[21]

To Joseph Holt, Washington, 13 February 1863[22]

Mr. Nicolay has the honor to accept Mr. Holt's kind invitation to dinner, on Thursday February 19th, at six oclock.

To Therena Bates, Washington, 15 February 1863[23]

. . . On Friday night *[I went]* first to a little reception given by Mrs. Lincoln to Tom Thumb and his bride,[24] then to Mrs. Speaker Grow's reception,[25] then to a party at Mrs. Bacon's, then to a large party given by the Russian Minister. . . .

We have no news from the war. We suppose Grant and Banks to be doing all they can, and must wait their efforts with patience.

To Col. James B. Fry, Washington, 23 February 1863[26]

Is this man's name among those who have been appointed?[27]

To William Henry Seward, Washington, 26 February 1863[28]

The President directs me to say that he has not time just now to read the enclosed, but that he sees no objection to its publication.

To Therena Bates, Washington, 1 March 1863[29]

. . . I have been quite busy again this week, but have the satisfaction of knowing that Congress must adjourn next Tuesday night. So much of the business of confirming appointments, however, has been left undone by the Senate that the President will have to call an extra session of that house, which will keep the members here a week or two longer. . . .

We have no additional war news as yet, although we are anxiously awaiting some.

To Edwin M. Stanton, Washington, 6 March 1863[30]

The President desired me to say that you may take the name of Sturgis off the list of Major Generals,[31] and substitute Parke or any one whom you and Gen. Halleck may think best.[32]

To Therena Bates, Washington, 8 March 1863[33]

. . . The telegraph brought us news night before last of another serious reverse in Tennessee—an entire brigade which Rosecrans sent out to reconnoitre having been routed, killed, and taken prisoner.[34] Of course carelessness or inefficiency must have been the cause. It is very hard not entirely to lose one's patience at this succession of adverse accidents which seems to have no end. . . .

To Therena Bates, Washington, 15 March 1863[35]

The Senate finally adjourned yesterday at two oclock, after a week's very constant and industrious work, and I have the hope of a little intermission in the hurry and confusion of the last three months. That I shall enjoy and appreciate it, there is no doubt. Taking the winter altogether I have gone through much more easily and comfortably than I expected to do at its beginning. I feel much fresher and stronger than I did at this time last year and have no doubt that I shall still greatly improve in this respect, with the leisure and mild weather of the Spring.

John Hay went to New York last Thursday, and goes from there sometime this week to Hilton Head, S.C. for a two or three weeks' visit to Gen. Hunter.[36] I see the newspapers report that he goes to accept a place on Gen. Hunter's staff, which is not correct. He does hope to help the General take Charleston, but in an amateur and not a professional capacity.

Our army news does not amount to much. We had an amusing letter from Commodore Porter, describing how he one night built an imitation "monitor" and floated it down past Vicksburg, which so frightened the rebels that they sent down a hurried order and blew up the Indianola lately captured from us. Chinese warfare seems to pay best, and I am getting decidedly of the opinion that we should give the Celestial tactics a fair trial. At any rate we are even with the rebels on "Quaker guns."[37]

To Therena Bates, Washington, 19 March 1863 [38]

Our reverses still seem to continue. Information received through rebel sources states that Admiral Farragut attempted to pass the batteries at Port Hudson with his fleet, but was disabled and driven back, one ship, the Mississippi being burnt to the waters edge.[39] As we knew previously that he intended to make the attempt to pass, the story has the air of credibility. We shall probably learn the truth more fully before a great while.

I had supposed our fleet would have made an attack on Charleston or Savannah before this, but the delays seem never-ending.

The spring weather has been so terribly bad that we need not expect a movement from the army of the Potomac yet a while. From Vicksburg we ought to hear something soon. . . .

To Therena Bates, Washington, 22 March 1863 [40]

So far the month of March has brought us the wintriest weather of the present winter. For the last two weeks we have had almost a perpetual snowstorm, with all its inclement attendings. This morning the sun smiles out again, but with a very feeble and sickly luster. Good roads are a thing we remember to have had, but so long since, that the imagination has lost its power to reproduce them.

The week has not brought any very important events, nor even foreshadowed any very important transactions, either military or political. The feeling of the country is I think every day becoming more hopeful and buoyant . . . a very healthy reaction against Copperheadism becoming everywhere manifest. They will yet be made to repent their treason in sackcloth and ashes. The country is waking up to an appreciation of the shameful dishonor which any cessation of the war would involve us in, that does not first accomplish the complete subjugation of the rebels. Illinois presents the paradoxical spectacle of being at the same time the most loyal and most disloyal northern state.[41] What a load of sin rests on the Democratic party for thus having misled her people!

But I dont dare trust myself either to talk or write about it. It should be a battle of swords not words.

To Daniel Ullman, Washington, 26 March 1863[42]

The name of the officer of whom I promised to remind you (who desires to command a negro regiment) is Capt. M. S. Littlefield; he is an energetic brave and experienced soldier.[43] If an opportunity to make him serviceable presents itself, please inform me.

To Therena Bates, Washington, 29 March 1863[44]

. . . There has been no special stir about anything. The war news has all been very meagre and that which did come, so generally unsatisfactory, that one did not care to look at or think of it a second time. The weather has been disgustingly bad all week, to add to the general uninvitingness of all matters.

This blankness of experience is becoming too intense, (if you will allow a paradoxical expression.) I am beginning to want to get away very badly—somewhere—anywhere almost, where I could have either more leisure or more excitement—something besides mere dull profitless labor, as this seems to be. Unfortunately John is just going to take his trip to South Carolina, which will take him a month or six weeks at least, and therefore I cannot even think of a furlough until he returns. . . .

To Therena Bates, Washington, 5 April 1863[45]

I am literally alone in the house here today. John Hay left last Thursday morning for New York, and sailed in the "Arago" yesterday morning for Hilton Head. He expects to help Gen. Hunter capture Charleston. I hope he may—but am afraid that Charleston problem is a harder one than we imagine.

The President and Mrs. Lincoln started away yesterday evening for a brief visit to the Army of the Potomac. They will be gone three or four days.[46]

If I were not of a very hopeful disposition I should feel blue about military affairs. Grant's attempt to take Vicksburg looks to me very much like a total failure, with the possible danger that the whole "Yazoo Expedition" may be cut off and captured.[47] At Port Hudson we are held at bay;[48] at Charleston our chances for success are too small;[49] and the Army of the Potomac, in addition to seeming <u>fated</u> never to accomplish anything even under the most favorable contingencies, is still hopelessly weather-bound. Do not understand that I am despairing. I only mean that the present programme looks unsatisfactory to me. But if the present programme fails, we will devise and try a new one. We <u>must</u> and <u>will</u> succeed. . . .

To Therena Bates, Washington, 9 April 1863[50]

I am still enjoying the quiet in the house produced by the President's absence. He has not yet returned from Fredericksburg, or rather Falmouth, and consequently the crowd that usually haunts the antechamber and my office keep at a distance. He will probably be back again by tomorrow, when they will once more swarm in upon us like Egyptian locusts. . . .

To William B. Edwards, Washington, 9 April 1863[51]

I am instructed by the President of the United States to acknowledge your favor of March 10th, enclosing the resolution passed by the Baltimore Conference of the M. E. Church, at its late session in Georgetown, and to thank you and them for their expression of piety and patriotism.

To John Hay, Washington, 10 April 1863[52]

. . . The President and Mrs. L. went to Falmouth last Saturday and are there yet. I guess the Tycoon has concluded to follow your example and go on Hooker's staff. . . .

To William Henry Seward, Washington, 12 April 1863[53]

The President will endeavor to call as you request.

To Therena Bates, Washington, 16 April 1863[54]

Since I wrote you, on Sunday last, we have received pretty full news from Charleston concerning the late fight there. The Admiral and other officers there the day after the attack came to the conclusion it was a failure and resolved to abandon it. I can hardly understand why they came to this determination so soon, for after all the damage done us was very slight (the Keokuk being a comparatively weak vessel, not built on the Monitor plan.)[55] To counterbalance the sinking of our ship and the trifling derangement of some of the Monitors, we had tested their comparative invulnerability and had found and secured possession of a safe and important anchorage inside Charleston Bar, from which we could greatly lessen the line of blockade, and more important than all it substantially commanded a part at least of Morris Island enabling us to gain a lodgment there by landing troops, and beginning a series of siege operations that might of themselves render Fort Sumpter untenable. This advantage was partially thrown away by the subsequent withdrawal of the whole iron-clad fleet, leaving the enemy undisturbed in the work of erecting new batteries, which they began, even before we left, to protect that only weak point in their defences. I am inclined to think Admiral Du Pont has ere this discovered that he made a mistake in thus leaving, and has gone back to renew operations to again secure the points named.[56] Morris Island may yet be found to be the "heel of Achilles." Nous verrons.

It has been raining for two days—again delaying our hopes of dry roads and a speedy movement of Hooker's Army.

To John Hay, Washington, 20 April 1863[57]

. . . The President and Secretary of War went off on a reconnaissance yesterday—I suppose to Acquia Creek but returned in the evening. What they did or saw has not transpired. . . .

To Therena Bates, Washington, 29 April 1863[58]

Very queer characters occasionally call on me here. That you may be reassured in the prospect of a speedy crushing out of the rebellion, I must inform you of a new leader and agency about to take part in the contest.

The other morning my doorkeeper brought in a plain-looking but also very rational-looking man, ordinarily dressed, appearing, perhaps more than anything else to be a farmer. I asked him to be seated, which he did, when he at once without circumlocution, and in a very matter-of-fact and business-like way stated the object of his call.

"I come here" said he "about the business of this war we are engaged in. I am commissioned from on high to take [the] matter in hand and end it. I have consulted with the Gov. of 'York state,' and he has promised to raise as many men of the militia of that State as I need. But as I didn't want to proceed without authority I came on here to see Gen. Halleck. I have had an interview with him and he told me that he could not give me any men or assistance, that nobody but the President had authority to act in the case. I have therefore come to see the President to obtain his consent to begin the work. Although no power is competent to stop or impede my progress, yet I desired to act with the approval of the authorities. I shall take only two thousand men, and shall go down South, and get Jeff Davis and the other leaders of the rebellion and bring them here to be put in the lunatic asylum—because they are plainly crazy, and it is of no use to be fighting with crazy men."

In reply I assured him that the President was so engaged that it would be impossible for him to gain the desired interview—that the President would give him no men, nor authority of any kind—and that whatever he did in the matter he must do on his own responsibility. He appeared to be satisfied that I properly represented the President, and went away saying that he should write at once to the Governor of "York State*["]* to raise and organize his force for him, and proceed with his work.

All this transpired with as much gravity and method as if it had been a little conference about any matter of routine business, and an observer would have thought that I was as crazy as the man himself, from the perfectly serious and natural manner in which both he and I talked the matter over. Lunatics and visionaries are here so frequently that they cease to be strange phenomena to us, and I find the best way to dispose of them is to discuss and decide their mad projects as deliberately and seriously as any other matter of business.[59] . . .

To Therena Bates, Washington, 3 May 1863[60]

The grand army of the Potomac, under Hooker's leadership is again in motion, having begun on Monday last, and crossed the Rappahannock both above and below Fredericksburg on Tuesday and Wednesday last. We know very little as yet as to what was attempted, or what has been accomplished, except that that part of it which crossed above has gained a very important and advantageous (apparently) position on the flank of the rebel position at Fredericksburg. Still the value of strategical positions after all depends on the final working out of the whole problem, in which the movements of the enemy plays a very prominent part. Hooker himself seems to attach a great deal of value to the success of his first movements for he issued a congratulatory order to his army, in which he stated that the enemy would be compelled to come out and fight. A dispatch from his chief of staff was received yesterday in which he incidentally remarks that they are having "a lively time." We infer from this that they perhaps had a battle yesterday, but of course cannot guess as to its extent or result. For the present we are obliged to content ourselves in patience, with a silent prayer for the success of our arms.

These impending or transpiring events of course absorb universal interest. The city is full of rumors, many of them very wild and extravagant, ranging from brilliant success to disastrous defeat, usually according to the wishes and sympathies of their retailers. Nothing reliable is known, however, beyond what I have stated, by any one. . . .

To Therena Bates, Washington, 4 May 1863[61]

We have been in a terrible suspense here for two days as to the result of the battle which Gen. Hooker is fighting on the Rappahannock, nor have we yet any definite information on the subject.[62]

His movement of last week had precisely the effect which he expected and intended viz: the enemy, finding him in position at Chancellorsville, were compelled to leave their entrenchments at Fredericksburg and come out and fight him. He maintained this fight, as we learned yesterday at about four o'clock for all of Saturday and half of Sunday (yesterday,) but at the time we received news, had been driven back from his position, and had lost several batteries of artillery. Sedgwick, who with a part of the force had crossed below Fredericksburg, had not come to his aid as he had expected, and he did not know where he was, nor when he could come.[63] He was however still in good spirits and "did not despair of success." This was the first news we received and made us feel very gloomy.

Very soon after however we began to hear that Sedgwick had come up the river to the town of Fredericksburg and had attacked and stormed the batteries and heights just back of it, (where Sumner was repulsed at the last battle,)[64] and that he had passed on over the hills and was several miles on his way on the direct road to Chancellorsville, to either fall upon the rear of the enemy or to join Hooker. This very welcome news was confirmed by messengers who had been lookers-on of the fight, and who came successively one at about 12 o'clock last night, and the other at three this morning. This last man had not slept for two nights and had a terrible haggard and staring look.

This morning at ten another man came through who left Hookers camp at nine P.M. last night, and says that there was fighting all yesterday afternoon, the advantage remaining with us.

Through last night and today boats have been from time to time coming up from Acquia Creek which have so far brought 800 to 1000 rebel prisoners captured by us at the storming of Fredericksburg heights on yesterday morning.

Today at three o'clock an officer comes up, who brings the body of Maj. Gen. Berry of Maine, killed in Hooker's fight,[65] and says he learned that the enemy have again recaptured the works and heights at Fredericksburg. We do not as yet however get any confirmation of the intelligence, which would be very bad if true.

As I write the funeral escort of Gen. Berry, infantry cavalry and artillery, with draped banners and bands playing dirges is passing along P*[ennsylvani]*a Ave.

In this way our news fluctuates from good to bad. We have no dispatch from Hooker, the understanding being that he will not report until he has results which he deems decisive. Nor do his officers telegraph. So we are compelled to pick up our news as we best can, and at this writing, 6 P.M. Monday we are about as much in the dark as to the final result as we were on Saturday night.

Wednesday, 6 May, 3 P.M.

I wrote the above expecting to send it yesterday, but the still undecided character of the news led me to defer it until we should hear something definite. I am pained to be compelled to add that the news after fluctuating all of yesterday and today between good and bad finally settled down into the disagreeable but stern fact that Hookers attempt to beat the rebel army is again a failure, and that he has felt himself compelled to recross to the north bank of the Rappahannock to save the army from danger of defeat. In the bitterness of disappointment I can add no comment*[.]*

To Ozias M. Hatch, Washington, 5 May 1863[66]

. . . Hooker has been fighting nearly a week on the Rappahannock, but as yet without any decisive results so far as we know. We have but little information beyond what you will find in the newspapers up to date.

To Ozias M. Hatch, Washington, 6 May 1863[67]

Your dispatch of March 9th recommending prov*[ost]* marshals reads ninth district Benj F Weist Pittsfield Ill Should it not be Benj F Westlake Ans*[wer.]*[68]

To Col. A. H. Bowman, Washington, 9 May 1863[69]

The President of the United States directs me to acknowledge the receipt of your letter of the 6th inst., reporting the completion and readiness of a large Map, illustrating the Campaigns of Napoleon, which you were kind enough to promise to have prepared for him, at the time of his visit to West Point *[in June 1862].*

He will be pleased to have you forward it to him here as you suggest.

To Therena Bates, Washington, 10 May 1863[70]

As soon as the President received the news that Hooker had returned to this side of the Rappahannock with his army he and Genl. Halleck at once went down there to satisfy himself as to its true condition.[71] Considering that the movement had taken him somewhat by surprise he came home tolerably well reconciled to it, although the information of the entire success of Stonemans cavalry expedition,[72] which we have since received makes it pretty plain that it would have been better for Hooker to have remained on the other side, and to have fought out the battle there—at least so it seems to me. Still Hooker did not have all these data to judge from and therefore perhaps decided rightly. It was however a great disappointment to the country, which is terribly impatient for military success.

The army is still in excellent condition. Only three of the seven army corps were much in the fight. . . . All the indications are that the enemy suffered much more severely than we in the conflict.[73] An intercepted dispatch from Lee to one of his subordinates in Western Virginia states that their loss was "fearful."

Exchanged prisoners who were in Richmond at the time, state that our cavalry penetrated within sight of the city, and the force, (some 400 strong) who were in that neighborhood could have easily gone into and captured it, or at least destroyed all the valuable rebel stores buildings and machinery, as there were no rebel soldiers left in it. It is a great pity the opportunity could not have been taken advantage of, but of course our troops had no means of knowing the fact.

Fortunately Porter and Grant seem to be making some headway on the Mississippi, one having captured Grand Gulf, and the other taken some guns and prisoners at Port Gibson, and that occupies and diverts public attention somewhat.[74]

To Therena Bates, Washington, 17 May 1863[75]

The past week has not brought us any remarkable occurrences, and therefore I have no special news to write. The old "all quiet on the Rappahannock" seems to be fully reestablished. . . .

The President has just been in my room for a little while, and among other things told me that Senators Wade and Chandler,[76] who returned from the army yesterday, report that it is in good spirits and courage, and that they think it would be able to cross and whip the enemy now. The pickets stationed along on each side of the Rappahannock have gone back to their old pastime of bandying wit and repartee across the river. "I say Yank," shouted over one of the rebels, "where is fightin' Joe Hooker, now?" "Oh, he's gone to Stonewall Jackson's funeral," shouted "Yank" in reply.

It is nearly time we were hearing something from Grant. At last accounts he had beaten the enemy handsomely at Port Gibson, and was moving toward the railroad bridge over the Big Black river in the rear of Vicksburg. It looks to us here very much as if that must bring on a decisive struggle there in which the enemy must either defeat us or we will defeat them. . . .

To Therena Bates, Washington, 25 May 1863[77]

The success of Grant's operations around and about Vicksburg is really glorious and inspires new satisfaction and hope among all. Our last news is to the effect that Grant after having fought a successful battle nearly every day for about a week, has finally invested Vicksburg itself with every favorable prospect of its capture. We are anxiously awaiting further news before we give full vent to our exultation, as we know from sad experience how often performance finally falls short of promise.[78] The praise of our western soldiers is on every lip, Illinois valor particularly receiving as it properly should, large honor. If, as we now fondly hope and pray, Grant can capture Vicksburg and the rebel army in it together, our pleasure will only be kept within bounds by the sorrowful recollection of how many of our brave boys have given their health and life to win the proud victory. Still I shall say the prize is worth the price. With their blood shall liberty cement her enduring foundations, and with the fire of their heroism feed forever the quenchless flame on her altar.

To Therena Bates, Washington, 31 May 1863[79]

It is Sunday again, and we are yet without our expected news of the capture of Vicksburg; though all our news indicates that the siege is progressing steadily and satisfactorily, and that the place must eventually fall. But so much depends upon our taking it speedily, that my impatience illy restrains itself. I think the rebels are preparing their minds to hear of its loss to them—at least so the tone of their papers and their studious silence indicates. . . .

I received a letter from John Hay yesterday saying that he would be home in a day or two.[80] I expect he finds it getting hot and disagreeable at Port Royal. . . .

To Joseph Holt, Washington, 1 June 1863[81]

If you can come over immediately this morning the President will endeavor to work a while on the Court Martial cases.

To Therena Bates, Washington, 4 June 1863[82]

. . . The siege of Vicksburg is progressing slowly, but yet as we think is making some headway. From New Orleans we also get news that Banks has invested Port Hudson[.][83] Meanwhile the rebels are gathering a force under Johns[t]on to menace Grant in rear and compel him to raise the siege.[84] The game is getting sufficiently complicated to excite our liveliest interest and anxiety. But we must wait.

To James R. Gilmore, *[Washington]* 14 June 1863[85]

The President has no objection whatever to your publishing what you propose concerning the negro insurrection, providing you do not in any way connect his name with it.[86]

To Edwin M. Stanton, Washington, 17 June 1863[87]

The President directs me to ask when and whether Frank E. Foster was appointed confirmed and commissioned an Additional Paymaster, whether he accepted or declined the appointment, and whether it would be competent now to assign him to duty under the same?[88]

To the *Chicago Tribune*, Washington, 19 June 1863[89]

Private

I have duly received your note of the 16th inst. in which among other things you say

"By the way, we are told the President said to Senator Sumner recently, that he had not seen a copy of the Chicago Tribune for four months. Now as it is mailed regularly we wish to know whether it is received at the White House. If it miscarries we will have that corrected. If he does not want it—declines to read it—we will discontinue sending it. Please answer. Yours Respectfully, Tribune Company"

To this let me answer:

The Chicago Tribune is received very regularly, opened and kept with other papers on the newspaper table in my office; it is very regularly examined by myself, and especially sought after by the Western men who happen here.

That so far from desiring to place the Tribune under ban in the Executive Mansion the President requests me to say that he will be very glad to receive it here so long as in your kindness you may please to send it.

And to this much from him let me add a word on my own responsibility. Excepting the Washington City Dailies, in which he carefully reads the telegraphic dispatches, the President rarely ever looks at any papers, simply for want of leisure to do so. In this the Tribune fares as well as, and no worse than all others. Still I think that during the two years of his stay here, he would have been attracted to your journal more frequently as to an old and familiar friend, if it had not in that time contained so much which he had a right to expect it would <u>at least have left unsaid</u>.[90]

I can assure you of what you ought to be able to guess—that the President's task here is no child's play. If you imagine that <u>any man</u> could attempt its performance, and escape adverse criticism, you have read history in vain, and studied human nature without profit. But was it not to be expected that those of the President's friends, who knew him long and intimately—who understood his integrity and his devotion to the country and the cause entrusted to his charge—would at least abstain from judging him in the blindness of haste, and condemning him in the bitterness of ill-temper? It does seem to me that this much was due to generosity and charity for the fiery trial which he is called upon to pass through here, if not to political or personal friendship.

Let me repeat that these are exclusively my own thoughts and not the President's, and even I would not have written them, if I could, without misconstruction have otherwise answered the implication in your note to which you specifically requested a reply.

Let me add that I desire to continue reading the Tribune—reserving only the privilege of finding as much fault with it as it finds with the Administration, which I know is unselfishly endeavoring to do its whole duty in the crisis.

To C. W. Hebard, Washington, 20 June 1863[91]

<u>Private</u>

I have the honor to acknowledge to *[the]* receipt of your letter of the 18th and the accompanying papers.

The mistake by which a pamphlet copy of the President's letter was sent to the Copperhead journal in your city was one committed through the inadvertence of another person, and overlooked by myself in the hurry of business.[92] Not only is there no disposition on my part to furnish these disloyal sheets with unusual facilities, but it has been my invariable custom to withhold from them the courtesies usually extended to the Press. I regret the present inadvertence.

As to the statement you make of this journal being borne on the Advertising list of the War Department, I find upon inquiry that it is not so borne. If it has received government patronage heretofore it has been given by subordinate officers of the service. Their orders at present however are to patronize no journals not specially indicated by the War Department for that purpose.

To Therena Bates, Washington, 21 June 1863[93]

. . . Since writing you last Pennsylvania and Maryland have had another "invasion" fright, and not without some reason, though I believe it is turning out to be only a raid.[94] Lee's army has moved up towards Harper's Ferry, though precisely where, or for what purpose, I think is not yet definitely settled. Hooker is on the alert, has moved his forces so as to keep within reach of him, ready to attack or defend as may become judicious. I do not think we are in the least danger here, or even in any danger of having our communications with the North interrupted. Copperheadism is silenced for the moment in the east by the raising of six months volunteers to defend Pennsylvania against invasion. Eternal disgrace ought to attach to the Democracy of Illinois for passing an anti-war resolution at their late State Mass Meeting on the 17th inst.[95] It does seem as if they were endeavoring to sound the lowest depths of infamy and moral treason[.]

To Therena Bates, Washington, 30 June 1863[96]

Stirring times seem to be upon us again. It appears pretty evident that Lee has taken the most of his army into Maryland and Pennsylvania, with perhaps the design of taking Baltimore or Washington—his object not being as yet sufficiently developed to say with any certainty what it is. At present the rebel army is scattered about over Pennsylvania gathering up forage and stealing supplies. That State is almost completely paralyzed by fear or entirely apathetic, and is moving in a very feeble way to help herself. Whether as the danger presses her she will arouse herself to more vigorous action is yet a problem.

The army of the Potomac has been constantly on the alert ever since Lee began his movement, and has been following him, watching an opportunity to strike him a blow. Hooker was at his own request relieved of its command on Sunday last and Gen. Meade appointed to succeed him.[97] He is a good officer so far as he has been tried; but as we have had six different commanders fail in the task he assumes it is idle to say in advance whether or not he will make the seventh.

On Sunday the rebels made a pretty daring raid into this vicinity, capturing a wagon train within ten or twelve miles of this city. It produced quite a little panic among the citizens when it became known. . . .

To Therena Bates, Washington, 5 July 1863[98]

Since writing to you last the army of the Potomac has met and measured strength with the enemy. On Wednesday the 1st our troops came up with the rebels at Gettysburg, where a considerable engagement ensued, without much advantage to either side. On Thursday and Friday the enemy again attacked Gen. Meade and were repulsed with great disaster to them. On yesterday there seems to have been no fighting. The enemy is giving way; but whether it is to be a regular retreat, or whether he is only falling back for a more advantageous position among the mountains we are not yet certain. We undoubtedly have a very great advantage as the case stood at last accounts; and the government here, and General Meade, as also Gen. Couch at Harrisburg are fully alive to the exigencies of the hour, and are doing everything that is possible to secure a great victory.[99] The issue looks more hopeful than it has ever done before with this army, and we are watching the final result with the most intense anxiety. The turning point of the whole war seems to be crowding itself into the present. It seems almost impossible to wait for the result. Hours become days and days become months in such a suspense.

To Therena Bates, Washington, 12 July 1863[100]

We have no news here today of any special importance except that Meade's army is perhaps today attacking the rebel force under Lee somewhere between Williamsport and Hagerstown. The two armies were very near each other on yesterday, and a battle must almost necessarily result. . . . If Meade can gain another decisive victory the rebel cause will hardly be able to recover from the disaster. Public feeling has been wonderfully improved and buoyed up by our recent successes at Gettysburg and Vicksburg, and we confidently hope for another victory in the coming fight. . . .

To Ozias M. Hatch, Pittsfield, Illinois, 24 July 1863[101]

I wish you would go over to the Post Office in Springfield, and pick a crow with *[postmaster]* John Armstrong for me. When there the other day I mailed a letter directed over here, franked, as usual in the following way:

"From the President of the United States
    Jno. G. Nicolay
    Priv. Sec."

Upon sending it, somebody in his office made the following endorsement on it:

"Frank Illegal

President not in this vicinity."

and marked 6 cents postage due upon it.

I want you to ascertain for me whether he did this himself or whether one of his clerks did it. If his clerk did it, then Armstrong ought to kick him out of the office. If Armstrong himself did it, then I intend to ask him officially his reasons therefor, and submit the question to the Postmaster General. . . .

To Ozias M. Hatch, Pittsfield, Illinois, 29 July 1863[102]

I do not know that I can do anything else with the enclosed case except refer it to you and ask you to advise Mr. Tuck about it. I shall start from here in a day or two and will of course be unable to look after it.[103]

To John Hay, Denver, 22 September 1863[104]

I start tomorrow morning Conejos-ward.[105] We go as far as Colorado City by the Santa Fe stage, where Gov. Evans will overtake us in his ambulance,[106] and convey us to our destination. We expect a huge pow-wow—the redskins it is said will be there in force 10,000 strong.

The boys here got up a nice dancing party at the Tremont last night where we "stripped the slight bombastic toe" until 3 A.M. and went home with the crinolined juveniles by the early starlight. The affair panned out big, and there is promise that the lead will be energetically worked during the winter.

Yours (till I transfer my affections to a native American copperhead.)

To President Lincoln, Denver, 12 October 1863[107]

Please delay any opinion as to Governor Evans until you hear from me

To Dr. E. M. Seeley, Washington, 14 November 1863[108]

Since my return from the west, where I learned that you had been taken prisoner, I have received letters from your wife and your other relatives in St. Louis, requesting me, if possible to send you money in Richmond, where they learned you were at present confined. Pursuant to this request I send you enclosed in this letter a U.S. Treasury note for twenty dollars ($20.00) I send only this small sum because the contingencies of transportation render it reaching you so uncertain, and will forward more immediately upon being notified by you that it has come safely to your hands.

Please acknowledge its receipt as soon as possible, and also inform me whether I can in any other way relieve any of your present or prospective necessities arising out of your imprisonment.

To Gen. Solomon A. Meredith, Washington, 14 November 1863[109]

Daniel H. Gilmer, who was Colonel of the 38th Regiment of Illinois Volunteers, led his Regiment into the battle of Chickamauga, and is among the <u>missing</u> of that fight.[110] The only intelligence concerning him is that he was seen during the fight to be wounded, but after the battle, although special search was made among the dead on the field, his body could not be discovered, nor has any mention been made as yet of his name, among the prisoners which are reported as having been taken by the rebels.

His friends still hope that he is living, and think that he is a prisoner confined somewhere in the South, in some prison from which a list of those held in confinement has not yet been published.

Do you know of any means of gaining any information concerning him, and if so, will you not be so kind as to interest yourself specially to obtain it and communicate it to me?

Memorandum, 6 December 1863[111]

Saw Colfax this morning and learned from him the particulars of Etheridge's plot to revolutionize the House.[112] E. insists that member's certificates which do not specify that they were elected "according to the laws of the State or of the United States" (quoting the language of the law*[)]*, are invalid. He therefore proposes to leave off the roll, as not having proper certificates the members from Vermont, Maryland, Missouri, Minnesota, California, Kansas, Oregon, Virginia and West Virginia.

When I returned home the President sent for Colfax. He showed him a blank certificate which he had two months ago sent to the Senators of the States, calling their attention to this law, to the probability that a contest would be made over the members certificates, and suggesting that they have them made in several different forms, so as *[to]* cover all the points which might probably be raised.[113] In some of the States it seemed that this precaution had been neglected, notwithstanding his warning.

"The main thing Colfax," said the President, "is to be sure to have all our men there. Then if Mr. Etheridge undertakes revolutionary proceedings, let him be carried out on a chip, and let our men organize the House. If the worst comes to the worst a file of 'Invalids' may be held convenient to take care of him.*["]*

Memorandum, 7 December 1863[114]

The President this evening read me a telegram from Foster saying that Sherman had reached and joined Burnside at Knoxville that Longstreet was in full retreat up the valley into Va.—that he Foster would obey orders received and vigorously follow up the pursuit &c.[115]

"Now" said the President, "if this Army of the Potomac was good for anything—if the officers had anything in them—if the army had any legs, they could move thirty thousand men down to Lynchburg and catch Longstreet. Can anybody doubt, if Grant were here in command that he would catch him? There is not a man in the whole Union who would for a moment doubt it. But I do not think it would do to bring Grant away from the West. I talked with Gen. Halleck this morning about the matter, and his opinion was the same.*["] ["]*But you know Mr President,*["]* said the General, *["]*how hard we have tried to get this army to move towards the enemy and we cannot succeed."

—"This" said the Prest. (referring to Sherman's junction with Burnside, and Longstreets retreat) *["]* is one of the most important gains of the war— the difference between Burnside saved and Burnside lost is one of the greatest advantages of the war—it secures us East Tennessee."

Memorandum, 8 December 1863[116]

Today while comparing the engrossed and printed copies of his message *[to Congress]*, the President, by way of comment on some part he was reading said:

"When the Missouri delegation was appointed and it was known they were coming to see me,[117] Seward asked that until I should hear and decide their case in my own mind, I would not say a word to him on the subject, or in any way ask his opinion concerning the controversy, so that hereafter we might both say that he had taken no part whatever in the matter; to which I agreed. Yet Wendell Phillips[118] said in a late speech that Seward had written the whole of that letter."[119]

Memorandum, 14 December 1863[120]

This morning early Edward[121] came into the President's office and announced that Mr. *[Fernando]* Wood was here to see him.[122] "I am sorry he is here," said the President. "I would rather he should not come about here so much. Tell Mr. Wood that I have nothing as yet to tell him, on the subject we conversed about when he was last here." Edward went out to deliver his message.

"I can tell you what Wood (F.) wants," said the President to me. "He came here one day last week to urge me to publish some sort of amnesty for the northern sympathizers and abettors of the rebellion, which would include Vallandigham,[123] and permit him to return; and promised that if I would do so, they would have two Democratic candidates in the field at the next Presidential election."

Memorandum, 15 December 1863[124]

Wade rode down with me in my carriage to his lodgings today—and the conversation turning on Chase's aspirations to the Presidency, by way of illustrating how long he had been planning and working for it, told me that at the beginning of the war when the new regiments were being officered, he (Wade) had got several second lieutenants appointed, but not paying further attention to them, he found that Chase got the commissions and forwarded them with letters claiming the merit of having attained the appointments.

To William Henry Seward, Washington, 17 December 1863[125]

The President will be pleased to see you immediately.

Memorandum, 19 December 1863[126]

Mr. *[Joseph R.]* Flannigan, editor of the Phila. News, which sometime since hoisted the name of Lincoln for the Presidency came in this afternoon, and not being able to see the President, sat down and talked politics with me. From what he says Chase is actively at work through his friends in Phila. F. says that he has been applied to, to do the press-work for two papers to be published in Chase's interest; one formerly an organ of the Union League, and a new one to be started by one of the Hardings of the Inquirer—both bought by Jay Cooke & Co.[127]

To J. B. Lippincott, Washington, 29 December 1863[128]

I beg leave to return you my sincere thanks for "Charles the Bold," and "Held in Bondage," which you were so kind as to send me on Christmas Eve. I shall examine them with more special interest since making your very agreeable personal acquaintance, and looking through your immense publishing house during my brief visit to Philadelphia.

If you should visit Washington during the winter I hope you will honor me with a call. Trusting that you enjoyed a "merry Christmas" and wishing you a "happy New Year" I remain

      Your obt servt

1864

To Therena Bates, Washington, 2 January 1864[1]

I have just run away a little while from the reception which is going on below (this being our New Years Day) to write you "A happy New Year," and to get a brief respite from the interminable crowd which is besieging the Presidential doors. I have not seen anything like it on New Years since I have been here. . . .

To Joseph Holt, Washington, 8 January 1864[2]

I do not find in my office the papers referred to in the enclosed note.
    Have you any memorandum of them on your books?[3]

To William Henry Seward, Washington, 8 January 1864[4]

The President will be pleased to see the members of the National Academy of Sciences at one o'clock P.M. today agreeably to your appointment.

To John Hay, Washington, 18 January 1864[5]

I have this morning procured from the Interior Dept. and mailed to you at Hilton Head, the laws of the 37th Congress, 3 Vols. in paper. I suppose they will contain what you want—they cost nothing.

—————— When I came to direct the cards for the dinner, I referred the question of *[the]* "snub" to the Tycoon who after a short conference with the powers at the other end of the hall came back and ordered Rhode Island[6] and Ohio[7] to be included in the list. Whereat there soon arose such a rampage as the House hasn't seen for a year, and I am again taboo. How the thing is to end is yet as dark a problem as the Schleswig-Holstein difficulty.[8] Stod*[dard]* fairly cowered at the violence of the storm, and I think for the first time begins to appreciate the awful sublimities of nature. Things have subsided somewhat, but a day or two must of course bring them to a head.

Sewards and Colfax's parties were both successes—Miss Dickinson made a telling harangue—complimented the President—and alluding to his prospective second term the house came down with continued and repeated rounds of applause.[9] It was a gratifying evidence of the strength of the tide here. . . .

To H. J. Alvord, Washington, 20 January 1864[10]

The President requests me to return his thanks to Mr. Clark and yourself for the present of White fish sent him this morning.

To John Hay, Washington, 29 January 1864[11]

I have been for a week trying to get time to write, and haven't yet succeeded. Between work which arises and pleasure which allures, minor duties are unceremoniously laid on the shelf. Congress sends up a hungrier swarm of gad-flies every morning to bedevil the President, and to generally retard and derange business[.] My subs are not yet well broken in and I must necessarily give everything my personal supervision.[12]

I came out of what Uncle Jesse calls the imbroligo of the Cabinet dinner with flying colors.[13] As I wrote before, after having compelled Her S*[atanic]* Majesty *[Mrs. Lincoln]* to invite the Spragues I was taboo, and she made up her mind resolutely not to have me at the dinner. She fished around with Stod to try to get posted about managing the affair: but I instructed Stod to tell her, 1st that there was no way of his obtaining the requisite information, and 2dly that if there were, yet as it was exclusively my business he could and would not do anything in the premises. Stod I think carried out my instructions faithfully[.] She expressed her great regret but still announced her determination to run the machine without my help. Things ran on thus till the afternoon of the dinner when Edward *[McManus]* came up to tell me that she had backed down, requested my presence and assistance—apologizing, and explaining that the affair had worried her so she hadn't slept for a night or two. I think she has felt happier since she cast out that devil of stubbornness. The dinner was got through with creditably. On Wednesday last she sent out cards for the Diplomatic Dinner. While she has not in all matters done so, she has in the main adopted my advice and direction in this.

Society flourishes—I couldn't begin to count the parties on all my fingers. They are beginning to double up. Phernandiwud *[Fernando Wood]* had a grand blow-out last night to which he didn't invite me. Bob *[Lincoln]* has been home about a week, and Neil Dennison is staying with him.

The Tycoon is taking the Arkansas matter in hand as you will see by the papers. I have not yet had time to get you Gantt's Address but will do so*[.]*[14]

But I must stop and go to the senate.

To John Hay, Washington, 10 February 1864[15]

Put crape on your hat. Tonight at about 8:30, while Cooper was gone to his supper, the stables took fire and burned down. The carriages & coupé alone were saved—everything else went—six horses, including the President's, ours, and Tad's two ponies, are "gone where the good horses go."[16] . . .

Tad was in bitter tears at the loss of his ponies, and his heaviest grief was his recollection that one of them had belonged to Willie.

Cooper thinks the stable must have been fired. He had not been away from it an hour, and feels sure all was right when he left it. Besides he says it was impossible for the fire to have caught from the gas. Mrs. L. had discharged her coachman today, and Bob who is here suspects him of the work. . . .

To Joseph Holt, Washington, 13 February 1864[17]

In answer to your note of this morning the President requests me to say that he will again take up the Court Martial Cases on Monday morning at nine A.M. if you will be so kind as to come at that hour.[18]

To Thaddeus Stevens, Washington, 15 February 1864[19]

In the discharge of my official duties as Private Secretary to the President of the United States, I have almost constant use for a carriage in which to carry messages from the President to Congress, and to visit the various Departments, &c. For this purpose, I have, since Sept. 11th 1861, kept a private carriage, the total original cost and expense of which, (including carriage, horses, harness, repairs, horsefeed, and coachman's wages,) up to Feb'y 1st 1864, have been $3060.49. Of this amount, I have been able to pay out of the public appropriations, viz: the deficiency and contingent funds for the Executive Office, only the sum of $1318.46, leaving more than one half, viz: the sum of $1742.03 to be defrayed out of my own private purse. As the government only pays me an annual salary of $2500—as I lost the horses in the late burning of the stables at the Executive Mansion,—and as the great rise in prices has so largely increased this class of expenses, I cannot longer afford to bear this private expense for the public service. All similar services are provided at the public cost, and it would be but simple justice for Congress to re-imburse me for the above amount already paid out of my own pocket; at all events I respectfully ask that an appropriation be made for this necessary expenditure in the future, the current rate of which will be, in addition to the cost of a new pair of horses, about one hundred dollars per month.

To John Hay, Washington, 17 February 1864[20]

I have been too infernally busy to write, which accounts for your not having received more letters from me. A note came here a day or two ago from Gen. Gillmore saying you had gone to Florida,[21] from which I infer that you are living in metaphorical clover while we poor devils are eating the husks of hard work in the national pig-sty. Kick up your heels while you may!

Although there is much doing in politics there is nothing decisive. The treasury rats are busy night and day and becoming more and more unscrupulous and malicious. They are circulating a scurrilous anonymous pamphlet to injure the Prest. and today I was shown a circular signed by Pomeroy as "Chairman of the National Executive Committee[*"]* proposing a Chase organization throughout the country.[22] The adherents of this faction in the House and Senate are malicious and bitter but as yet dare not openly attack the Tycoon[*.]* Winter Davis showed his teeth in the House yesterday, but got no backing except from two or three members.[23] Things have been drifting along chaotically for two or three weeks but active work must begin soon[*.]* Defrees has gone to Indiana to look after matters there and we shall probably have a good endorsement there.[24]

Corruption intrigue and malice are doing their worst, but I do not think it is in the cards to beat the Tycoon.

To Therena Bates, Washington, 21 February 1864[25]

. . . I have had the blues badly several times this past week. It seems as if the circumstances surrounding my position were getting worse day by day. I am beginning seriously to doubt my ability to endure it a great while longer. . . .

To Col. James B. Fry, Washington, 25 February 1864[26]

The President of the United States has received, signed, and sent to the State Department an act entitled "An Act Entitled an Act to amend an act entitled 'An act for Enrolling & calling out the National Forces & for other purposes, approved March Third Eighteen hundred & sixty-three."

To Therena Bates, Washington, 28 February 1864[27]

. . . The interest of the week has been centered in political matters almost entirely. Chase as you know would like to be the next candidate for the Presidency, and has I think for a year or more past been working to that end. Notwithstanding he made but little headway, he still persevered, and succeeded during this winter in enlisting a few malcontents in the Republican party actively in his behalf. They organized a committee, and have issued one or two documents designed mainly to damage Mr. Lincoln; and about a week ago a Secret Circular signed by Senator Pomeroy as Chairman of the Committee, disparaging Mr. Lincoln and lauding Mr. Chase found its way into print.[28] The Circular I suppose was not issued with Mr. Chase's knowledge or consent; but being circulated by his active friends, is nevertheless connected in the public mind with Mr. Chase's known aspirations to the Presidency and consequently he is, whether justly or unjustly, charged with its responsibility. The effect has been very seriously to damage what very slight prospect he had because it has stirred up all Mr. Lincoln's friends to active exertion, and already four States have chosen and instructed their delegates for him. Nothing, as things look now, can prevent the renomination and re-election of Mr Lincoln, except serious military disasters during the Spring campaigns and which of course we do not look for.

Still they sometimes come and a very disagreeable one has within a day or two been reported to us in Florida. Gen. Seymour it seems, neglected Gillmore's instructions to stay in his position and wait for the enemy; but went out to find him and has lost a battle, 800 or a thousand men and five guns.[29] Our first information about it came from Hay, although I infer from his letters that he was not in or near the fight.

Tonight the city is full of rumors that the Army of the Potomac is in motion but the President has no reliable information about it.

To Edwin M. Stanton, Washington, 2 March 1864[30]

The President has received the telegram of the Governor of Illinois to the Secretary of War, giving notice of an insurrection in Edgar County in that State, and which you have referred to him for instructions.[31] He directs me to request that you will please consult with the General-in-chief and to comply with the request of Governor Yates, if that shall be the most expeditious and feasible plan

To Therena Bates, Washington, 8 March 1864[32]

. . . At the date of my last letter Kilpatrick was on his way to try to reach and liberate our Union prisoners in Richmond,[33] but failed in the main enterprise. From information received within a day or two we fear that Col. Ulric Dahlgren has been killed.[34] He was decidedly the most gallant and daring cavalry officer of the war and his loss will be mourned here as widely and deeply almost as was Ellsworths. . . .

Memorandum, Washington, 8 March 1864[35]

In obedience to an invitation from the Sec of War, Gen Grant reached the city at about 5 P.M. By some sort of negligence there was no one at the Depot to receive him but he found his way to Willards with the two members of his staff who accompanied him.

———— Reception tonight. The weather was bad; but the "Republican" having announced that Grant would attend the reception it brought out a considerable crowd. At about 9 1/2 P.M. the General came in—alone again excepting his staff—and he and the President met for the first time. The President expecting him knew from the buzz and movement in the crowd that it must be him; and when a man of modest mien and unimposing exterior presented himself, the President said "This is General Grant, is it?" The General replied "Yes!" and the two greeted each other more cordially, but still with that modest deference—felt rather than expressed by word or action—so appropriate to both—the one the honored Ruler and the other the honored Victor of the nation and the time. The crowd too partook of the feeling of the occasion—there was no rude jostling—or pushing or pulling, but unrestrained the circle kept its respectful distance, until after a brief conversation the President gave the General in charge of Seward to present to Mrs L. at the same time instructing me to send for the Secretary of War. After paying his respects to Mrs. Lincoln the General was taken by Seward to the East room where he was greeted with cheer after cheer by the assembled crowd, and where he was forced to mount a sofa from whence he could shake hands with those who pressed from all sides to see him. It was at least an hour before he returned, flushed heated and perspiring with the unwonted exertion.

After a promenade in the East Room—the Prest with Mrs Seward and

Gen Grant with Mrs L.*[—]*the party returned to the Blue Room and sat down. The President went up stairs and returning in a little while sat down near where the General the Sec of War and myself were sitting*[.]*

"Tomorrow," said the Prest to the Genl. "at such time as you may arrange with the Sec of War, I desire to make to you a formal presentation of your commission as Lieut. Genl. I shall then make a very short speech to you, to which I desire you to reply, for an object; and that you may be properly prepared to do so I have written what I shall say—only four sentences in all—which I will read from my MSS. as an example which you may follow and also read your reply, as you are perhaps not as much accustomed to speaking as I myself—and I therefore give you what I shall say that you may consider it and from *[form]* your reply. There are two points that I would like to have you make in your answer: 1st To say something which shall prevent or obviate any jealousy of you from any of the other generals in the service, and secondly, something which shall put you on as good terms as possible with this Army of the Potomac. Now consider whether this may not be said to make it of some advantage; and if you see any objection whatever to doing it be under no restraint whatever in expressing that objection to the Secretary of War who will talk further with you about it."

The General asked at what time this presentation should take place.

"The Secretary of War and yourself may arrange the time to suit your convenience. I am all ready, whenever you shall have prepared your reply."

"I can be ready in thirty minutes" said the General.

One oclock tomorrow was finally fixed as the hour, after which the General took his leave, accompanied by the Sec of War.

———— The President, as I learned in reply to a question to him, is contemplating bringing the General east to see whether he cannot do something with the unfortunate army of the Potomac.

———— During the reception a dispatch was brought to me announcing that the Union ticket had been today carried in N.H. by 3,000.

Memorandum, 9 March 1864[36]

The Presentation ceremony of Gen. Grant's commission as Lieut General, took place today at 1 P.M. in the Cabinet chamber. The newspapers give the proceedings and addresses in full. Both the President and the General read their remarks from MSS.[37] The General had hurriedly and almost illegibly written his speech on the half of a sheet of note paper, in lead pencil, and being quite embarrassed by the occasion, and finding his own writing so very difficult to read, made rather sorry and disjointed work of enunciating his reply. I noticed too that in what he said, while it was brief and to the point, he had either forgotten or disregarded entirely the President's hints to him of the night previous.

—— During this afternoon, Gov. Chase sent the President a copy of his letter to Judge Hall of Ohio withdrawing his name from the Presidential canvass.[38]

To Charles G. Halpine, Washington, 11 March 1864[39]

I have been too busy sooner to answer your note of the 4th. I have not been under such a pressure of work since in Washington as during the last six weeks. . . .

To Therena Bates, Washington, 21 March 1864[40]

I have been quite as much occupied as ever during the week past, although the work has not been quite as hard and fatiguing. Hay has not yet returned, but as he has not written for some time I expect he is on the way. I think he is a good deal annoyed at the way his name has been bandied about in the newspapers when there was not a shadow of foundation for it all.[41] . . .

There is no news. The armies are of course standing still until Grant shall get his new harness well on. He is expected here tonight. Congress is driveling its time away luckily not doing much harm if it is doing no good. Chase having retired from the Presidential contest, the tide continues to set as strongly as ever to Lincoln, and politicians therefore have but little to intrigue about. A few malcontents in the Republican party are stewing around, trying to make Butler, Fremont, or anybody they can get, the nucleus of a little faction in opposition to Lincoln, but there is not the remotest prospect that their eggs will hatch. It is a time of general calm— most likely a calm before a storm—for we shall undoubtedly have events and excitements enough during the year.

To John Evans, Washington, 22 March 1864[42]

Colorado Enabling Act was signed yesterday by the President.

To Therena Bates, Washington, 25 March 1864[43]

I start in half an hour from now (6 1/2 P.M.) for a few days trip to New York. Hay reached home yesterday morning, looking very well and having had rather an agreeable trip down south. He will remain on duty here in his old position for the present. . . .

To President Lincoln, New York, 30 March 1864[44]

<u>Private.</u>

Mr. Weed was here at the Astor House on my arrival last Saturday morning, and I gave him the note you sent him.[45]

He read it over, carefully once or twice and then said he didn't quite understand it. He had written a letter to Judge *[David]* Davis, which the Judge had probably shown you, but in that he had said nothing except about Custom House matters.[46]

He said that all the solicitude he had was in your behalf. You had told him in January last that you thought you would make a change in the Collectorship here, but that thus far it had not been done. He had told you he himself had no personal preference as to the particular man who is to be his successor. He did not think Mr. Barney a bad man but thought him a weak one.[47] His four deputies are constantly intriguing against you. Andrews is doing the same.[48] Changes are constantly being made among the subordinates in the Custom House, and men turned out, for no other real reason than that they take active part in primary meetings &c., in behalf of your re-nomination.

His only solicitude he said, was for yourself. He thought that if you were not strong enough to hold the Union men together through the next Presidential election, when it must necessarily undergo a great strain, the country was in the utmost danger of going to ruin.

His desire was to strengthen you as much as possible and that you should strengthen yourself. You were being weakened by the impression in the popular mind that you hold on with such tenacity to men once in office, although they prove to be incapable and unworthy. This feeling among your friends also raises the question, as to whether, if re-elected, you would change your Cabinet. The present Cabinet is notoriously weak and inharmonious—no Cabinet at all—gives the President no support. Welles is a cypher, Bates a fogy, and Blair at best a dangerous friend.

Something was needed to reassure the public mind and to strengthen yourself. Chase and Fremont, while they might not succeed in making themselves successful rivals might yet form and lead dangerous factions. Chase was not formidable as a candidate in the field but by the shrewd dodge of a withdrawal is likely to turn up again with more strength than ever.

He had received a letter from Judge Davis, in which the Judge wrote him that he had read his (Weed's) letter to you, but that you did not seem ready to act in the appointment of a new Collector, and that he (the Judge) thought it was because of your apprehension that you would be merely getting "out of one muss into another."

A change in the Custom House was imperatively needed because one whole bureau in it had been engaged in treasonably aiding the rebellion.

The ambition of his life had been, not to get office for himself, but to assist in putting good men in the right places. If he was good for anything, it was as an outsider to give valuable suggestions to an administration that would give him its confidence. He feared he did not have your entire confidence—that you only regarded him with a certain degree of leniency; that you only regarded him as being not quite so great a rascal as his enemies charged him with being.

The above are substantially the points of quite a long conversation. This morning I had another interview with Mr. Weed.

He had just received Gov. *[Edwin D.]* Morgan's letter informing him of the nomination of Hogeboom[49] to fill McElrath's place,[50] and seemed quite disheartened and disappointed. He said he did not know what to say. He had assured your friends here that when in your own good time you became ready to make changes, the new appointments would be from among your friends; but that this promotion of one of your most active and malignant enemies left him quite powerless. He had not yet told any one, but knew it would be received with general indignation, &c &c.

I shall remain here a day or two longer.

To President Lincoln, New York, 30 March 1864[51]

I called on Gen Schurz on my arrival here last Saturday, and have also seen him twice since. I found him very cordial, very friendly towards yourself, quite reasonable in his own wishes and requests, and liberal in his appreciation of the troubles and difficulties with which you have to contend. According to his own statements there is evidently a serious misapprehension, or misunderstanding about his alleged order interrupting the transportation of troops last fall, which at least deserves investigation before permanent blame is attached to him. I have promised to look into the matter for him when I return to Washington. I enclose his memorandum on the subject.[52]

He also sends a letter on general matters, noting some few points about which we talked, and which I will explain more fully when I return.

He is under impression that the German movement for Fremont is earnest and will be pretty strong, and that they seriously intend to run him as a third candidate—that *[Samuel C.]* Pomeroy, *[B. Gratz]* Brown & Co have transferred their strength from the Chase movement to this, and are bent upon defeating you at all events.

To John Hay, New York, 30 March 1864[53]

Please hand the enclosed to the President, except the memorandum concerning Col. Bourry, which keep until I can look after it on my return.[54]

To John Hay, New York, 1 April 1864[55]

I had determined to start home tonight, but reading the villainously unfair and untrue editorial in the Tribune of this morning,[56] I have determined to stay till I can have another talk with Greeley and Gay,[57] and tell them a fact or two, so that if they print misrepresentations in the future they should do so knowingly. As Mr. Greeley only comes to his office very late in the evening I do not know how soon I may be able to get off.

—— Please attend to the matter of the flowers for me without fail as I have promised Miss Stevens that they shall be here. Let the gardener send them as cut flowers, unless he thinks he can send them more conveniently made up into one or two bouquets. The Express companies dead-head *[ship free of charge]* articles for the fair so that I suppose there will be no demand for bucksheesh there.[58] Inquire as to how the trains run, so that if possible the flowers may be cut and packed very early Monday morning and got through here by Monday night.

—— Leavitt Hunt wrote to Webster of the State Dept for some important autograph MSS. to be sold at the fair,[59] and Webster sent him the MSS. of the Presidents Thanksgiving Proclamation, which was written by Seward and is in his handwriting.[60] Hunt was under *[the]* impression that it was the President's MSS. and was about to advertise it as such when I happened to see him and explained the matter to him whereupon he deferred the notices of it, I agreeing to write to you to go and see Webster *[and ask]* why he sent that particular thing, which cannot be palmed off as the President's MSS. and yet which cannot be advertised as Sewards. It is of no serious consequence in any event and yet it will be a pestiferous annoyance to have the newspapers gossip and wrangle about it.

Go and see Webster, and try to gather from his conversation whether it was meant as a trick by which to inform the public that Seward wrote a document usually ascribed to the President. If so then we had better have it announced that the document is Sewards composition and so end all controversy at once. If that was not Websters purpose then he had better send some other MSS. which may be announced as Sewards and thus avoid all speculation and gossip about it on the part of the public.

To Therena Bates, New York, 1 April 1864[61]

. . . I have been mainly occupied with seeing and talking with politicians in regard to the next Presidential election, about which there seems to be more diversity of views and interests here than anywhere else in the country, although the general fact that Lincoln's re-nomination and re-election is considered almost a foregone conclusion even by those who are dissatisfied with that result and who therefore adopt the belief very reluctantly and unwillingly. . . .

To William Dennison, Washington, 7 April 1864[62]

The President thinks he cannot safely write that class of letters.[63]

To Salmon P. Chase, Washington, 8 April 1864[64]

In answer to your note of today the President directs me to say that the order concerning the exportation of salted provisions has not yet been issued.[65] It was merely printed and sent to you for examination and will not be issued before a full consultation with yourself.

To Therena Bates, Washington, 10 April 1864[66]

. . . But little that is of interest has transpired here, except that the Senate the other day by a vote of 38 to 6 passed the resolution proposing an amendment to the Constitution of the United States abolishing slavery; and that on Friday and Saturday the House of Representatives was disgraced by the treasonable utterances of two of its members, Long of Ohio[67] and Harris of Maryland[68]—and doubly disgraced that a two-thirds vote could not be obtained to expel Harris. Long's case comes up on Monday, but taking yesterday's vote as a criterion I fear his name is also yet destined to remain a blot upon the rolls. . . .

To James R. Gilmore, Washington, 11 April 1864[69]

I brought your letter to the notice of the President as requested. He said he no longer distinctly remembered what he said to you at the interview referred to, and that he could better answer your question, if you were to write out and submit to him, what you propose to publish, concerning the same.[70]

To Joseph Holt, Washington, 13 April 1864[71]

The President will endeavor to take up the Court Martial cases at nine o'clock tomorrow morning, if you will please be here.

To Therena Bates, Washington, 17 April 1864[72]

All my good intentions to write you two letters this past week again came to nothing in the multitude of little things that absorbed my attention. I really don't know what becomes of all the time—at the end of a week I can't see that I have accomplished much, and yet there is never an opportunity for doing the things I have most at heart. This everlasting frittering away of hours and days is one of the many very disagreeable features of life here. . . .

The news for the week is neither important, nor very good what there is of it. I have not yet seen the official dispatches (if there be any) concerning the capture of Fort Pillow by the rebels but I suppose the fact, while not absolutely dangerous, is seriously disgraceful, and will create much uneasiness in Kentucky and Tennessee.[73]

The case of the traitor Long was disposed of by Congress. The Democratic party virtually defended his treason, on the plea of defending the right of free speech. Colfax seeing that he could not pass his resolution of expulsion by the requisite two-thirds vote changed it to one of censure, which passed by only ten majority, all the Democrats voting against it. Congress is timid, vacillating and idle—to say nothing of its being selfish and corrupt. It is fortunate that the fate of the country does not hang entirely on its action. . . .

To Benjamin F. Butler, Washington, 19 April 1864[74]

Private

I find the following statement floating about the newspapers.

["]Mrs. J. Todd White, a sister of Mrs. President Lincoln, was a rebel spy and sympathizer. When she was passed into the confederacy a few days ago, by way of Fortress Monroe, she carried with her in trunks all kinds of contraband goods, together with medicines, papers, letters, etc., which will be doubtless of the greatest assistance to those with whom she consorts.

["] When Gen. Butler wished to open her trunks, as the regulations of transit there prescribe, this woman showed him an autograph pass or order from President Lincoln, enjoining upon the federal officers not to open any of her trunks, and not subject the bearer of the pass, her packages, parcels or trunks, to any inspection or annoyance.

*["]*Mrs. White said to General Butler, or the officers in charge there, in substance, as follows: 'My trunks are filled with contraband, but I defy you to touch them. Here,' (passing it under their noses), 'here is the positive order of your master!'

*["]*Mrs. White was thus allowed to pass without the inspection and annoyance so peremptorily forbidden by President Lincoln in an order written and signed by his own hand, and to-day, the contents of his wife's sister's trunks are giving aid and comfort to the enemy—nor least is the shock which these facts will give to the loyal hearts whose hopes and prayers and labors sustain the cause which is thus betrayed in the very White House.*["]*

Now the President is not conscious of having given this lady a pass which permitted her to take anything more than the ordinary baggage allowed, nor which exempted her from the existing rules of inspection. He certainly gave her no such extraordinary privileges as are above described and implied.

Will you please inform me whether Mrs. White presented to you what purported to be anything more than the usual pass on which persons have been sent through our lines, or which purported to entitle her to carry more than ordinary baggage?

2d Did she take with her more than ordinary baggage?

3d Was or was not her baggage inspected?

4th Did she use the language alleged in the above statement?[75]

P.S. Are such passes usually taken up by our offices? If so please send me this pass, or a copy of it.

To Jackson Grimshaw, Washington, 22 April 1864[76]

. . . There is but little stir in politics here just now. A few discontented Radicals in New York are agitating in Fremont's behalf, but they are a skeleton organization and have no public sentiment at their back. In this city, a few original Chase men, chagrined that their favorite gave out so early in the Presidential race, still live in hope that something may turn up to their advantage in the Baltimore Convention,[77] and to this end also echo and magnify the mutterings of the Fremonters. The Fremont movement has no substantial foundation outside of the State of Missouri, except so far as Republicans at other points sympathize with the supposed wrongs of the Missouri

Radicals—wrongs which are entirely suppositious, and exist only in the scheming brains of factious and selfish and faithless Missouri politicians of the Gratz Brown school, who avow "rule or ruin" as their principle of action.[78]

But their whole scheme will come to nothing. Mr. Lincoln will be re-nominated, and re-elected unless there should be an unexpected and surprising revolution in politics before November next.

To Joseph Holt, Washington, 25 April 1864[79]

The President thinks it will be impossible for him to take up the Court Martial cases today. To-morrow morning at nine, however, he will endeavor to do so.

To Horace Greeley, Washington, 25 April 1864[80]

Private

Will you be so kind as to publish the enclosed, or its equivalent, in the editorial columns of The Tribune?[81]

The silly story which it contradicts, was vouched for in the Washington Correspondence of The Tribune on March 28th last. On that authority the Copperhead newspapers are circulating it. As the whole story was from the first without truth or foundation, it is but fair also to publish the correction through The Tribune.[82]

To Benjamin F. Butler, Washington, 28 April 1864[83]

I thank you for your kind letter of the 21st inst., answering my inquiries in the case of Mrs. *[Martha Todd]* White.[84] I sent the enclosed brief editorial to the N.Y. Tribune, which appeared in its issue of yesterday. I felt myself that the whole *canard* was too silly and trivial to merit an official contradiction, but thought that a correction in this shape was due and proper, and troubled you with the matter only that I might get the exact facts, to have them put in as few words as possible.

To James R. Fry, Washington, 30 April 1864[85]

The President cannot promise to come. Will write you today.[86]

To Therena Bates, Washington, 1 May 1864[87]

. . . I see no early prospect of getting out West on a visit. Congress is not making any headway with its work, and it is but little over a month now until the Baltimore Convention.

I think Grant is on the eve of important movements, but do not know what they are to be. As we have been doing for three years past we can only wait patiently and hope for a signal victory. Our Spring campaigns however have so generally been failures that people are beginning to feel superstitious about them, and therefore hardly trust themselves to expect decided success. . . .

Nicolay's recollection of 3 May 1864, contained in a letter to Edgar T. Welles[88]

On the 3d of May 1864 Mr Lincoln called a cabinet meeting for the discussion of the question what course the Government should take in regard to the massacre of colored soldiers at the capture of Fort Pillow by the rebels on April 12.

I will be glad if you can send me any extracts from your father's *[Gideon Welles's]* diary in reference to that cabinet meeting, and the subject discussed. I judge that the matter was not disposed of for some days, and am inclined to think that it was at last allowed merely to drop out of sight because of the greater interest in Grant's campaign which was about beginning.[89] . . .

To Therena Bates, Washington, 8 May 1864[90]

We have been in another week of terrible suspense. Grant began moving last Wednesday morning, and beyond learning that he had succeeded in crossing the Rapidan without serious opposition, we were without any information from him for two or three days. And indeed we know comparatively little yet of his operations, beyond the fact that he has fought one or more severe battles, and which information we pick up from the dispatches of others. The latest and most specific news that we have is that eight to ten thousand wounded are being sent back—that the Chief Quartermaster of the Army is telegraphing for a large supply of grain—and that he says "the enemy is said to be retiring." This you see does not furnish much data from which to draw conclusions.[91]

Meanwhile General Butler has gone up the James River with transports and gunboats, and landed at City Point, just above the mouth of the

Appomattox River, where he menaces Petersburg, and where he is in a position to advance upon Richmond should that become expedient.[92]

In the West Sherman started from Chattanooga for Dalton, at the same time that Grant moved, but we have heard nothing further from him.[93] . . .

To Albert G. Riddle, Washington, 10 May 1864[94]

Confidential Yours of the 7th is received. The President himself has no very distinct recollection of what transpired at the interview named. He thinks, however, that nothing was said, which at the time he would not have been entirely willing to have had written or repeated.

Whether or not you should write out your recollection of the interview, is a question he leaves entirely to your own wish; and if you conclude to do so, he will not consider that you have any unfriendly motive in it.[95]

My own suggestion is that if you write such a statement, it would be well to send it here to me to look at before you mail it to the parties desiring it.

To Samuel Burnham, Washington, 11 May 1864[96]

Your note of May 4th, addressed to the President of the United States was duly received.[97] I enclose a copy of the reply of Prof. Henry to an inquiry on the subject of your request, which the President directed me to make.[98] While it is not practicable for the Institution to present you a full sett of the "Contributions," Prof. Henry states that "parts of volumes, or single memoirs are sometimes given to aid special studies.["]

To Ozias M. Hatch, Washington, 14 May 1864[99]

Private When you see Judge Kellogg of Fulton,[100] or Mr. Green of Menard,[101] you are authorized to say to them that the President would be pleased to have them assist you and my other friends in making me a delegate for the 9th District. If they were here, he would say this much to them; but having up to this time written nothing whatever bearing even remotely upon the subject of his own re-nomination, he does not wish to say it by letter.[102]

To Col. E. D. Townsend, Washington, 14 May 1864[103]

Does not General Order No. 191 answer the accompanying note?[104] If so, please send me a copy that I may mail it in reply.[105]

To Therena Bates, Washington, 15 May 1864[106]

. . . I think the crisis of this campaign was passed, when Grant determined to keep on fighting, after the battles of Thursday and Friday, of week before last (May 7th & 8th.) Following his usual tactics, Lee had thrown almost his whole force against ours hoping to divide and beat Grant's army; the battles were fierce and bloody, and especially on Friday evening the enemy gained some temporary advantage. There was just about the same state of things, under which our army has always previously retreated and given up the contest, and indications which we get here, lead us to believe, that the same thing would have occurred this time but for Grant's presence. He went to the front himself, and became satisfied from a personal inspection that no serious disaster had taken place; and on that knowledge announced his determination to stay and fight it out. His judgment was confirmed by the fact, that the next morning the enemy had retired from our front.

Since then he has been following up the rebels, cautiously but energetically, fighting them almost every day, constantly forcing them back, and on Thursday the 12th, winning a very decided victory, in the capture of many prisoners, guns, and officers. Again the enemy abandoned their positions and works in the night, and again he followed them up. At last reports from him (yesterday morning*[)]*, he was preparing to make another demonstration upon them, to see whether they were making a decided stand, or whether they were merely attempting to cover their retreat.[107]

The whole situation is so encouraging, that we hope he may be able to totally destroy the rebel army, and capture Richmond. If he can have the same general success, which he has had for ten days past, that result is almost sure. Were this accomplished, it would be but the work of time to finish up the rebellion

Because this prospect is at present so cheering and this hope so promising of fulfillment, I think I have been more nervous and anxious during the week past, than for a year previous, lest some unexpected and untoward accident should prevent its realization*[.]*

The President is cheerful and hopeful—not unduly elated, but seeming confident; and now as ever watching every report and indication, with quiet, unwavering interest.[108] If my own anxiety is so great, what must be his solicitude, after waiting through three long, weary years of doubt and disaster, for such a consummation, to see the signs of final and complete victory every day growing so bright and auspicious! . . .

To James R. Gilmore, Washington, 20 May 1864[109]

This morning I gave to the President the copy of "Harper" which you left with me. He said he should take pleasure in looking over your article.[110]

In answer to your question he asked me to write to you that he thinks the publication talked of had on the whole better not be made.[111]

I forward herewith a letter for you addressed to my care, which arrived last night.

To Therena Bates, Washington, 22 May 1864[112]

When I wrote you last Sunday, I supposed the great events then in progress would have reached some culminating point before this, but the contrary has occurred. Rains and storms came on, making the movements of great armies very difficult, and at last accounts, Grant and Lee were substantially in the positions they then respectively occupied. Still there seems to be constant activity—Grant's wounded are being taken care of, and his reinforcements are arriving, which will about replace his losses in the late battles, and we may any day hear that another great battle is being fought. In the southwest meanwhile, the rebels are constantly giving way before Sherman's advance, indicating that they are either not strong enough to fight, or that they are stripping that region of troops to reinforce Lee. It is a good sign, that all officers as well as civilians who come back here after visiting the Army of Grant, uniformly mention the confidence expressed by all the generals and men, that they will win the next battle. Whether the confidence be well or ill founded does not matter much, it is a great point that they possess it. . . .

In less than three weeks the Baltimore Convention will have decided who is to be the next President. The indications all are that Mr. Lincoln will be re-nominated with scarcely a dissenting voice. . . .

To Horace Greeley, Washington, 26 May 1864[113]

Private

In "The Tribune" of yesterday the Washington Correspondent,[114] writing under date of the 24th inst., says:

"The subject of arbitrary arrests was incidentally discussed in cabinet council today. Mr. Chase manfully denounced them. The suppression of the New York papers,[115] and extradition of Arguelles were both condemned by him,[116] as devoid of policy, and wanting law. The defense of these measures was more irritable than logical and assured."

I do not know what Mr. Chase's views may be on these subjects; but the statement that he expressed them as alleged, is untrue. Mr. Chase did not attend Cabinet meeting on the day mentioned; these subjects were not discussed at that Cabinet meeting; nor has there been any conference about the matter between the President and Mr. Chase, at any other time.

Knowing that you wish to be fair and just in your criticisms of the conduct of the administration, I take the liberty of bringing this matter to your notice, as one of many instances of the reckless misstatements and unfounded imputations of your Washington Correspondent.

To Therena Bates, Washington, 29 May 1864[117]

. . . I have but little news in detail from the army. Gen. Grant is still driving ahead towards Richmond. Up to this time, his uniform strategy has been to flank Lee on the right, and fight wherever it became necessary. His latest flanking march was to withdraw all his force north of the North Anna, and then march rapidly to the southeast on the north bank, until he was able to cross the Pamunkey River just below the junction of the North and South Anna. By this movement he has by an almost complete surprise and with scarcely any opposition gained a position at Hanover Court House, between Lee and Richmond. What will result from this we cannot of course yet tell.

If any doubt remained before, about the certainty of Mr. Lincoln's renomination, it has been pretty well dispelled by the action of the State Conventions of New York, Ohio, and Illinois during the past week, all of which have elected delegates favorable to him, and passed resolutions recommending his renomination. I suppose a similar unanimity has not occurred during the whole history of the country.

To John Hay, Baltimore, 5 June 1864[118]

Arrived here safely—find quite a number of delegates already in, but have not yet talked much with them.

One of the first men I met was B. C. Cook, who stands at the head of our Illinois delegation, and had quite a long and confidential talk with him.[119] He told me he had thought of going to Washington tomorrow, but seeing me he concluded he could sufficiently post himself.

He premised by telling me that the milk-and-water Lincoln resolution which was first reported to the Illinois State Convention, was cooked up by a few plotters, to the utter surprise and astonishment of nine-tenths of the Convention, and by only a part of the Committee, and was with the others reported to the Convention when there was but a small attendance, it being late at night, but that the Convention very handsomely repudiated them, referred them to a new Committee, which introduced and passed others of the right stripe.[120] Cook does not seem to know thoroughly who were at the bottom of the matter. He thinks Turner was the chief manager.[121] Medill is understood to have declared himself opposed to the resolution in Committee but seems to have contented himself with the mere expression of his dissent, after which he went away without further active opposition.[122] Strangely enough one or two men have told me that Wm A Grimshaw,[123] either of his own volition or under the influence of others, was in the scheme. Jack*[son Grimshaw]* on the contrary, Cook told me, was open and hearty for Lincoln.

Cook says there will be three or four disaffected members in the delegation from Illinois, but that nevertheless the delegation will vote and act as a unit, under the instructions of the Convention and also the will of the large majority of the delegation. He says the delegation will in good faith do everything they can for Lincoln that is in arranging the Vice P., the Committees, Platform &c. taking his own nomination of course as beyond question.

What transpired at home, and what he has heard from several sources, have made Cook suspicious that Swett may be untrue to Lincoln.[124] One of the straws which lead him to this belief is that Swett has telegraphed here urging the Illinois delegation to go for *[Joseph]* Holt for Vice President.

I told Cook that I thought Lincoln would not wish even to indicate a preference for V.P. as the rival candidates were all friendly to him.

There will be some little trouble in arranging the matter of the contested seats from Missouri. The Radicals seem to have the technical right to be admitted. They threaten to withdraw from the Convention if the Conservatives are also admitted; but promise to abide *[by]* the action of the Convention if they (the Radicals) obtain the seats. Cook says they intimated to him that they would even promise to vote for Lincoln in the Convention, for the promise of an admission to seats.[125]

Whitelaw Reid is here and told me this evening that the Radicals conceded Lincoln's re-nomination, but their present game was to make a very radical platform.[126]

Cook wants to know confidentially whether Swett is all right—whether in urging Holt for V.P. he reflects the Presidents wishes—whether the President has any preference, either personally or on the score of policy—or whether he wishes not even to interfere by a confidential indication. Also whether he thinks it would be good policy to give the Radical delegates from Missouri the seats, on their promising to vote for him.

Please get this information for me, if possible. Write and send your letter by express so that it will reach me by the earliest practicable hour on to-morrow (Monday). This will go to you by express by the 7 A.M. train tomorrow so that you ought to have it by ten A.M.

Address me at Eutaw House.[127]

To John Hay, Baltimore, 6 June 1864[128]

Things all going off in best possible style. There is not even a shadow of opposition to the President outside the Mo. Radical delegation, and I think even they if they get seats will go for him. Blow is understood to say that he will not take his seat in the Convention but will support Mr. Lincoln if nominated.[129]

Hamlin will in all probability be nominated V.P.[130] New York does not want the nominee—hence neither Dix[131] nor Dickinson[132] have any backers. Andy Johnson seems to have no strength whatever; even Dr Breckenridge and the Kentuckians oppose him.[133] Cameron received no encouragement outside of Pennsylvania, and he is evidently too shrewd to beat an empty bush. The disposition of all the delegates was to take any war Democrat, provided he would add strength to the ticket. None of the names suggested seemed to meet this requirement, and the feeling therefore is to avoid any weakness. It strikes everybody that Hamlin fills this bill, and Pennsylvania has this afternoon broken ground on the subject by resolving, on Cameron's own motion to cast her vote for him. New York will probably follow suit tonight, which will virtually decide the contest[.]

The delegations being so unanimous for Lincoln are in a great measure indifferent about the other matters. All the day, every body has been asking advice—nobody making suggestions. The Convention is almost too passive to be interesting—certainly it is not at all *[as]* exciting as it was at Chicago. . . .

To John Hay, Baltimore, 7 June 1864[134]

The Convention met at noon today and organized by making Dr Breckenridge of Ky. temporary chairman. He is a poor presiding officer—has a weak voice and is somewhat slow. But the Convention was good natured and tractable, and he managed to get through the session, not however without wasting a couple of hours of time. In the stormy seas of the Chicago Wigwam he could not have lived fifteen minutes.

But the Convention had ample compensation for his other disqualifications, in the fact that he made a splendid, straight-out radical speech. It was clear earnest and forcible and will make an invaluable campaign document— I doubt whether we get a better one during the whole campaign. The Convention adjourned to seven this evening after appointing Committees on Credentials, Organization, and Resolutions.

The Vice Presidency goes a-begging. Yesterday as I wrote you the current set towards Hamlin. But New England does not support Hamlin or at least Massachusetts does not, because, it is shrewdly suspected, she hopes something may turn up in a new deal which would enable her to push *[John A.]* Andrew. New York leaned decidedly to Hamlin yesterday evening; but the main thing New York wants is <u>not</u> to have the V.P. because that would obstruct Seward's future. So this morning, New York, fearing that through Hamlin's failure Dickinson might succeed determined to go for Johnson. So the matter drifts. . . .

To John Hay, Washington, 11 June 1864[135]

The President desires you to bring the papers which Capt. J. N. Brown herewith encloses, to his special notice.[136]

To John Hay, Baltimore, 12 June 1864[137]

. . . Before leaving, I instructed Neill[138] to open such letters addressed to me as came from any of the Departments, as they were likely to be on office business. . . .

To Edward D. Neill, Baltimore, 12 June 1864[139]

If Mr. *[Simon P.]* Hanscome, the editor of the Republican comes up tomorrow morning, let him copy and publish the within notice of my departure if he wishes—on reflection I think you had better make two copies of it yourself and give one to him and the other to the "Star" Reporter.

To John Hay, St. Joseph, Missouri, 29 June 1864[140]

Confidential

During my few days' sojourn here, I have been looking a little into "the situation:"

If Missouri be not "governed too much," it is at least governed by too many different and conflicting authorities. For instance: Gen. C. B. Fisk is in command of this District, comprising all the Counties of the State lying north of the Missouri River, exercising all the usual functions and authority of a District Commander.[141] But his is not the only military authority in the District. There is in addition, a system of military provost marshals (not those appointed under the enrol*[l]*ment law) but appointed under the orders of Gen. Rosecrans, and governed, regulated, and instructed by Col. *[John P.]* Sanderson, of Gen. Rosecrans staff, who is the Provost Marshal General, of that system. This military district commanded by Gen. Fisk, is subdivided into nine subdistricts, each of which has a provost marshal, appointed nominally by Rosecrans, but really by Sanderson, to whom they report, and under whose direction they gather information, make arrests, issue orders and do various acts, all independently of, and in many instances without the knowledge of Gen. Fisk the District Commander.

This is still not all. Under existing laws and orders, the Governor of Missouri controls certain organizations of State Militia, and again independently of the other military authorities of the State. That is: he may at his own option call and put certain militia into service, or being in service, he may relieve it from service, and disband it, he alone being the judge of the necessity of doing either. Using this District then, as an illustration, there are three distinct sources of military authority here, all independent of each other, viz

1 The District Commander

2 Sanderson's Provost Marshals

3. The Governor as Com. in Chief of the State Militia.

It is easy to see that perpetual confusion and conflict of authority, and especially conflict of policy grows out of this state of things, and I have no doubt that many of the Missouri troubles grow solely out of this confusion.

One of the most serious of the late affairs in this district, grew directly out of this independent police system of Sanderson's.

A detective or scout named Truman went to Sanderson and Rosecrans, and professed to be able to ferret out a great conspiracy which had for its object the capture of Hannibal, Quincy and other points by guerrillas. They believed him, and sent him up here with directions to detail a squad of soldiers to go with him under his orders, who were to disguise themselves as guerrillas, and thus spy out and punish the plotters. Truman however seems to have been a very bad character, illiterate, intemperate, immoral, and subsequently criminal. Gen. Fisk suspected him from the first, and soon becoming convinced after he had started on his scout that his suspicions were true, ordered him to report himself to Sanderson at St. Louis. Truman however, instead of obeying the order, telegraphed to Sanderson and Rosecrans, asking permission to "stay in the field a week longer," saying it was a "military necessity." Sanderson and Rosecrans answered his telegram and told him to "go ahead." He went ahead and in a few days summarily shot and hung <u>seven</u> men, whom he took from their houses and farms, and who were not at the time in arms or engaged in overt acts of treason. This occurred in Chariton county. Of course it produced a reign of terror there. Everybody took to the brush, and since that time, <u>thirteen</u> Union men have been murdered in retaliation. Altogether it was a most terrible affair. Truman was promptly arrested, and is now in confinement here for trial.[142]

The Governor's independent action in Militia matters is a great source of difficulty to the District Commander here. In counties where the force is very much needed, the Governor has neglected to commission the officers which have been chosen, while in others he has relieved and disbanded the militia already serving. Since I have been here, one company in Ralls Co. and another in Pike Co have been thus relieved from duty, the first notice the District Commander had of it, being the petitions and protests of the Union men there, not to be left unprotected at the mercy of the bushwhackers. Of course politics has much to do with all these local movements and changes. In this district as elsewhere in the State, the feuds are bitter and unrelenting and the language and acts of men intemperate and rash. I do not pretend to say who is right or who is wrong; the point I make is, that the division and conflict of authority as it now exists, is powerless for good and potent for mischief.

Gen. Fisk, the District Commander here, whom the President personally knows is, I am convinced, an able, prudent and sagacious officer. His policy has been to conciliate—to induce men to cease wrangling and fighting, and to promote peace and quiet, by laboring together for the re-establishment of courts, schools, churches, and engaging in philanthropic enterprises, and pursuing the cultivation of their farms—so that the whole military power of the district could be used to put down the actual bushwhackers and guerrillas. To his appeals in this behalf he has met most encouraging responses from the people of the District; but his pacific efforts have been in a measure prevented and neutralized by the disadvantageous division and conflict of authority under which he has been compelled to labor.

To John Hay, St. Joseph, Missouri, 29 June 1864[143]

<u>Confidential</u> Please lay the enclosed before the President, if he can find time to read it.

Sanderson's Chariton Co. Affair has a very bad look about it now—I don't know how it may develop itself on the trial. Both he and Rosey [*Gen. Rosecrans*] seem to have been miserably duped by the man Truman. Gen. Fisk seems to think that Sanderson is in a state of chronic stampede, while Gov. Hall curses him black and blue.[144] I doubt whether he is the proper man for inquisitor-general for this State. This affair greatly shakes my faith in the truth of his Val[*landigham*] conspiracy.[145] There is suspicion among some here that Sanderson runs too much of the machine in this State, while Rosey idles away valuable time inventing coal oil lamps.[146]

I think Gen. Fisk is a quiet shrewd and able man, who manages affairs here as well as is possible under his embarrassments. But with Sanderson on one flank, Gov. Hall on the other, the bushwhackers in front and his paw-paw militia in the rear, he has a hard row to hoe. He asked yesterday to be relieved from duty here. For his own sake I could wish him to succeed in this, but for the sake of the service I think he ought to stay. I doubt whether any one else could so well do his work. So far as I can learn he satisfies the people, which is a great thing in itself.

He has been very kind to me here, and should he come to Washington during my absence, please give whatever facilities and assistance you can, on my behalf.

To John Hay, St. Joseph, Missouri, 2 July 1864[147]

I see by the dispatches of yesterday that Chase has resigned, and Gov. Tod has been appointed to succeed him.[148] What's up?

If things break loose generally so as to make my presence desirable at home, telegraph me to Fort Kearney, and Cottonwood Springs.

We had another delay this morning, and it is now 1 o'clock P.M. but I think we shall get across the river and started in an hour or two.

To Therena Bates, Washington, 5 August 1864[149]

I am safely back here again. . . . I find Hay well, and the work in the office going along comfortably. . . .

To John McMahon, Washington, 6 August 1864[150]

The President has received yours of yesterday and is kindly paying attention to it.[151] As it is my business to assist him whenever I can, I will thank you to inform me, for his use, whether you are either a white man or a black one, because in either case you cannot be regarded as an entirely impartial judge. It may be that you belong to a third of fourth class of <u>yellow</u> or <u>red</u> men, in which case the impartiality of your judgment would be more apparent.

To Therena Bates, Washington, 14 August 1864[152]

The staple topic of all conversation here—viz the heat—must also be the staple subject for letters if it continues at its present intensity—for there is literally no escaping from it day or night, and however stale or disagreeable and it is both, it will continue to force itself upon everybody's attention. It is found here I think in its most inevitable, and most subduing and oppressive form, anywhere between this and Fort Kearney, St. Jo. not excepted. Still, I came back here so much refreshed and reinvigorated by my trip, that I am enduring the baking and stewing to which I am at present subjected with a reasonable degree of patience and philosophy.

Hay left day before yesterday on a trip to his home in Warsaw, on which he expects to be gone some five or six weeks.

There is no news except the report of Farraguts successful operations in Mobile Bay. I suppose we shall be able to get and hold Forts Morgan and Gaines (the latter of which surrendered according to rebel reports) and will thus be able to relieve a large number of our blockading vessels.[153] But I doubt whether we shall immediately succeed in capturing the city because the channel is so shallow that our vessels cannot approach near enough to it to bombard it.

To Clinton B. Fisk, Washington, 14 August 1864[154]

. . . Although the country generally is in a feverish and unsatisfied condition, at our failure to obtain great military successes thus far during the season, the President is as ever, patient, plucky and confident. . . .

To George W. Bridges, Washington, 18 August 1864[155]

If Governor Andrew Johnson thinks execution of sentence in case of Wm. R. Bridges should be further suspended, and will request it, the President will order it.[156]

To Daniel S. D. Baldwin, Washington, 19 August 1864[157]

The President never interferes with the details of Army organization,[158] and the note of Hon. D. S. Dickinson, accompanying your application of the 17th inst. is returned, as it is presumed it will have as much weight with

General Patrick,[159] as if it were directed to him, instead of Major Gen. Burnside.

To William Henry Seward, Washington, 19 August 1864[160]

The President directs me to send you the enclosed letter and to request you to consider its suggestions.[161]

To Mrs. John Tyler, Washington, 19 August 1864[162]

I am directed by the President of the United States, to acknowledge the receipt, of your letter of the 15th inst. requesting that your home on the James River, may be restored to the charge of your manager, Mr J. C. Tyler.

The President directs me to say in reply, that military considerations must of course control the decision of your request, and that the subject is therefore referred to Major General Butler.

To Therena Bates, Washington, 21 August 1864[163]

. . . The week has passed again without any remarkable event. There is rather a bad state of feeling throughout the Union party about the political condition of things. The want of any decided military successes thus far, and the necessity of the new draft in the coming month, has materially discouraged many of our good friends, who are inclined to be a little weak-kneed, and croakers are talking everywhere about the impossibility of re-electing Mr. Lincoln, "unless something is done." What that precise something is to be they don't very distinctly define. I think however, that it is mainly anxiety and discouragement and that they will recover from it, after the Democrats shall have made their nominations at Chicago, and after the active fighting of the political campaign begins. The Democrats are growing bold and confident, and will be very unscrupulous, but I still *[do]* not think they can defeat Mr. Lincoln in any event. . . .

To William T. Otto, Washington, 22 August 1864[164]

In accordance with our conversation of today, I will be obliged if you will have an appointment made out for Edward D. Neill of Minnesota to be Secretary to the President to sign Land Patents.

I enclose the resignation of Mr. Neill as a Second Class Clerk in your Department, and respectfully ask that you appoint Charles H. Philbrick, of Illinois, to fill this vacancy, as soon as he shall arrive here.[165] I have written him today to come.

To Horace Greeley, Washington, 23 August 1864[166]

I will be very glad to see the friend whom you mention in your note of the 21st inst., which is just received.[167] Please give him a letter of introduction to me.

To William S. Rosecrans, Washington, 24 August 1864[168]

David D. Mills, Private Co. B 1st Iowa Cavalry, in Myrtle St. Prison, St. Louis, writes that he is condemned to be executed Sept. 2, 1864, and asks executive clemency.

The President requests that you will please examine the case.[169]

To William Henry Seward, Washington, 24 August 1864[170]

The President desires me to send to you, the enclosed letter of Mr Ward Hunt,[171] with the request, that you will, after perusal, return it.[172]

To Simon Cameron, Washington, 24 August 1864[173]

The President desires me to write, that your letter of the 22nd inst, with the enclosures, has been duly received.[174]

To John Hay, Washington, 25 August 1864[175]

Hell is to pay. The N.Y. politicians have got a stampede on that is about to swamp everything. Raymond and the National Committee are here today. R. thinks a commission to Richmond is about the only salt to save us— while the Tycoon sees and says it would be utter ruination. The matter is now undergoing consultation. Weak-kneed d——d fools like Chas. Sumner are in the movement for a new candidate—to supplant the Tycoon.[176] Everything is darkness and doubt and discouragement. Our men see giants in the airy and unsubstantial shadows of the opposition, and are about to surrender without a fight.

I think that today and here is the turning-point in our crisis. If the President can infect R. and his committee with some of his own patience and pluck, we are saved. If our friends will only rub their eyes and shake themselves, and become convinced that they themselves are not dead we shall win the fight overwhelmingly.

To William Dorsheimer, Washington, 27 August 1864[177]

Your letter of the 24th inst. was not received until this morning*[.]* [178] The President directs me to thank you for your kind offers, and suggestion, but thinks the step you propose had better not be taken, because the danger of complication from it is much greater than the promise of any good results.

To Edward D. Neill, Washington, 28 August 1864[179]

I start tonight to New York, to be gone two or three days.

Take charge of the office, and get along with the work as well as you can.

Where business can be deferred, defer it till my return.

To Edward D. Neill, Washington, 28 August 1864[180]

Save all the Chicago papers so that we may have a full report of the *[Democratic]* Convention.

To Therena Bates, Washington, 28 August 1864[181]

. . . I have been rather expecting to make another visit to the West in September, but it is rendered somewhat doubtful by the present rush of affairs. I think Hay will be back by the middle of September, but it may take both of us to keep the office under proper headway.

I wrote to you that the Republican party was laboring under a severe fit of despondency and discouragement. During the past week it reached almost the condition of a disastrous panic—a sort of political Bull Run—but I think it has reached its culmination and will speedily have a healthy and vigorous reaction. It even went so far as that Raymond, the Chairman of the National Executive Committee wrote a most doleful letter here to the President, summing up the various discouraging signs he saw in the country, and giving it as his deliberate opinion that unless <u>something</u> was done, (and he thought that "something" should be the sending Commissioners to Richmond to propose terms of peace to the Rebels, on the basis of their returning to the Union) that we might as well quit and give up the contest.[182] In this mood he came here to Washington three or four days ago to attend a meeting of the Executive Committee of the National Committee. The President and the strongest half of the Cabinet—Seward, Stanton and Fessenden,[183] held a consultation with him, and showed him that they already thoroughly considered and discussed his proposition; and upon showing him their reasons, he very readily concurred with them in the opinion that to follow his plan of sending Commissioners to Richmond, would be worse than losing the Presidential contest—it would be ignominiously surrendering it in advance.

Nevertheless the visit of himself and committee here did very great good.

They found the President and Cabinet wide awake to all the necessities of the situation, and went home much encouraged and cheered up. I think that immediately upon the nominations being made at Chicago (it seems now as if McClellan would undoubtedly be the nominee) the whole Republican Party throughout the country will wake up, begin a spirited campaign and win the election.

To Reverdy Johnson, Washington, 28 August 1864[184]

Telegram has been sent to Gen. Wallace.[185]

To Charles J. M. Gwynn, Washington, 28 August 1864[186]

Telegram has been sent to Gen. Wallace.[187]

To President Lincoln, New York, 29 August 1864[188]

I did not reach here until noon today, in consequence of the late train of last night coming no farther than Philadelphia.

I have seen no one yet but Mr. Raymond and Mr. Weed, and several influential men from the country, who were in Mr. Raymond's office when I went there.

Raymond is still of opinion that the changes contemplated should be made at once, although he does not seem to have conferred with any one, except Weed, who joins him very decidedly in the same belief. I myself asked Mr. Weed the distinct question whether the change ought to be made now, or after the election, and he answered, <u>now</u> by all means.

The conference of Raymond and Sherman[189] with him this morning of course apprised him that the step was in contemplation. I do not know through whose instrumentality it was, but somehow Mr. Draper[190] has been informed that you were thinking of appointing him Surveyor, and he and some of his friends are stirring up a new difficulty by announcing and insisting that he will decline it. I enclose a letter to you on the subject from Draper's bosom friend, Moses H. Grinnell,[191] who had just brought it to Mr. Weed to be forwarded to you when I saw him.

There is however still a chance that Draper will re-consider this determination. If he does not then I advise, on the strength of what I have heard today, that you accept his declension as final, and leave him out in the cold until he becomes more tractable. I will write more fully of this tomorrow.

I hope Fenton may come on tonight, as he thought he would, so that I may have his advice in the matter tomorrow.[192]

To President Lincoln, New York, 30 August 1864[193]

Mr. Fenton arrived here this morning and had a conversation with Weed, in which he urged upon Weed his reasons in detail <u>against</u> any changes in the Custom House at this time. Mr. Weed heard him through, admitted there was much force in what he said, but was not convinced. In a conversation with me afterwards, Mr. Weed repeated what he said to me yesterday, that changes were absolutely necessary and would be productive of much good. Delafield Smith,[194] and Mr. Evarts[195] also concur with Weed. Gov. Morgan was here at the Astor House a little while this evening. I talked with him on the subject, and while he seemed to have no definite impressions as to what really was best to be done, he said he would stand by whatever you might do. I saw Greeley yesterday and today; I did not talk very fully with him on this matter but gathered from what he said, that while he did not see much good likely to result from changes, yet that Barney was not good for anything.

On the whole I have concluded that I will endeavor to see Barney and Andrews as early as I can tomorrow, if they are in the City, and ask them for their resignations in accordance with your instructions.

Almost all those with whom I have consulted, however, unite in saying that, excepting the Collector and Surveyor, there should be very few, <u>if any</u> other changes in their subordinates. Those who are in should have the hope of being <u>kept</u> in as a motive for work, while those who are out should have the hope of being <u>put</u> in to prompt them. The new appointees of Collector and Surveyor should receive instructions from yourself on this point.

Mr. Evarts is very earnest that Draper should be made collector instead of Wakeman.[196]

Gov. Morgan and Senator Morrill have been through most of the New England States.[197] They report an improved state of feeling in all respects, and say we will certainly *[carry]* Maine at the approaching September election, by a good majority.

In my conversation with Mr. Greeley I urged upon him the necessity of fighting in good earnest in this campaign. He said in reply "I shall fight like a savage in this campaign. I hate McClellan."

Mr. Weed and Gov Morgan concur in the opinion that Preston King will not take the Post Office in this city.[198] Gov. Morgan suggests James Kelley instead.[199]

I send this by Robert *[Todd Lincoln]*. If I get matters arranged satisfactorily I may start home tomorrow night—if not I will stay another day unless you telegraph for me.

To President Lincoln, New York, 31 August 1864[200]

Confidential I called on Mr. Barney today and gave him your message. He said he desired a few days of time in which he might prepare his papers, accounts &c for the change, and suggested that he would tender his resignation today to take effect on the 5th of Sept., to which I agreed, and he has forwarded the resignation to the Secretary of the Treasury by tonights mail. He was at first a little surprised and disposed to temporize about it—suggesting that he would like to go to Washington to confer with you on the subject, &c—but at length acquiesced very cheerfully, saying that he should still do all he could for you and the cause, and should retain all his personal friendship and esteem for you.

Mr. Andrews whom I have also seen did not accede to your request. He spoke of it as a sacrifice demanded by Mr. Weed to gratify his personal ill-will towards him—said you were mistaken in supposing Mr. Weed controlled the politics of the State—said that if you would wait until after the coming State Convention, and were not convinced that he (Andrews) carried the Convention against Weed he would willingly resign &c.[201]

He finally left me without saying what he would do, but afterwards sent me the letter which I enclose.

He said however that even if you removed him, he should support yourself and the ticket.

My impression tonight is that you will do best to adhere to your original programme, although Mr. Weed and some of his friends have mooted the proposition to make Dennison collector,[202] Draper Naval Officer, and Wakeman Surveyor. Weed told me this afternoon that he thought Draper would agree to this. I am also informed that Wakeman would be satisfied with it.

But I still think that if you adhere to the original plan, Mr. Draper will finally acquiesce, although he now seems firm in his determination to decline.

I shall stay here over tomorrow. Shall I come home tomorrow night, or shall I remain longer, to look after this and other matters? Please telegraph.

To President Lincoln, New York, 31 August 1864[203]

I was in a great hurry when I closed the letter which I forwarded by the 7 1/2 train this evening, and forgot to enclose Mr. Andrews' letter to which I referred. I enclose it herewith and send it by the train which will reach Washington by noon tomorrow.

To Therena Bates, Washington, 4 September 1864[204]

I returned on yesterday from New York, where I have been since last Monday, on a mission from the President in connection with some changes in the custom house officials, which the President deemed advisable and necessary. It was a very delicate, disagreeable and arduous duty, but I think my visit had a beneficial influence, and assisted in bringing about some much needed reforms.

Our friends in New York were much dispirited when I went there, and evidently gave up all hope of Republican success in this fall's election. But several circumstances—the fall of Mobile, the Chicago nominations and Platform, &c. &c.—occurred while I was there, and gave them new hope and courage and I think we shall have no similar despondency during the campaign. While it is utterly impossible to harmonize all the New York factions, I think they will generally acquiesce in the new appointments the President will make there, and work earnestly for success in November. . . .

The political condition has very much improved since I last wrote to you. The depression under which our friends were everywhere laboring, is undergoing a very decided and healthy reaction; the surrender platform which the Chicago Convention made is disgusting very many honest War Democrats, and the fall of Fort Morgan and capture of Atlanta by Sherman of which we received news here yesterday morning,[205] will stimulate it into a very potent enthusiasm. If things continue as favorable as they seem today we shall beat Little Mac very handsomely. When I left New York the feeling against the Chicago Platform was so strong that the universal rumor was that he would take grounds in favor of the prosecution of the War in his letter of acceptance.[206] I do not think however that that will save him. In a conversation with a Democratic friend there I told him that I thought Little Mac's blanket was too short—if he pulled it up over his head his feet would stick out—if he kept his feet covered he would have cold ears. Unless the Republicans are recreant to every sentiment of duty and honor we shall send this Chicago programme to a speedy oblivion. The Lord preserve this country *[from]* the kind of peace they would give us. It will be a dark day for this nation if they should elect the Chicago ticket, and purchase <u>peace</u> at the cost of Disunion, Secession, Bankruptcy and National Dishonor, and an "ultimate" Slave Empire. I cannot think that Providence has this humiliation or disgrace and disaster in store for us. . . .

To William Henry Seward, Washington, 6 September 1864[207]

Should the enclosed be acknowledged, and if so how?

To Theodore Tilton, Washington, 6 September 1864[208]

<u>Confidential</u> There is no truth whatever in the report that Mr. Lincoln said he was "a beaten man." I felt quite sure of it when I saw you, though of course I could not positively know the fact as I do now. We have encouraging news from all quarters. The Atlanta victory alone ought to win the Presidential contest for us.[209]

To Therena Bates, Washington, 11 September 1864[210]

While the week just passed has brought us no event of startling nature or great magnitude, there have been some lesser ones that are gratifying, and which assist materially in improving the general feeling of the country, and especially the political situation.

1st Sherman's Victory at Atlanta, according to the details received proves in every way as effective and important as was expected from the first and incomplete report.

2d McClellan having written and published his letter of acceptance, and having attempted in it to ignore and dodge the question presented by the platform whether he was for war or peace, finds the difference of opinion on this point, in his party, irreconcilable, and has developed a row in the happy Democratic family which promises to be serious—two influential New York papers having already repudiated him. "Go it husband, go it bear."[211]

3d The publication of Grant's letter in which he gives an encouraging view of the military situation, and tells the country the true road to peace is through hard fighting till the rebellion is put down.[212]

4th The Vermont election which shows from 3 to 5000 gain on her former Republican majority.

5th The ready acceptance by the moneyed men of the new 30 Million Loan recently offered by Fessenden, about three times the amount having been bid for.

Altogether the results of the week are most cheering and inspiring. The political situation has not been as hopeful for six months past as it is just now. There is a perfect revolution in feeling. Three weeks ago, our friends everywhere were despondent, almost to the point of giving up the contest in despair. Now they are hopeful, jubilant, hard at work and confident of success.

We are anxiously awaiting the result of the election in Maine day after tomorrow, which will have a very decided influence on the campaign. Our friends there are sanguine of success.

Hay has not yet returned and I cannot yet decide whether or when I will come west.

To James C. Conkling, Washington, 12 September 1864[213]

Private

Your two letters of the 5th & 6th Inst giving information about the proposed Cincinnati Convention have been duly received by the President.[214] We had also had previous notice of the movement from other sources. From all I have learned about it, I do not think that it has at any time been formidable. Not more than two or three men of any preeminence or influence have openly avowed their support of it. Some others secretly sympathised with it, but very soon they became convinced that it was utterly futile, and for at least two weeks past, have abandoned all expectations that it would result in anything whatever, and have since that time given an efficient, if not a willing support to the President. I think our friend need be under no apprehension that any other than he will be our Presidential candidate. The chances are much greater that Fremont will be withdrawn, and that his supporters will unite with us, than that any new candidate will be further urged by those who are dissatisfied with the President. Our news from all quarters is very encouraging. I hope you will succeed in making a vigorous campaign in Illinois. If you have time, please keep me posted as to its progress.

To Simon Cameron, Washington, 14 September 1864[215]

Private

Your note of yesterday came duly to hand.[216] When last I heard from General Schurz he was making preparations with the expectation of making a speech at Philadelphia. I suppose you can learn his whereabouts and engagements by writing to Mr Raymond.

The President yesterday made an order in reference to Major Taggart.[217] The Lehigh matter is being looked after. It was necessary to make some enquiries by letter there.

To Horace Greeley, Washington, 15 September 1864[218]

Private

In furtherance of the idea you suggested to me when in New York, I send you enclosed a copy of the letter of Col. Markland Special Mail Agent, who has under Mr Blair's instructions, made arrangements for the distribution of such newspapers, or other political matter, as the National Committee may determine to circulate in the Army of the Potomac.[219] Will you please show it to Mr Raymond and confer with him further on the subject?

Your late letter,[220] enclosing one from Col Conkling was duly received,[221] and shown to the President. Col. Phillips' papers were specially referred by the President to the Secretary of War.[222] Our news from all quarters is very encouraging.

To Therena Bates, Washington, 18 September 1864[223]

Hay returned home this morning—that is to say returned here. . . .

Maine, which voted on Monday last, went handsomely in our favor, giving about her full majority of last year. Should the same general result prevail throughout the country as did last year, and the result*[s]* in Vermont and Maine are very strong indications that such will be the case, then Mr. Lincoln will receive a very large majority of the Electoral votes. The next important elections that are to come off are those in Indiana and Pennsylvania, which occur on the 11th of October next. From all I can learn the result in both these States is somewhat doubtful, that in Indiana most so because of the absence of her soldiers in the field who are not permitted to vote. Should Indiana and Pennsylvania go decidedly for us, the Democrats will have but very little courage and hope left for the remainder of the campaign; on the contrary, should they go against us, the Democrats will take great encouragement, and we great despondency from the result, and then the campaign will become very desperate, doubtful, and fierce on both sides, with the largest chances in our favor. At all events the contest will be short, and we shall soon know whether the country is to be saved under Lincoln or lost under McClellan

To Leonard Grover, Washington, 19 September 1864[224]

Presented your matter at Treasury Department. They say the matter lies exclusively within the discretion of Collector at New York. He will probably admit them at once.

To President Lincoln, New York, 22 September 1864[225]

I found Mr Weed absent when I arrived here, and although he was expected this morning, he has not yet returned.

A friend of his telegraphed him today that I was here, and wished to see him, and he thinks he will be here tomorrow.[226]

To William E. Chandler, Washington, 28 September 1864[227]

Private

Your telegram of this morning, announcing that the Supreme Court of your State has unanimously decided your Soldiers' Voting Bill to be a law, has been duly received by the President who expresses his great satisfaction thereat.

I take this opportunity to apologize for and explain my seeming neglect of the letter you wrote to me in connection with this matter, asking my certificate as to the usual mode of presenting bills to the President.[228] At the time your letter reached me I was too sick to do any work. The papers were on my table to be attended to among the first things I should do, but before I got well, I went off quite suddenly to New York on a mission for the President, from which I only returned on Monday morning last, and since which time until the receipt of your dispatch, I have scarcely been strong enough to write a letter. I beg that you will not think that the matter was neglected from any indisposition on my part to assist you as far as possible in reaching a right determination of the case, but charge it to the account of unavoidable delays, from which fortunately in this case, no adverse results have come.

To Hanson A. Risley, Washington, 1 October 1864[229]

If you should be passing by the Executive Mansion before 4 1/2 P.M. today will you please call up and see me a moment?

To Therena Bates, Washington, 2 October 1864[230]

I have but little to write to you in the shape of news except that Sheridan seems to have made very sure work of his recent victory in the Shenandoah Valley,[231] and that Grant, by way of preventing Lee's sending any fresh forces against Sheridan, has again been attacking Lee's army in front of Petersburg and Richmond, and thus far with very fair success, having captured fifteen guns in one assault.[232] I do not yet know whether it be merely a demonstration, on his part, or whether he intends to make a real attempt to take one or both places. A day or two more I suppose will develop his purpose.

The political news from all directions is very encouraging. In Indiana and Pennsylvania the contest has been very closely fought, and the result at the elections to be held on the 11th inst. is still in some doubt, though our friends are very hopeful of carrying both by a small majority. But whether we carry them or not, it is very generally conceded that the President will be re-elected in November unless the popular feeling should greatly change in the interim. . . .

To Therena Bates, Washington, 4 October 1864[233]

Quite unexpectedly to myself, the President this morning asked me to go out to St. Louis to attend to some matters there for him. . . .

To Horace Greeley, Washington, 4 October 1864[234]

Confidential

I brought to the President's notice, your suggestion about the matter of exchange of prisoners, and learned from him, the reason why nothing can be done about it at present. The reason is <u>conclusive,</u> as you would at once appreciate, and admit if I could see and tell you.

All our political news continues good.[235]

To Capt. Edward G. Bush, Washington, 5 October 1864[236]

Planters House until 3 P M this 28th Oct.

To President Lincoln, St. Louis, 10 October 1864[237]

I reached here safely on Saturday last at about noon. Since then I have seen and talked with a number of gentlemen, but up to this time rather with a view of getting at the precise state of <u>feeling</u> they entertain, than in the way of suggestion to any of them. Things are in a pretty bad tangle, but I think they are gravitating towards an understanding—temporary at least if not permanent—which will unite the vote of all the union men on the electoral and State ticket. But I shall look farther, and talk more, tomorrow, and will report progress as soon as any is made.

To President Lincoln, St. Louis, 12 October 1864[238]

Confidential

General Rosecrans this morning asked me to obtain for him, a copy of his official report of the battle of Rich Mountain, together with the supplementary reports of the Regimental commanders, and also your permission that he may make the same public.[239]

His object in this is to controvert McClellan's Report of that battle, in which he thinks McClellan has done him (Rosecrans) injustice.[240]

Without having heard the General say directly, that he was for you, all his language to me leaves no other inference, and I am sure that the foregoing request is made with a view to make a publication that shall assist your election.

As some of our friends here suspect him of sometimes talking a little on the other side, I think it most advisable to furnish him as promptly as possible, the means and occasion of defining his position in such a way that it may no longer be misunderstood, as he has of his own accord requested it.

He says that at the time he made the report it was forwarded to Washington so promptly that he had no opportunity of keeping a copy.

I do not see that any harm can result from giving him one, and at the same time it will gratify him and assist the common cause.

To President Lincoln, Springfield, Illinois, 18 October 1864[241]

I arrived here last night, having left St. Louis yesterday morning. I was there over a week, and talked very fully with our friends of all the different factions, and have I think as full and fair an understanding of their quarrels as one can get in such brief time.

My conclusion is, that there is little else than <u>personal animosity</u>, and the usual eagerness to appropriate the spoils, that is left to prevent a full and harmonious combination of all the Union voters of Missouri. Even these obstacles are fast giving way before the change and pressure of circumstances, and the mere lapse of time.

Of the Claybank faction,[242] but little is left in point of numbers. Such portion of them as did not go to the Democracy (where they originally came from) are fusing with the Radicals, until but a small nucleus, consisting of the office-holders, and a few old personal friends of Frank Blair, remains as a distinct and separate organization. They are held aloof more by pride and personal feeling, I think, than anything else.

A few days before my arrival in St. Louis, Mr. *[William L.]* Avery, the Secretary of the Western branch of the Union National Committee, had called a meeting of men belonging to the different factions, with a view of bringing about united action, and also to devise measures for a more active campaign. The meeting was well attended, and the talk was conciliatory. A committee was appointed; when it met, Hume offered a resolution to raise a finance committee to collect funds,[243] and Foy offered a substitute,[244] proposing to vote for all candidates that would support Lincoln and Johnson, and that the primary meetings, conventions &c. for the selection of candidates should be called simply "Union" meetings. The Radicals would not consent to strike the word "Radical" from their party title, and voted down

Foy's substitute, whereupon he and others withdrew from the Committee. A number of Claybanks, however, took part in the primary meetings and conventions for nomination of the County ticket, and two or three Claybanks were put on the ticket.

Foy and Blair both told me that the only test they desired to make was that candidates, whether State, Congressional or County, should avow themselves for you. That the man who would not avow himself for you when the choice was only between yourself and McClellan, was clearly not your friend; and that you certainly could not wish your friends to vote for your enemies. While I was in St. Louis, the Claybanks held a caucus, to which I was invited, where the same sentiments were expressed, and at which a committee was appointed to address a letter to the various candidates, asking them the direct question whether or not they intended to support you. So much for the Claybanks.

As to the Radicals, Hume called on me the day after my arrival, and told me that he had some weeks before interrogated Fletcher, the Radical candidate for Governor,[245] and had received his private assurance that he would support you, but that he did not then deem it politic to declare his purpose, because such avowal would be almost certain to alienate from him a large number of Germans who were yet bitterly hostile to you, and who in such event would take measures to set up a ticket of their own. Afterwards I saw Fletcher, who had the evening before made a little reception speech at Barnum's Hotel, in which, while announcing his determination not to vote for McClellan, he had not said anything about voting for you. Fletcher told me that when he arrived, he had made up his mind to announce his purpose to vote for you; but that at Barnum's he had found the letter of the Claybank Committee (which I have previously mentioned,) and that he concluded he would not be coerced into an explanation; but that in the course of a week or ten days he would take occasion to declare himself for you. Meanwhile primary meetings had been held, and on Monday Oct 10th the County Convention was held and a ticket nominated. The Convention did not adopt a resolution endorsing the national ticket. On the same day the Congressional Convention for the second District was held, and nominated Blow. He has not yet, even in private, admitted that he would vote for you. On the 12th, the Congressional Convention for the 1st District met. Knox[246] was the candidate of the "Democrat" Office clique[247]—C. P. Johnson[248] was the candidate of those against the Democrat. Johnson was nominated; but the Knox men contended that the nomination was unfair, and have bolted, and when I left were obtaining signatures requesting Knox to run independent. As that however would most likely insure the election of a Democrat, efforts were also being made to induce both Johnson and Knox to withdraw, and to combine the Union vote on Judge *[Samuel T.]* Clover *[Glover]*. The indications were when I came away that this would be done in a day or two.

I gave Mr. Foy your message and learned from him that he and the other office-holders are entirely willing to acquiesce in your wishes. They claim they have always been ready to support the ticket as soon as candidates were ready to declare themselves for you. I am satisfied that the indisposition on the part of both radicals and claybanks to come forward in a manly spirit and heal their dissensions, is due entirely to the long and chronic character of the quarrel, and that in the very nature of the case the reconciliation will be somewhat slow, although it seems to be going on pretty satisfactorily now.

It seems to be very well understood that with the exception of very few impracticables, the Union men will cast their votes, for you, for the radical Congressmen, for the Emancipation candidates for the State Legislature and the State Convention, so that in practice nearly everybody is right and united, while in profession everybody is wrong, or at cross purposes. I do not see that anything but time will abate the disorder.

When I arrived, Gen. Rosecrans had not yet issued his order about the election, and the radicals were very apprehensive, and anxious about that— more so than about their own factious quarrels, or the distribution of patronage. They said, "a good election order is the main thing we want. That, and that alone will enable us to carry the State." Rosecrans issued his order and they expressed themselves entirely satisfied with it.[249] They said I might assure you that you would carry the State.[250] Fletcher, who knows more of the other parts of the State than of the City, seems confident of the same result. He thinks he will be elected by ten thousand majority. I think he is perhaps too sanguine, but he seems pretty confident, and as he has lately been a good deal among the people, his judgment ought to be pretty good.

I urged upon the factions in the 1st Congressional district, that their quarrel ought not to be permitted to lose us the Congressman there—that if we continued to make gains as we had done in Indiana, Ohio and Pennsylvania we should get a two-thirds vote in the House and thus be able to pass the Constitutional Amendment about Slavery.[251] They acknowledged the importance of the matter and will I think unite on a third candidate and elect him.[252]

**To President Lincoln, Springfield, Illinois,
8 November 1864**[253]

Springfield township gives twenty 20 maj*[ority]* for Lincoln

**To President Lincoln, Springfield, Illinois,
10 November 1864**[254]

Few & scattering returns from the State received as yet but they show a pretty uniform union gain in the vote of eighteen sixty 1860.

**To President Lincoln, Springfield, Illinois,
10 November 1864**[255]

Reported vote of forty four 44 Counties gives Lincoln twenty five thousand majority a gain of four thousand two hundred on your vote of sixty *[1860]* in the same Counties. Both branches Legislature & ten union Congressmen

To Therena Bates, Washington, 4 December 1864[256]

. . . Although the session of Congress begins tomorrow comparatively few members have yet arrived in the city so that I doubt whether a quorum will be on hand. The President's message is finished and printed, but he thinks he will not send it in before Tuesday, which will give me more time to have the MSS. copies prepared and to get ready to deliver it.

Hay and I were invited to attend some private theatricals at the Navy Yard on Thursday night last, which went off very creditably; and last night we went to a gentleman's party given by Forney at his rooms on Capitol Hill.[257] . . .

To Therena Bates, Washington, 8 December 1864[258]

. . . Congress met on Monday but the President did not get the message ready until Tuesday, when it was sent in, and at the same time he sent in the nomination of Chase as Chief Justice of the Supreme Court. Probably no other man than Lincoln would have had, in this age of the world, the degree of magnanimity to thus forgive and exalt a rival who had so deeply and so unjustifiably intrigued against him.[259] It is however only another most marked illustration of the greatness of the President, in this age of little men. . . .

To Therena Bates, Washington, 11 December 1864[260]

Scarcely anything of interest transpired during the last half of the week just past. Congress, following its usual habits of indolence and of letting everything take its own time at the beginning of a session, adjourned over from Wednesday afternoon until tomorrow, the Monday following. The only news we have from Sherman's army is that furnished us by the rebel newspapers, that he concentrated his army at Millen, and was making his way towards the coast, intending it was supposed to come out somewhere near Beaufort, S.C. if he could manage to cross the Savannah river, which the rebel papers predicted he would most likely be unable to do. They promise their people every day that he is to be stopped, and surrounded, and annihilated, but do not indicate how or where. . . .

To Therena Bates, Washington, 16 December 1864[261]

. . . About three days of the week have been taken up with a row with my particular feminine friend here *[Mary Todd Lincoln]*, but I have got through it without any serious damage, or even loss of temper.

The news this morning is very encouraging from all quarters. Sherman is before if not in Savannah,[262] and Thomas seems to have defeated Hood at Nashville.[263] The Anaconda is beginning to squeeze the rebellion, and even our Canadian neighbors are beginning to show alarm lest the rebel raiders in their midst shall stir up a warmer hornets' nest on our northern borders than they may be able to bear.

In the House of Representatives yesterday Henry Winter Davis made one of his malignant but covert onslaughts on the Administration, but was promptly squelched by the House.

To Nathaniel P. Banks, Washington, 17 December 1864[264]

Permit me herewith to introduce my friend, Hon. S. M. Cullom Republican Member of Congress elect from the President's District in Illinois, who wishes to see you.[265]

To Therena Bates, Washington, 18 December 1864[266]

. . . General Thomas seems to have won a glorious and decisive victory at Nashville which substantially annihilates the last army the rebels had in the west. Sherman is before Savannah and will take the place I think at his leisure. There remains but the army of Lee to be caught and overcome, and the military strength of the rebellion is at an end. I think this result will almost certainly come within the next year, and I hope that we may even gladden our next fourth of July with the rejoicings over the great event.

To Simon Cameron, Washington, 23 December 1864[267]

Private

After pretty mature deliberation I am ready to join you and others in the enterprise of buying and publishing the "Baltimore Sun," if it can be obtained on the terms you mentioned to me. Before completing the arrangement, however, I want to talk over the matter fully with you.

Will you be here soon? or if not, when can I find you at home by coming to Harrisburg—or better still, could you not come to Baltimore?

Please write or telegraph me, as you think best.

P.S. Please say nothing to any one at present about my proposed connection with the affair.[268]

To Therena Bates, Washington, 24 December 1864[269]

. . . Congress has adjourned and the eagerness with which the members rush off to their several homes is a good indication that they expect a happier Christmas there, than they could by any possibility find in this labor-ridden and care-burdened town, whose very atmosphere seems infected with some subtle poison fatal to all peace of mind or repose of body. Sometime in the future years, when war and sorrow shall have lifted their shadow from the land, we may perhaps hope to establish the holidays here by Act of Congress or some equally potent authority, that shall compel us to garnish our lives at least for one week with the outward symbols of rejoicing, even if the heart shall find no cause to be glad. . . .

To William P. Fessenden, Washington, 29 December 1864[270]

The President of the United States will be pleased to receive the Members of the Cabinet, and their families on New Years Day (Monday January 2, 1865) at twelve oclock M. precisely.

To John M. Palmer, Washington, 30 December 1864[271]

I have duly received your letter of the 22d inst., and read the same to the President, as you desired me to do.[272]

In reply, the President requested me to say to you that you were not mistaken in the kindness and regard he entertains for you, and that he desired you to follow the course you had indicated in your letter, until you should hear from him.

To Therena Bates, Washington, 30 December 1864[273]

. . . I am kept pretty hard at work—that is about all the news I have to report—but well, and suffer in nothing but my temper.

We had the news of the fall of Savannah to cheer us on Christmas morning—or rather on Monday morning, which was kept as Christmas. We had hoped that we should be able to celebrate our New Years with re-joicings over the fall of Wilmington, but that expedition turns out a failure[.][274] . . .

1865

To William Henry Seward, Washington, 3 January 1865[1]

Mr. Robert Lincoln and myself will accompany you to Philadelphia and Trenton, to attend the funerals of Ex-Vice President Dallas,[2] and Minister Dayton[3] in accordance with your invitation of this morning.

To Therena Bates, Washington, 6 January 1865[4]

I have been absent three days on a trip to Philadelphia and Trenton, where I went in company with Mr. Seward, and Robert Lincoln, to attend the funerals of Mr. Dallas, Vice President under Polk, and Mr. Dayton—the President deeming that this mark of respect was due to these deceased gentlemen for their eminent worth and high public service. . . .

To H. A. Swift, Washington, 12 January 1865[5]

The President does not remember the case of the petition of Gen. H. Barnes, mentioned in your telegram. Pardons are usually made out formally and transmitted through official channels. The President's mere signature on a petition would not be a pardon, unless it was signed to an explicit order for one. I cannot send a more definite answer to your question unless it is stated more in detail.

To Therena Bates, Washington, 15 January 1865[6]

. . . The city is dull—and has been so, all during the past month. Events that are really important do not seem to make much impression upon the public mind. Sherman's advent in Savannah,[7] Butlers failure at Wilmington, the Debate in Congress on the Constitutional Amendment,[8] all excite but a momentary ripple of attention. I supposed the arrival of the gay season would make some little stir; but now after a week's experience that too seems to be going along without any real vitality. The President's public reception last Monday night, Mrs. Lincolns afternoon reception on yesterday, and Speaker Colfax's reception on Friday night last were well attended; but the other affairs of the week were all dull and spiritless—Mrs. *[Kate Chase]* Sprague's reception yesterday afternoon and Mrs. Seward's last night being both positive failures.

I do not know to what to ascribe this state of things unless it be to the reaction which follows the intense popular interest in the last Presidential election. Public feeling, though silent, was highly wrought up about that, and having safely passed that crisis I have no doubt is now in the condition of the most indifferent <u>laissez aller</u>. Whether or not it will recover, seems yet uncertain. . . .

Memorandum, 18 January 1865[9]

I went to the President this afternoon, at the request of Mr. Ashley,[10] on a matter connecting itself with the pending Amendment of the Constitution. The Camden & Amboy interest promised Mr. Ashley that if he would help postpone the Raritan Railroad Bill over this session,[11] they would in return make the N.J. Democrats help about the amendment either by their votes or absence.[12] Sumner being the Senate champion of the Raritan bill, Ashley went to him to ask him to drop it for this session. Sumner however showed reluctance to adopt Mr. Ashley's suggestion, saying that he hoped the amendment would pass anyhow, &c. Ashley thought he discovered in Summer's manner two reasons 1st that if the present Senate resolution were not adopted by the House, the Senate would send them another, in which they would most likely adopt Sumner's own phraseology, and thereby gratify his vanity and ambition; and 2d that Sumner thinks the defeat of the Camden & Amboy monopoly would establish a principle by legislative enactment, which would effectually crush out the last lingering relics of the States' Rights dogma. Ashley therefore desired the President to send for Sumner, and urge him to be practical and secure the passage of the amendment in the manner suggested by Mr. A.

I stated these points to the President who replied at once

"I can do nothing with Mr. Sumner in these matters. While Mr. Sumner is very cordial with me, he is making his history in an issue with me on this very point. He hopes to succeed in beating the President so as to change this government from its original form, and making it a strong centralized power."

Then calling Mr Ashley into the room, the President said to him, "I think I understand Mr. Sumner; and I think he would be all the more resolute in his persistence on the points which Mr. Nicolay has mentioned to me if he supposed I were at all watching his course on this matter."[13]

To Therena Bates, Washington, 26 January 1865[14]

. . . The city has been full of rumors about the peace negociations of the elder Blair, who has gone to Richmond a second time, but as the matter now stands I do not think anything is likely to come of it*[.]*[15]

Our armies are everywhere active, and military operations will be pushed ahead as fast as the winter weather will possibly permit. The whole military situation has been so much simplified and contracted by Sherman's successful march to Savannah that we all look forward to an early overthrow of the rebel armies with most sanguine hopes.

To President Lincoln, Washington, 31 January 1865[16]

Constitutional amendment just passed by 119 for to 56 votes against.[17]

To Lew Wallace, Washington, 31 January 1865[18]

Your second dispatch in regard to Waters is received.[19] The President's dispatch of this morning did not refer to Levin T. Waters, but to a man who it was represented had been convicted by a military commission of unlawful trade with the rebels or something of that kind, and was to be sent this morning to the Albany Penitentiary.[20] His name was given as Chas. E. Waters. If such prisoner is on his way north let him be brought back and held as directed in the President's dispatch.

To John A. Andrew, Washington, 1 February 1865[21]

The President of the United-States has just signed the Resolution of Congress submitting to the legislatures of the several States a proposition to amend the Constitution of the United States.

To Richard J. Oglesby, Washington, 1 February 1865[22]

Your dispatch received.[23] The Resolution of Congress submitting to the legislatures of the States a proposition to amend the Constitution of the United-States, was signed by the President today.

To Therena Bates, Washington, 4 February 1865[24]

. . . The excitement of the week has been the peace rumors and proceedings growing out of Blair's two trips to Richmond, which I mentioned in a former letter. The substance of what he accomplished was to get from Jeff Davis on the one hand, and the President on the other an expression of willingness to send or receive commissioners or persons who should be permitted to hold an informal conference about matters with a view to reaching a peace.

In pursuance of this willingness so expressed, Jeff. Davis, some days since sent Stephens,[25] Hunter[26] and Campbell[27] to our lines to hold such a conference. They were permitted to come to Fortress Monroe, where Seward went to meet them on Wednesday, and the President also went down on Thursday[.] They had on yesterday, a four hours' interview with them. It was a long and rambling talk, entirely friendly and courteous, and also entirely informal. Nothing was written.

Of course it would be impossible to give an outline of a four hours conversation; but substantially the talk amounted to this: the President told them that he could not entertain any proposition, or conversation which did not concede and embody the restoration of the national authority over the states now in revolt. That he could not recede in the least from what he had publicly said about slavery; and that he could *[not]* concede or agree to any cessation of hostilities, which was not an actual end of the war and a disbandment of the rebel armies.

They on their side neither offered nor declined any distinct point or proposition; but the drift of all their talk was that they desired a cessation of hostilities, or armistice, or as they phrased it "a postponement of the issue." So the conference broke up without any result or conclusion, or even without broaching or debating any points or propositions.

I ought to have mentioned at the beginning of this, that I was present at the House of Representatives on Tuesday last when the Constitutional amendment *[abolishing slavery]* was passed. It was a scene of great interest, and the announcement was greeted with loud and long applause. . . .

To Mark Hoyt, Washington, 8 February 1865[28]

The President has received your dispatch asking an interview.[29] He cannot appoint any specific day or hour, but your delegation may come at their own convenience and he will see them as soon as he possibly can after their arrival.

To John A. Andrew, Washington, 9 February 1865[30]

The President has today sent a dispatch ordering that the execution of Hugh F. Riley, Eleventh Mass. Vols. be suspended until further orders and the record forwarded for examination[31]

To Therena Bates, Washington, 10 February 1865[32]

Do not think that because I have written nothing about it, I have not been engaged in considering the question as to where I shall stay and what I shall do after next fourth of March. I have thought about the matter almost constantly ever since we talked it over . . . last fall; but I have not as yet reached any definite conclusion.

As the case now stands, I am pretty well resolved not to remain here in my present relation after that time, and I think the chances are also against my remaining in Washington. This feeling does not result from any talk with the President about the matter, although I have once or twice alluded to the subject in our conversation, but from other causes and considerations.[33] I think he does not now wish to be troubled with the question in any way, and therefore I do not repeat it to him. After his inauguration, however, other changes will necessarily take place, and after which I will probably be able to determine my own course. So I remain as patient as I can, three or four weeks longer.

We have had no special excitement this week. The President today sent a message to Congress in which he publishes the letters and telegrams preliminary to the late Peace conference at Fort Monroe. I think it will satisfy all the country, including even the grumblers that he is the wisest and safest man the nation could have at its head at the present time.

To James Speed, Washington, 22 February 1865[34]

Please let the enclosed be placed on file in your Department.

To Gustavus V. Fox, Washington, 24 February 1865[35]

In reply to your letter of the 22d inst., the President requests me to say that he thinks no record was kept here of the orders given to Lieut. D. D. Porter, in regard to his confidential mission to Pensacola in the U.S.S. Powhatan, in 1861. The President however remembers that Lieut. Porter was selected at the suggestion of Brevet Maj. Genl. (then Captain) Montgomery C. Meigs, who, he thinks may be able to inform you where the records or memoranda you desire were kept.[36]

To Therena Bates, Washington, 26 February 1865[37]

I have again been too busy since last Sunday to write to you. The demands upon my time seem to increase day by day, and if they were so to continue for any length of time, I should soon need a private secretary myself.

The news has been rather stirring during the week, and has brought us constant tidings of victory. Charleston, Fort Anderson, and Wilmington have successively fallen into our hands,[38] and though gained without serious battle or loss, are yet in every respect as important and valuable acquisitions as if we had taken them after sanguinary struggles. The impression begins to gain ground that Lee must abandon Richmond and endeavor to make a stand somewhat further south. Rebeldom seems to be losing and suffering in all quarters, and the Richmond papers are getting decidedly blue, notwithstanding they whistle most violently to keep off the ghosts. . . .

To Therena Bates, Washington, 5 March 1865[39]

Inauguration week is happily over, and with it most of the hard work of the winter. Lent has substantially stopped the gaieties; the House of Representatives adjourned and only the Senate remains in Special Session. The office-seekers will swarm in upon us like Egyptian locusts for two or three weeks; but I do not think the President intends to give them much encouragement, and without that the extravagant hotel bills here will exhaust their pockets in a very short time and send them home where they can find cheaper living.

The ceremonies passed off yesterday in as pleasant a manner as was possible. The morning was very dark and rainy, and the streets were very muddy. Nevertheless large crowds were out, in the procession and at the Capitol. I think there were at least twice as many at the Capitol as four years ago. Just at the time when the President appeared on the East portico to be sworn in, the clouds disappeared and the sun shone out beautifully all the rest of the day. We had a reception here at night, which was without exaggeration the largest crowd that has been here yet. The doors were closed at eleven o'clock and great numbers went away who had been unable to get in. . . .

To Therena Bates, Washington, 12 March 1865[40]

You have probably already seen from the despatches that I was on yesterday appointed and confirmed as Consul to Paris. The salary is $5000 per annum.[41]

I have not yet fully matured my future movements. The probability however is that I will not start there for two or three months yet, and that meanwhile I shall see you and ask you to be ready to go with me. . . .

I think of starting day after tomorrow on a short trip to Charleston, and after my return, may possibly make a trip to Kansas before I see you; but as I wrote above my plans are not entirely matured. . . .

To Charles L. Wilson, Washington, 22 March 1865[42]

. . . While I shall undoubtedly have plenty of work to do as Consul at Paris, the change from the trying duties of this position will I hope nevertheless prove agreeable and beneficial to me. . . .

To Therena Bates, Washington, 26 March 1865[43]

. . . I had a visit this morning from Mr. and Mrs. Clark Chapman, from Pittsfield. . . . As the President, Mrs. Lincoln and "Tad," are all away on an excursion to the Army of the Potomac, I was enabled to show them through the rooms in the house and also to take them into the greenhouse.[44] The expressions of enthusiastic wonder and delight to which Mrs. C. gave vent, at the sight of what she evidently considered so much stately magnificence, were truly fresh and interesting, and almost enough to make me forget for the moment what an ill-kept, inconvenient, and dirty old rickety concern it really is, from top to bottom. I wonder how much longer a great nation, as ours is, will compel its ruler to live in such a small and dilapidated old shanty and in such a shabby-genteel style. . . .

To Charles A. Dana, Washington, 27 March 1865[45]

The bearer Thomas Cross, a colored servant in the Executive Mansion,[46] desires a pass for a nephew of his (also colored) to go to Savannah, Ga. I know nothing of him personally, but venture to recommend that it be granted him, on the statement of the bearer Thos. Cross, who is a reliable and industrious servant, provided it conflicts with no regulations, civil or military.

To Frank Moore, Washington, 28 March 1865[47]

I start this morning on a trip to Charleston, Savannah, and Havana, to be gone about three weeks. . . .

**To Therena Bates, aboard the *Santiago de Cuba*
in the Chesapeake Bay, 17 April 1865**[48]

We have arrived this far on our return voyage in safety and good health. Last night as we passed Cape Henry, and took a pilot on board to enter Hampton Roads, we had from him the first news of the terrible loss the country has suffered in the assassination of the President. It was so unexpected, so sudden, and so horrible even to think of, much less to realize, that we <u>could</u> not believe it, and therefore remained in hope that it would prove one of the thousand groundless exaggerations which the war has brought forth during the past four years. Alas, when we reached Point Lookout at daylight this morning, the mournful reports of the minute guns that were being fired, and the flags at half-mast left us no ground for further hope. I went on shore with the boat to forward our telegrams and there found a Washington paper of Saturday, giving us all the painful details.

I am so much overwhelmed by this catastrophe that I scarcely know what to think or write. Just as the valor of the Union arms had won decisive victory over the rebellion, the wise and humane and steady guidance that has carried the nation through the storms of the past four years, is taken away, and its destiny is again shrouded in doubt and uncertainty. My own faith in the future is not shaken, even by this sad event; but will the whole country remain as patient and as trusting, as when it felt its interests safe in the hands of Lincoln?

It would seem that Providence had exacted from him the last and only additional service and sacrifice he could give his country—that of dying for her sake. Those of us who knew him will certainly interpret his death as a sign that Heaven deemed him worthy of martyrdom.

You will readily infer that my own personal plans may be entirely changed by this unlooked for event. We hope to reach Washington by 4 P.M. today. I will write again as soon as I can, but may not learn anything definite for some days.

To Therena Bates, Washington, 18 April 1865[49]

Our ship arrived safely at the Navy Yard at about 2 1/2 P.M. yesterday. I cannot describe to you the air of gloom which seems to hang over this city. As I drove up here from the Navy Yard through the city, almost every house was draped and closed, and men stood idle and listless in groups on the street corners. The Executive Mansion was dark and still as almost the grave itself. The silence and gloom, and sorrow depicted on every face are as heavy and ominous of terror, as if some greater calamity still hung in the air, and was about to crush and overwhelm every one.

This morning the house is deeply draped in mourning, and the corpse is laid in state in the East Room where great crowds are taking their last look at the President's kind face, mild and benignant as becomes the father of a mourning nation, even in death. The funeral will take place tomorrow.

To Andrew Johnson, Washington, 20 April 1865[50]

The death of President Lincoln having terminated the necessity for my temporary continuance in the discharge of its duties, I respectfully ask permission to resign the office of Private Secretary to the President of the United States. . . .

To Andrew Johnson, Washington, 24 April 1865[51]

James Johnson, the colored man who is the bearer of this, asks me *[to]* give him this note to you, and to say that he has been one of the late President Lincoln's body servants for two years past.[52]

I do this very cheerfully and also add my own personal testimony to his faithful service in that capacity, and my own knowledge of his skill in his occasional attendance on Major Hay and myself.

To Therena Bates, Washington, 24 April 1865[53]

After the funeral of the President on Wednesday last, I felt entirely too depressed in spirits to write you a letter.[54] Words seemed so inadequate to express my own personal sorrow at the loss of such a friend as the President has been to me, and my deep apprehension of the new troubles and difficulties in which it would involve the country, that I could not bring myself up to the task of attempting to portray them in language.

I think that I do not yet, and probably shall not for a long while, realize what a change his death has wrought in my own personal relations and the personal relations of almost every one connected with the government in this city who stood near to him, and this state of feeling is very much enhanced by the unsettled condition of the country. . . .

Major Hay and I are still here arranging the papers of the office, which has kept us very busy.

Notes
Index

Notes

The following abbreviations for frequently cited sources are used in the notes:

AL MSS   Abraham Lincoln Papers
Basler, *CWL*   Roy P. Basler et al., eds., *The Collected Works of Abraham Lincoln*, 8 vols. plus index (New Brunswick, N.J.: Rutgers University Press, 1953–55)
DLC   Library of Congress
IHi   Illinois State Historical Library, Springfield
JGN MSS   John G. Nicolay Papers
LM   Lincoln Museum, Fort Wayne, Indiana
OMH MSS   Ozias M. Hatch Papers

Introduction

1. Nicolay, 1898 speech to high school students, quoted in David McWilliams, "Personal Recollections of Mr. Lincoln," *Northwestern Christian Advocate,* n.d., reprinted in the *St. Louis Globe Democrat,* 12 Feb. 1901.

2. Therena Bates of Pittsfield, Illinois, was born in Pittsfield, Massachusetts, on 31 May 1836, wed Nicolay on 15 June 1865, and died on 25 November 1885. Her brother, Dorus E. Bates, was a blacksmith who served as a captain in the Union army, lost an arm at Vicksburg, and became the model for Tillman Joy in John Hay's poem "Banty Tim."

3. Henry B. Van Hoesen, "Lincoln and John Hay," *Books at Brown* 18 (1960): 155–56.

4. On Lincoln as a father figure to Nicolay and Hay, see Michael Burlingame, *The Inner World of Abraham Lincoln* (Urbana: University of Illinois Press, 1994), 77–79.

5. Helen Nicolay to Richard Watson Gilder, Washington, 19 Jan. 1908, Century Collection, New York Public Library. Gilder feared correctly that "the caution he must have exercised may have taken the snap out of the letters." Gilder to Helen Nicolay, New York, 21 Jan. 1908, JGN MSS, DLC.

6. Notes by Helen Nicolay, enclosed in Helen Nicolay to James G. Randall, Washington, 7 Mar. 1931, James G. Randall Papers, DLC.

7. Nicolay to Therena Bates, Springfield, 9 Dec. 1860, JGN MSS, DLC.

8. Helen Nicolay, *Lincoln's Secretary: A Biography of John G. Nicolay* (New York: Longmans, Green, 1949).

9. John G. Nicolay and John Hay, *Abraham Lincoln: A History,* 10 vols. (New York: Century, 1890).

10. Charles M. Segal, ed., *Conversations with Lincoln* (New York: Putnam's, 1961).

11. Don E. Fehrenbacher and Virginia Fehrenbacher, comps. and eds., *Recollected Words of Abraham Lincoln* (Stanford: Stanford University Press, 1996).

12. Roy P. Basler et al., eds., *The Collected Works of Abraham Lincoln,* 8 vols. plus index (New Brunswick, N.J.: Rutgers University Press, 1953–55).

13. Genealogical notes by Helen Nicolay, JGN MSS, DLC. He had three brothers—Frederick Lewis (?–1872), John Jacob (1819–89), and John—and one sister, Catherine (?–1867). Frederick Lewis had emigrated to the U.S. before the rest of the family. Much of the following account is based on H. Nicolay, *Lincoln's Secretary,* 3–45, and a draft of that volume in the JGN MSS, LM.

14. *Illinois State Journal* (Springfield), 14 Mar. 1861; *Pike County Republican* (Pittsfield, Ill.), 31 Mar. 1943; H. Nicolay, *Lincoln's Secretary,* 5–6.

15. The merchant was Aaron Reno, whose daughter, Carrie Reno Brooks, told this story to Goyne S. Pennington. Pennington to the editor, Pittsfield, 7 June 1910, "Hon. John Nicolay," *Pike County Democrat* (Pittsfield, Ill.), 29 June 1910.

16. Autobiographical sketch by Nicolay, dictated to his daughter Helen, 14 Oct. 1897, scrapbook, box 1, JGN MSS, DLC; Goyne S. Pennington to the editor, Pittsfield, 7 June 1910, "Hon. John Nicolay," *Pike County Democrat,* 29 June 1910.

17. H. Nicolay, *Lincoln's Secretary,* 3–8; draft of Helen Nicolay's biography of her father (hereafter referred to as "Helen Nicolay, draft"), typescript, 11–12, JGN MSS, LM; Thomas Hall Shastid, *My Second Life* (Ann Arbor, Mich.: George Wahr, 1944), 63; *Pike County Republican,* 31 Mar. 1943; Milo L. Pearson, article on Ozias M. Hatch, *Pike County Republican,* 6 Feb. 1957. Garbutt told the story of the abusive woman (who may have been the wife of the relative he lived with) to one R. Monroe Worthington. *Pike County Republican,* 8 Mar. 1905, quoted in the same newspaper, 10 June 1942. The story was "universally accepted" in Pittsfield. In the twentieth century, it was told by the descendants of Col. A. C. Matthews, Dr. Benjamin E. Norris, Joseph Heck, Capt. Watson Goodrich, and many others. See Jesse M. Thompson, "Lincoln-Douglas-Hay-Nicolay," *Journal of the Illinois State Historical Society* 18 (1925): 734–35, and Shastid, *My Second Life,* 63. On many occasions, Shastid heard this story from Mrs. Garbutt, Nicolay's virtual foster mother. Curiously, Nicolay did not become a naturalized citizen of the United

States until 12 October 1870. Certificate of naturalization, scrapbook, box 1, JGN MSS, DLC; *Pike County Republican,* 12 July 1933.

18. Reminiscences of Z. N. Garbutt, told to R. Monroe Worthington, *Pike County Republican,* 8 Mar. 1905, copied in the same newspaper, 10 June 1942; Nicolay to Ella M. Orr, Washington, 27 Jan. 1896, in Helen Nicolay, draft, 18–19, JGN MSS, LM.

19. *Pike County Republican,* 10 June 1942; *Washington Times-Herald,* n.d., copied in *Pike County Republican,* 8 June 1949; H. Nicolay, *Lincoln's Secretary,* 9–10.

20. Autobiographical sketch by Nicolay, dictated to his daughter Helen, 14 Oct. 1897, scrapbook, box 1, JGN MSS, DLC; H. Nicolay, *Lincoln's Secretary,* 5. In an unpublished autobiographical novel, Nicolay described a log cabin school vividly (quoted in Helen Nicolay, draft, 5, JGN MSS, LM).

21. Nicolay, address given 4 July (no year given), quoted in Helen Nicolay, draft, 10, JGN MSS, LM.

22. Autobiographical sketch sent by Nicolay on 17 Nov. 1887 to the editors of the *Dizionario Bigraphico degli Scrittori Contemporanei,* copy, JGN MSS, DLC. Nicolay described primitive country schools in amusing detail in an autobiographical novel, a portion of which is quoted in Helen Nicolay, draft, 6–7, JGN MSS, LM. A memo among Nicolay's papers indicates that the newspaper was owned by Garbutt and J. M. Parkes (7 Sept. 1848–25 Apr. 1849); Parkes (26 Apr. 1849–13 May 1853); Parkes and Nicolay (14 May 1853–19 Apr. 1854); and Parkes (20 Apr.–13 Sept. 1854). Nicolay took over as sole proprietor on 14 September 1854. JGN MSS, DLC.

23. Obituary of Nicolay in the *Washington Evening Star,* undated clipping, LM. The *Pike County Free Press* (Pittsfield, Ill.) published several of his poems. See scrapbook, box 1, JGN MSS, DLC.

24. Shastid, *My Second Life,* 72n. Shastid's father, John Greene Shastid, had known Lincoln in New Salem before moving to Pittsfield in 1836. Article by Joseph C. Shastid, *Illinois State Journal,* 12 Feb. 1939.

25. Goyne S. Pennington to the editor, Pittsfield, 7 June 1910, "Hon. John Nicolay," *Pike County Democrat,* 29 June 1910.

26. Thompson, "Lincoln-Douglas-Hay-Nicolay," 735; *Pike County Republican,* 6 Oct. 1937, 10 June 1943.

27. Helen Nicolay to Richard Watson Gilder, Washington, 27 Apr. 1903, JGN MSS, LM. Hay evidently assisted Nicolay in editing the *Pike County Free Press.*

28. *Pike County Republican,* 8 Feb. 1939.

29. Nicolay interviewed by Edward Marshall, 6 Feb. 1894, *The Press* (New York), 11 Feb. 1894. The rally took place on 27 October. Nicolay had invited Richard Yates to speak at it. Nicolay to Yates, Pittsfield, 22 Oct. 1856, Yates Family Papers, IHi. He later invited Yates to lecture to the Pittsfield Library Association. Nicolay, John Weed, and William Ross to Yates, Pittsfield, 4 Dec. 1856, Yates Family Papers, IHi.

30. J. W. Wheeler to Nicolay, Chicago, 23 Mar. 1857, scrapbook, box 1, JGN MSS, DLC.

31. Agreement regarding the *Missouri Democrat,* 3 July 1857, in Basler, *CWL,* 2:410.

32. Memo by William McKee and George W. Fishback, St. Louis, 3 Sept. 1857, scrapbook, box 1, JGN MSS, DLC. Lyman Trumbull recommended that Nicolay try to line up subscribers to the *Missouri Democrat* in counties where the *Washington National Intelligencer* circulated most widely. Ozias M. Hatch to Trumbull, Springfield, 29 Oct. 1857, Lyman Trumbull Papers, DLC.

33. Nicolay to Lyman Trumbull, Springfield, 20 Dec. 1857, Trumbull Papers, DLC.

34. In December 1857, Trumbull wrote to Nicolay:

> I am glad to know that so much was done for the Mo. Democrat, & shall expect good fruit from the seed already sown. Of course it would have been more grati-fying had more been accomplished, but you who were on the ground & in the service were best able to judge whether anything would have been gained by pressing the matter just now, & have probably acted wisely in the course adopted. I have great faith . . . in the efficacy of newspapers. The Republican party being as I believe the advocates of a righteous cause, the better our posi-tion is understood, the stronger we shall be.

Trumbull to Nicolay, Washington, 26 Dec. 1857, JGN MSS, DLC.

35. William McKee and George W. Fishback to Ozias M. Hatch, St. Louis, 6 Dec. 1857, OMH MSS, IHi. Charles D. Hay evidently took over Nicolay's job of lining up subscribers for the *Missouri Democrat* in southern Illinois. C. D. Hay to Lyman Trumbull, Newton, Ill., 9 Nov. 1857, Trumbull Papers, DLC.

36. Nicolay was asked to replace Charles Philbrick as Hatch's clerk. In the fall of 1857, Hatch reported that Jesse K. Dubois "says it would be better to keep him *[Nicolay]* here all the time, and employ some one else, who has more determina-tion to work for the Democrat. Beside Nicolay can lend a hand occasionally to the Journal men." Hatch to Lyman Trumbull, Springfield, 23 Nov. 1857, Trumbull Papers, DLC.

37. *Pike County Republican,* 6 Feb. 1957; Helen Nicolay, draft, 26–29, LM.

38. Shastid's recollections, paraphrased in *My Second Life,* 71; "Lincoln in Early Life, Colonel Nicolay's Reminiscences," Washington correspondence by C., *Chicago Herald,* 4 Dec. 1887; undated memorandum by Nicolay, "dictated to Helen M. Hough," JGN MSS, DLC.

39. Robert Todd Lincoln to Isaac Markens, Manchester, Vt., 4 Nov. 1917, Robert Todd Lincoln Papers, Chicago Historical Society.

40. Milo Pearson, Jr., article on Ozias M. Hatch, *Pike County Republican,* 11 Feb. 1959.

41. Caroline Owsley Brown, "Springfield Society Before the Civil War," *Journal of the Illinois State Historical Society* 15 (1922): 492.

42. Helen Nicolay, draft, 29–30, JGN MSS, LM.

43. Anna Ridgely Hudson, "Springfield, Illinois, in 1860, by a Native Springfielder," typescript dated Dec. 1912, John Hay Papers, Brown University.

44. Lincoln to Greeley, Springfield, 8 Nov. 1858, in Basler, *CWL,* 3:336; Nicolay to O. M. Hatch, Columbus, 21 Dec. 1859, JGN MSS, DLC; George M. Parsons to Lincoln, 17 Jan. 1860, AL MSS, DLC.

45. *Pike County Republican,* 12 July 1933.

46. Diary of Anna Ridgely Hudson, entry for 5 July 1869, IHi.

47. *Pike County Republican,* 12 July 1933; the text appears in Paul Findley and Warren Winston, "The Great Triumvirate" (pamphlet) (Pittsfield: *Pike County Republican* Office, 1973), 15–16.

48. In the spring of 1860, Nicolay had negotiated for a clerkship with Pascal P. Enos of Springfield. When he asked for a salary of $1,200, Enos balked. Nicolay to Ozias M. Hatch, Pittsfield, 6 Apr. 1860, OMH MSS, IHi.

49. Nicolay interviewed by Edward Marshall, 6 Feb. 1894, *The Press* (New York), 11 Feb. 1894; undated memorandum by Nicolay, "dictated to Helen M. Hough," JGN MSS, DLC; A. S. Chapman, "The Boyhood of John Hay," *Century Illustrated Monthly Magazine,* n.s., vol. 46 (July 1909): 452; "Lincoln in Early Life, Colonel Nicolay's Reminiscences," Washington correspondence by C., *Chicago Herald,* 4 Dec. 1887.

50. William O. Stoddard, Jr., ed., *Lincoln's Third Secretary: The Memoirs of William O. Stoddard* (New York: Exposition Press, 1955), 64–65; Stoddard to William H. Herndon, Champaign, Ill., 27 Dec. 1860, AL MSS, DLC; Stoddard to Lyman Trumbull, Champaign, Ill., 27 Dec. 1860, Trumbull Papers, DLC.

51. Donald W. Riddle, *Lincoln Runs for Congress* (New Brunswick, N.J.: Rutgers University Press, 1948), 81–90.

52. James to Lincoln, Chicago, 27 Sept. 1860, AL MSS, DLC.

53. Henry C. Whitney to William H. Herndon, 23 June 1887, in Douglas L. Wilson and Rodney O. Davis, eds., *Herndon's Informants: Letters, Interviews, and Statements about Abraham Lincoln* (Urbana: University of Illinois Press, 1998), 619.

54. Kreismann to Charles H. Ray, Washington, 16 Dec. 1860, Charles Henry Ray Papers, Huntington Library, San Marino, Calif.

55. Smith to Charles Henry Ray and Joseph Medill, [Washington,] 4 Nov. 1861, Ray Papers, Huntington Library.

56. Whitney to Herndon, 23 June 1887, in Wilson and Davis, *Herndon's Informants,* 619.

57. Whitney to Herndon, Chicago, 18 July 1887, in Wilson and Davis, *Herndon's Informants,* 622.

58. William O. Stoddard, "White House Sketches," *New York Citizen,* 25 Aug.

1866, in Stoddard, *Inside the White House in War Times,* ed. Michael Burlingame (Lincoln: University of Nebraska Press, 2000), 151, 57.

59. Robert Colby to Lincoln, New York, 18 May 1861, AL MSS, DLC.

60. A. K. McClure, *Abraham Lincoln and Men of War-Times,* 4th ed. (Philadelphia: Times, 1892), 461.

61. Charles Hay to his sisters, Warsaw, Ill., 20 Feb. 1863, Charles Hay Papers, IHi. Russell described Hay as "very agreeable and lively." Russell, *My Diary North and South,* ed. Eugene Berwanger (New York: Knopf, 1988), 51.

62. Noah Brooks, Washington correspondence, 7 Nov. 1863, *Sacramento Daily Union,* 4 Dec. 1863, in Michael Burlingame, ed., *Lincoln Observed: Civil War Dispatches of Noah Brooks* (Baltimore: Johns Hopkins University Press, 1998), 83. Brooks said that Nicolay, Hay, and Stoddard "are all young men, and the least said of them the better, perhaps." Burlingame, *Lincoln Observed,* 84.

63. Weed to John Bigelow, New York, 26 Apr. 1865, in John Bigelow, *Retrospections of an Active Life,* 5 vols. (Garden City, N.Y.: Doubleday-Page, 1909–13), 2:521.

64. John Russel Young, "Lincoln as He Was," *Pittsburgh Dispatch,* 23 Aug. 1891.

65. John McWilliams, *Recollections of John McWilliams: His Youth, Experiences in California and the Civil War* (Princeton: Princeton University Press, [1919?]), 113.

66. Stoddard, "White House Sketches," *New York Citizen,* 25 Aug. 1866, in *Inside the White House in War Times,* 151, 57.

67. John Hay to James A. Garfield, Washington, 16 Feb. 1881, James A. Garfield Papers, DLC.

68. Copied in the *Washington Sunday Chronicle,* 2 Apr. 1865.

69. Stoddard, "White House Sketches," *New York Citizen,* 25 Aug. 1866, in *Inside the White House in War Times,* 151, 57.

70. William O. Stoddard, typescript of memoirs, 2:429, William O. Stoddard Papers, Detroit Public Library.

71. See "Mary Todd Lincoln's Unethical Conduct as First Lady," in Michael Burlingame, ed., *At Lincoln's Side: John Hay's Civil War Correspondence and Selected Writings* (Carbondale: Southern Illinois University Press, 2000), 185–203.

72. Nicolay to Therena Bates, Washington, 16 Dec. 1864, *infra.*

73. Anson G. Henry to his wife, Washington, 13 Mar. 1865, in Harry E. Pratt, ed., *Concerning Mr. Lincoln: In Which Abraham Lincoln Is Pictured as He Appeared to Letter Writers of His Time* (Springfield: Abraham Lincoln Association, 1944), 117.

74. Noah Brooks, Washington correspondence, 7 Nov. 1863, *Sacramento Daily Union,* 4 Dec. 1863, in Burlingame, *Lincoln Observed,* 87–88.

75. Philbrick to Ozias M. Hatch, Washington, 4 Apr. 1865, OMH MSS, IHi.

76. Brooks to Isaac P. Langworthy, Washington, 10 May 1865, in Burlingame, *Lincoln Observed*, 196.

77. Nicolay interviewed by Edward Marshall, 6 Feb. 1894, *The Press* (New York), 11 Feb. 1894.

78. In 1872, Robert Todd Lincoln wrote to Justice David Davis of the Supreme Court: "I wished particularly to say a word for our good friend Mr. Nicolay. I sincerely trust you can find it possible to aid him. You as well as nearly all the Justices knew him when he was here with my father, & I think no one could question his great personal fitness for the place. In so far as my poor word could assist him, I give it with the earnest hope he may succeed." Lincoln to Davis, Washington, 28 Nov. 1872, David Davis Papers, IHi. Nicolay crowed when he received the appointment: "Hurrah! Lucky as usual. I was today elected Marshal of the Supreme Court, after having made a hard fight during the two weeks past, against three or four strong candidates who had got the start of me by several months. . . . The place is as I am told one of the most comfortable about the city—salary $3,500—office in the Capitol, and work easy, with a good share of leisure." Nicolay to Ozias M. Hatch, Washington, 4 Dec. 1872, OMH MSS, IHi.

79. Nicolay, speech to high school students, quoted in David McWilliams, "Personal Recollections."

80. Autobiographical sketch by Nicolay, dictated to his daughter Helen, 14 Oct. 1897, scrapbook, box 1, JGN MSS, DLC.

1860

1. Lincoln's Secretariat Collection, LM. William E. Norris lived in Pittsfield, Illinois.

2. Trumbull Papers, DLC. Lyman Trumbull (1813–96) represented Illinois in the U.S. Senate (1855–73).

3. Simon Cameron (1799–1889), a prominent Republican leader in Pennsylvania, became Lincoln's secretary of war (1861–62).

4. JGN MSS, DLC.

5. AL MSS, DLC. A Virginia-born physician, George M. Harrison (1813–73) had served with Lincoln in the Black Hawk War of 1832 and provided William H. Herndon a full account of his reminiscences of that event. Wilson and Davis, *Herndon's Informants*, 327–30, 519–20, 553–56.

6. Trumbull Papers, DLC.

7. Draft, AL MSS, DLC. In March 1860, the firm of Follett, Foster and Co. in Columbus, Ohio, had published the Lincoln-Douglas debates. The proprietors were Oran Follett (1798–1894), a founder of the Republican party in Ohio, and his son-in-law, Frank E. Foster.

8. In 1860, Follett and Foster published William Dean Howells's *Lives and*

Speeches of Abraham Lincoln and Hannibal Hamlin. James Quay Howard (1836–1912), a graduate of Marietta College, was a friend of Howells, who hired him as a research assistant for the campaign biography. In May 1860, Howard traveled to Springfield, where he interviewed some of Lincoln's friends. After helping Howells get his book out, Howard wrote another campaign biography of Lincoln, which Follett and Foster released a month after Howells's volume appeared (J. Q. Howard, *The Life of Abraham Lincoln: with Extracts from His Speeches*). On 18 May, Follett, Foster and Co. asked the presidential nominee to suggest an author for their projected campaign biography. Telegram, Chicago, 18 [May] 1860, AL MSS, DLC. Horace White was a leading candidate for that honor. White to Lincoln, Chicago, 18 May 1860, AL MSS, DLC.

9. Among those receiving copies of biographical information about Lincoln were David W. Bartlett, William Dean Howells, and John Locke Scripps. Nicolay to Jesse W. Weik, Washington, 13 Feb. 1895, copy, JGN MSS, DLC. Follett and Foster were "greatly surprised" by Nicolay's telegram and protested that Lincoln himself had written them saying that the matter of the biographer would be discussed by the Illinois State Central Committee on 31 May. Follett and Foster to Nicolay, Columbus, 15 June 1860, AL MSS, DLC.

10. Lincoln himself emphatically protested against the claim that Follett and Foster published an "authorized" biography. Lincoln to Samuel Galloway, Springfield, 19 June 1860, in Basler, *CWL*, 4:79–80.

11. The same day that Nicolay wrote this letter, the following editorial appeared in the *Illinois State Journal*:

> We observe that various publishing houses in different parts of the country are advertising the "Life of Mr. Lincoln as nearly ready," "in press," etc., and prefacing their announcements with the statement that theirs is the "authorized" or the "only authorized," or "the only authentic and authorized" edition. Now there has been great competition for the publication of Mr. Lincoln's biography, and various parties have been here procuring the materials for such a work, but it is unnecessary, we presume, for us to say that none of them are "authorized" by Mr. Lincoln. He is ignorant of their contents, and is not responsible for anything they may contain.

12. Draft, AL MSS, DLC.

13. Richard Yates (1815–73) was the Civil War governor of Illinois.

14. John Todd Stuart (1807–85) was Lincoln's first law partner.

15. From 1837 to 1842, Lincoln boarded at the home of William Butler (1797–1876).

16. Rudd and Carleton published *The Life, Speeches, and Public Services of Abram [sic] Lincoln, Together with a Sketch of the Life of Hannibal Hamlin: Republican Candidates for the Offices of President and Vice-President of the United States* (New York, 1860).

17. JGN MSS, DLC.

18. In an essay, Nicolay explained why he visited Terre Haute:

About the middle of July, and while the presidential campaign seemed to be progressing in a way reasonably satisfactory to Republicans, Mr. Lincoln received intimations that Hon. Richard W. Thompson of Terre Haute Indiana (afterwards Secretary of the Navy under President Hayes) very much desired a private interview with him. Mr. Lincoln was well acquainted with Mr. Thompson; he knew him to be an astute politician who had formerly been an ardent Whig, but since the dissolution of that party had become affiliated with the "Know Nothings" or "Americans," and now represented perhaps more than any other western man, what remained of the strength and vitality of that faction, which, though no longer an influential third party, as in the preceding presidential election, was yet supposed to possess an important minority effectiveness that might control the result in a few States. While it was important to secure these little balances of power for the Republican ticket, there was on the other hand danger that too open an alliance might drive off an equal or greater number of foreign voters to whom the "Know Nothing" principles and objects were exceedingly obnoxious. The greatest caution was therefore necessary, for Democratic newspapers had been industriously charging Mr. Lincoln, not only with "Know Nothing" tendencies, but with being actually a member of a "Know Nothing" lodge—a charge however which he explicitly denied in a confidential letter to a friend.

Mr. Lincoln therefore, instead of inviting Mr. Thompson to Springfield, sent the writer to hold an interview with him at Terre Haute, giving him the following brief written instructions for his guidance:

Ascertain what he wants.

On what subject he would confer with me.

And the particulars, if he will give them.

Is an interview indispensable?

And if so, how soon must it be had?

Tell him my motto is "Fairness to all."

But commit me to nothing.

Nicolay, "Lincoln in the Campaign of 1860," in Michael Burlingame, ed., *An Oral History of Abraham Lincoln: John G. Nicolay's Interviews and Essays* (Carbondale: Southern Illinois University Press, 1996), 93–94. Cf. Thompson to Lincoln, Terre Haute, 6 July 1860, AL MSS, DLC, and Lincoln to Thompson, Springfield, 10 July 1860, in Basler, *CWL,* 4:82–83.

19. Fell Papers, DLC. Jesse Wilson Fell (1808–87) was born in Chester County, Pennsylvania, and became a leading citizen of Bloomington, Illinois.

20. In 1859, Lincoln gave Fell an autobiographical statement that Joseph Jackson Lewis (1801–83), a Republican politician from West Chester, Pennsylvania,

used to write a biographical sketch of Lincoln for a local newspaper, the *Chester County Times*. Lewis served as U.S. commissioner of internal revenue (1863–65).

21. Ives Autograph Book, A. K. Smiley Public Library, Redlands, Calif.

22. JGN MSS, DLC.

23. Goyne S. Pennington, a friend of Nicolay's, later recalled this event:

> I went with Mr. Nicolay in a buggy to attend the first political meeting in Springfield, the first great rally of the Wide Awakes of Illinois at the old Fair Grounds in 1860. It was estimated that 75,000 people were in attendance. We drove in the grounds through the gate and stopped in the rear of the speaker's stand. Mr. Grafton, a liveryman, drove in soon after, with a closed carriage—the only occupant of which was Mr. Lincoln. There were but few people in the rear of the stand, but thousands in front. . . . As soon as Mr. Grafton stopped some ten or twelve men recognized Mr. Lincoln seated in the carriage. They unhitched the horses and lifted the carriage up, and carried it on their shoulders. Mr. Lincoln, good naturedly admonished them, "Let her down easy boys!" He opened the carriage door and shook hands with them and made a bee-line for the speaker's stand, where he adroitly climbed up from the rear and took a seat. He was immediately recognized by the vast multitude who gave him a salute of welcome that shook the earth. Mr. Lincoln arose, bowed and resumed his seat. As soon as the tumult subsided, he motioned to Mr. Nicolay to come to him, and upon his return to the buggy, he said to me, "Mr. Lincoln wants to go back with us." I could see that haste was necessary, and that Mr. Lincoln did not want to get mixed up in that vast concourse of people, so I drove the rig, turning the front to the gate entrance.
>
> Mr. Lincoln dropped down suddenly from the rear of the speaker's stand and made a rapid bee-line to our buggy. As I was getting out, Mr. Nicolay said, "Goyn, you can go back in Mr. Grafton's carriage."
>
> "No," said Mr. Lincoln, "young man, you just stay in and go back with us. I shall not deprive you of your seat." I held up the reins and giving the horse the whip, I lit out to escape the big crowd approaching, and I got through the gate in good shape. Mr. Lincoln remarked that I was a good reinsman.
>
> As we rode along, . . . Mr. Lincoln was speaking of the great demonstration and wild enthusiasm of so large a crowd. He said, "Nicolay, I was afraid of being caught and crushed in that crowd. The American people remind me of a flock of sheep."

Pennington to the editor, Pittsfield, 7 June 1910, "Hon. John Nicolay," *Pike County Democrat*, 29 June 1910.

24. JGN MSS, DLC.

25. John Henry Brown (1818–91) of Philadelphia specialized in miniature portraits.

26. Republican John M. Read (1797–1874), justice of the Pennsylvania Supreme Court, championed the anti-slavery cause.

27. Brown reached Springfield on 12 August. The following morning, he told Read, "I called at Mr Lincolns house" and found that

he had already left home and Mrs Lincoln was too unwell to see me. I then went to the Executive Chamber where I had the pleasure of seeing Mr Lincoln. He at once consented to sit & proposed having the Daguerre taken immediately. We walked together to a Daguerrian room.

He enquired about you particularly & expressed pleasure to hear from you.

Mr Lincoln must be seen & known to be properly appreciated. Ten minutes after I was in his presence I felt as if I had known him for years, *[for]* he has an easy frankness & charm of manner which made me comfortable & happy while in his presence. . . .

I commenced his picture on Tuesday morning *[14 August]*, he gave me a sitting today in the State library room. I handed to him today, the engravings from your picture, for which please accept his thanks. He will retain one for himself & give the other to the Secretary of State. . . .

I do not think, that any painter can do him full justice. He is of a gay & lively disposition, laughs & smiles a great deal & shows to most advantage at such times, but of course cannot be painted so.

Brown to John M. Read, Springfield, 16 Aug. 1860, Read Family Papers, DLC.

In his diary, Brown noted that Lincoln sat for him on 16, 20, 22, 24, and 25 August. When the portrait was completed on that last day, Mary Lincoln spoke of it "in the most extravagant terms of approbation." The following day Brown recorded in his diary:

At church. Saw Mrs. Lincoln there. I hardly know how to express the strength of my personal regard for Mr. Lincoln. I never saw a man for whom I so soon formed an attachment. I like him much and agree with him in all things but his politics. He is very kind and sociable, immensely popular among the people of Springfield; even those opposed to him in politics speak of him in unqualified terms of praise. . . . There are so many hard lines in his face that it becomes a mask to the inner man. His true character only shines when in an animated conversation or when telling an amusing tale, of which he is very fond. He is said to be a homely man. I do not think so. . . .

Rufus Rockwell Wilson, *Lincoln in Portraiture* (New York: Press of the Pioneers, 1935), 109–10.

28. Read Family Papers, DLC.

29. Copy enclosed in Frederick G. Weiser to Marion Bonzi, Glen Ellyn, Ill., 27 Jan. 1948, reference files of the Abraham Lincoln Association, "Weiser" folder, IHi. Hall lived in Elmira, New York.

30. Lincoln's Secretariat Collection, LM. Bourne was a labor organizer in New York. On 12 September, he sent Lincoln some articles he had written on Stephen A. Douglas with the request that they be reprinted in Republican newspapers in the west. Bourne to Lincoln, New York, 24 September 1860, AL MSS, DLC.

31. AL MSS, DLC. Attorney Rufus L. Miller lived in Keokuk, Iowa. See Miller to Lincoln, 20 July 1864, AL MSS, DLC.

32. Robert B. Rutledge (1819–81) knew Lincoln well in New Salem in the 1830s and shared his reminiscences of those days with William Herndon. He was a brother of Ann Rutledge, whom Lincoln loved. Wilson and Davis, *Herndon's Informants,* 769.

33. Read Family Papers, DLC.

34. An envelope endorsed "John M. Read?" and postmarked Philadelphia, 2[0?] Oct. 1860, in the AL MSS, DLC, contains clippings from the *Philadelphia Inquirer* and pamphlets, including a series of six letters "To the People of Pennsylvania," dated between 22 September and 18 October.

35. JGN MSS, DLC.

36. President William Henry Harrison died a month after taking the inaugural oath in 1841. President Zachary Taylor died in 1850, a little more than a year after he had assumed office.

37. An example of such warnings is Zenas Wood to Lincoln, Montpelier, Vt., 5 Nov. 1860, AL MSS, DLC.

38. JGN MSS, DLC.

39. Benjamin Welch (1818?–63) was commissary general for the state of New York and later became an aide to Gen. John Pope.

40. Ohio governor Salmon P. Chase (1808–73) served as Lincoln's secretary of the treasury (1861–64). He had been elected to the Senate by the Ohio legislature in 1849.

41. JGN MSS, DLC.

42. Henry Shelton Sanford (1823–91) of Derby, Connecticut, had been chargé d'affaires in Paris under President Taylor; Lincoln named him U.S. minister to Belgium. Sanford later described this interview to John Hay, calling it

> an interesting conference with Mr Lincoln on the eve of the Election, when, just landed from South America, & from the midst of Revolutionary movements there, I was so impressed with the certainty of the impending uprising, that, armed with a letter from my friend Truman Smith, I went to Springfield to urge on the future President the Expediency of a speech or letter for the public the day after his election, which should strengthen the hands of the Union men *[in the]* South, & give the lie to the Revolutionists, insisting his feeling & purpose was, to break down & destroy "the Institution" in the Southern States by violating constitutional guarantees & thus help the loyal men resist the rising tide of Rebellion. He certainly entertained the idea for a time, but when I came back

from St Louis by appointment after the election (the night of it) the excitement was too overwhelming & the cry "who's afraid" was too strong. And it was better so—the time had come for the problem to be solved violently better than not at all. I have, nevertheless, often regretted I did not, at least, draw up the proposed paper, when, after long discussion, he asked me to do *[so]* then & there, in the room he was occupying in the State House. When I next met him (as President), he recollected me at once, & his remark "well, you see nobody's hurt yet" lead me to imagine his eyes were not yet opened to the full gravity of the crisis. . . .

Sanford to Hay, Gingelom, Belgium, 23 Nov. 1887, Hay Papers, Brown University. Perhaps in response to Sanford's appeal and Truman Smith's letter, Lincoln around 9 November wrote a statement saying he was "not insensible" to the anxieties of businessmen but was unwilling to make a public declaration. Basler, *CWL*, 4:138. Cf. Lincoln to G. T. M. Davis, Springfield, 27 Oct., to Truman Smith, Springfield, 10 Nov., and to Nathaniel P. Paschall, Springfield, 16 Nov., in Basler, *CWL*, 132–33, 138, 139–40.

43. U.S. Senator William Henry Seward (1801–72) of New York, a leader of the national Republican party, became Lincoln's secretary of state (1861–65).

44. JGN MSS, DLC.

45. JGN MSS, DLC.

46. It has been inaccurately suggested that Nicolay wrote for the *New York Tribune* an account of Springfield events on 6 November. Robert S. Harper, *Lincoln and the Press* (New York: McGraw-Hill, 1951), 65–66. See "Lincoln in 1860," an unidentified clipping, dated 1888, LM, containing the reminiscences of an unnamed journalist who covered Lincoln in Springfield for the *Tribune*.

47. JGN MSS, DLC.

48. Scott to Lincoln, New York, 29 Oct. 1860, AL MSS, DLC.

49. Lincoln's letter to Scott is in Basler, *CWL*, 4:137 (9 Nov. 1860).

50. JGN MSS, DLC.

51. JGN MSS, DLC.

52. JGN MSS, DLC.

53. JGN MSS, DLC.

54. Daniel Breck (1788–1871) of Richmond, Kentucky, was a conservative Whig who wed Mary Todd Lincoln's aunt. He had served on the Kentucky State Supreme Court (1843–49) and in the U.S. House of Representatives (1849–51).

55. Cassius Marcellus Clay of Kentucky (1810–1903) was a fiery anti-slavery leader whose reputation as an extremist hurt him politically. During the Civil War, he served as U.S. minister to Russia.

56. JGN MSS, DLC.

57. The American House was a large hotel built in 1838 by Elijah Iles at Sixth and Adams Streets.

58. JGN MSS, DLC.

59. The picture appeared in *Frank Leslie's Illustrated Newspaper,* 24 Nov. 1860.

60. John Milton Hay (1838–1905) was to become Nicolay's assistant in the White House (1861–65).

61. JGN MSS, DLC.

62. South Carolina seceded on 20 December. The Georgia Convention met on 14 December and on 19 January voted to secede.

63. JGN MSS, DLC.

64. JGN MSS, DLC.

65. JGN MSS, DLC.

66. Solomon Meredith (1810–75) of Cambridge, Indiana, was to achieve fame in the Civil War as the general commanding the "Iron Brigade."

67. Attorney William Tod Otto (1816–1905) of Indiana became assistant secretary of the interior under Lincoln.

68. Caleb Blood Smith (1808–64) was a prominent Indiana Republican who served as Lincoln's secretary of the interior (1861–63).

69. Schuyler Colfax (1823–85) was an Indiana politician who aspired to a seat in Lincoln's cabinet. He was beaten out by his fellow Hoosier, Caleb B. Smith.

70. Henry Smith Lane (1811–81) became governor of Indiana on 14 January 1861 and resigned two days later to accept a seat in the U.S. Senate.

71. H. Nicolay, *Lincoln's Secretary,* 56.

72. William Kellogg (1814–72) represented an Illinois district in the U.S. House of Representatives (1857–63).

73. The Committee of 33 was established by the U.S. House of Representatives on 4 December to devise a compromise settling differences between the North and South. Alexander R. Boteler (1815–92) represented a Virginia district in the U.S. House (1859–61).

74. Lincoln's letter to William Kellogg, Springfield, 11 Dec. 1860, is in Basler, *CWL,* 4:150.

75. John Sherman Papers, DLC, reel 1 of supplementary papers.

76. JGN MSS, DLC.

77. Francis P. Blair, Jr. (1821–75), helped lead the anti-slavery forces in Missouri. During the Civil War, he served both in the House of Representatives and in the army.

78. Edward Bates (1793–1869) was Lincoln's attorney general (1861–64). Born in Virginia, he moved to St. Louis in 1814 and became a leading Whig politician as well as a lawyer. Lukewarm on the slavery issue, he was a militant defender of the Union.

79. Horace Greeley's editorials in the *New York Tribune* urged that seceding states be allowed to "go in peace."

80. JGN MSS, DLC.

81. JGN MSS, DLC.

82. Francis P. Blair, Jr., to Lincoln, St. Louis, 12 Dec. 1860, telegram, AL MSS, DLC.

83. JGN MSS, DLC.

84. JGN MSS, DLC.

85. Millard Fillmore (1800–1874), a conservative Whig, had been president of the U.S. (1850–53).

86. Cf. Bates's description of this interview in Howard K. Beale, ed., *The Diary of Edward Bates, 1859–1866* (Washington: U.S. Government Printing Office, 1933; vol. 4 of the Annual Report of the American Historical Association for the Year 1930), 164–65 (entry for 16 Dec. 1860). A gentleman who spoke with Bates the afternoon after his morning conversation with Lincoln reported that "he talked very freely about the state of affairs at the present time. He says that he is decidedly in favor of preserving the Union at all hazard and at any expense. He deprecates civil war of course but wishes to test the question whether this govt has strenght *[sic]* enough to sustain itself or not. His feelings & views coincide with Mr. Lincoln*[']s* expressed to me since I have been here." Silas Noble to E. B. Washburne, Springfield, 17 Dec. 1860, E. B. Washburne Papers, DLC.

87. John A. Gilmer (1805–68) represented a North Carolina district in the U.S. House (1857–61). Thomas Corwin (1794–1865) of Lebanon, Ohio, represented his district in the U.S. House (1830–40, 1859–61) and served as U.S. minister to Mexico (1861–64). He was also a U.S. Senator from Ohio (1845–50).

88. Lincoln to Gilmer, Springfield, 15 Dec. 1860, in Basler, *CWL,* 4:151–53.

89. JGN MSS, DLC.

90. Mississippi seceded on 9 January.

91. The St. Nicholas was a Springfield hotel built in 1856 by J. D. Freeman.

92. JGN MSS, DLC.

93. Robert Anderson (1805–71) commanded the small Union garrison at Charleston, South Carolina, at the time that state seceded. Fearing that his troops were vulnerable in Fort Moultrie, on the mainland, Anderson moved them the day after Christmas to Fort Sumter in the middle of the harbor.

94. Lincoln wrote to Elihu B. Washburne of Galena, Illinois, on 21 December. Basler, *CWL,* 4:159. Washburne (1816–87) served in the U.S. House (1853–69). He was a staunch supporter of Lincoln's two bids for the U.S. Senate and labored mightily for him in the 1860 canvass. During the Civil War, he became the foremost champion of his constituent Ulysses S. Grant. Winfield Scott (1786–1866), commanding general of the U.S. Army, was a firm Unionist who took great precautions to assure that Lincoln would be peaceably inaugurated. He stepped down in November 1861 to make way for George B. McClellan.

95. William Henry Herndon (1818–91), Lincoln's third and final law partner (1844–61), was also his biographer.

96. JGN MSS, DLC.

97. Johnson's building was owned by Joel Johnson. In 1855, John W. Chenery

bought the City Hotel on West Washington Street, remodeled it, and changed its name to the Chenery House.

98. Joshua R. Giddings and George W. Julian Papers, DLC. The Radical Republican George W. Julian (1817–99) represented an Indiana district in the U.S. House (1861–71).

99. AL MSS, DLC, in the hand of Lincoln.

100. AL MSS, DLC, in the hand of Lincoln.

1861

1. JGN MSS, DLC.

2. JGN MSS, DLC.

3. The anniversary celebrated on the 8th was that of the battle of New Orleans, which had been fought on 8 January 1815.

4. On 10 December 1832, President Jackson issued a proclamation denouncing the South Carolina nullification movement as treasonous and warning that he would use all means necessary to enforce the laws.

5. JGN MSS, DLC.

6. Mississippi seceded on 9 January, Florida on 10 January, and Alabama on 11 January.

7. On 9 January, when the side-wheeler *Star of the West,* which the U.S. government had rented, approached Charleston harbor with provisions for the Union troops in Fort Sumter, South Carolina forces opened fire on it; the troops in Fort Sumter did not return the fire.

8. John Jones Pettus (1813–67) was governor of Mississippi.

9. In December and early January, secession-sympathizers Howell Cobb, John B. Floyd, and Jacob Thompson resigned from Buchanan's cabinet and strong Unionists Edwin M. Stanton, Jeremiah Black, Joseph Holt, and John A. Dix joined it.

10. Buchanan's special message was submitted to Congress on 8 January.

11. JGN MSS, DLC.

12. JGN MSS, DLC.

13. AL MSS, DLC. Wilson was the adjutant general of Pennsylvania.

14. Wilson replied on 30 January, offering to consult with the president-elect about the dangers he might encounter on his trip to Washington. Wilson to Lincoln, Erie, Pa., 30 Jan. 1861, AL MSS, DLC.

15. JGN MSS, DLC.

16. Copy, AL MSS, DLC.

17. Copy, AL MSS, DLC.

18. Tillman to Lincoln, Detroit, 24 Jan. 1861, AL MSS, DLC.

19. Elmer E. Ellsworth Papers, Brown University. Ellsworth's undated reply to

this letter is in the JGN MSS, LM. Ellsworth (1837–61) was a close friend of Lincoln, Nicolay, and Hay. In May 1861, he was shot to death immediately after removing a Confederate flag from atop a hotel in Alexandria, Virginia. Ruth Painter Randall, *Colonel Elmer Ellsworth: A Biography of Lincoln's Friend and First Hero of the Civil War* (Boston: Little, Brown, 1960).

20. Copy, AL MSS, DLC. Edwin D. Morgan (1811–83), governor of New York (1859–62), became U.S. senator from that state (1863–69).

21. Copy, AL MSS, DLC.

22. JGN MSS, DLC.

23. JGN MSS, DLC.

24. JGN MSS, DLC.

25. An 1822 graduate of West Point, David Hunter (1802–86) had been invited to join Lincoln on the trip to Washington after writing him about secession rumors in Kansas, where he had been stationed.

26. JGN MSS, DLC.

27. In 1847, Edwin D. and Henry A. Willard took over Fuller's City Hotel, which stood two blocks from the White House at 14th Street and Pennsylvania Avenue, remodeled it, and named it the Willard Hotel. Nathaniel Hawthorne said that "it may much more justly be called the center of Washington and the Union than . . . the Capitol, the White House, or the State Department."

28. Lyman Trumbull, E. B. Washburne, and other Republican members of Congress arranged to rent a house for the president-elect during the period between his arrival in Washington and his inauguration. Washburne went to some trouble to make arrangements in the hopes of saving money and making life more comfortable for Lincoln and his family. At the last minute, Mary Lincoln objected, and the presidential party went to Willard's Hotel instead. Washburne to Lincoln, Washington, 19 Feb. 1861, AL MSS, DLC; Thurlow Weed to Willard, Albany, 19 Feb. [1861], and Erastus Corning to Colonel [E. V.] Sumner, Washington, 20 Feb. 1861, Ward Hill Lamon Papers, Huntington Library; *Hartford Courant,* 21 and 23 Feb. 1861.

29. Telegram, OMH MSS, IHi. Hatch (1814–93) was secretary of state of Illinois and Nicolay's boss from 1857 to 1860.

30. Crosby N. Boyd Collection, DLC. Enclosed was a printed copy, with many emendations in Lincoln's hand, of the president's inaugural address.

31. JGN MSS, DLC.

32. JGN MSS, DLC.

33. OMH MSS, IHi.

34. Among the most conspicuous of the disappointed Illinois office seekers was Jesse K. Dubois, who complained in 1865 that

Lincoln is a singular man and I must Confess I never Knew him: he has for 30 years past just used me as a plaything to accomplish his own ends: but the moment he was elevated to his proud position he seemed all at once to have entirely changed his whole nature and become altogether a new being—Knows no one and the road to favor is always open to his Enemies whilst the door is systematically sealed to his old friends. I was not as much disappointed as my friends were at my late defeat as I never did believe Lincoln would appoint me although he time and again urged I had more talent than any of them. But I was his old friend and I could afford to be disappointed.

Dubois to Henry C. Whitney, Springfield, 6 Apr. 1865, in Wilson and Davis, *Herndon's Informants*, 620. While pondering his choice for an important government post, Lincoln reportedly told Dubois, "Uncle Jesse, there is no reason why I dont want to appoint you, but there is one why I can't—you are from the town I live in myself." Dubois allegedly replied: "Well, Abe, it's all right. If I were President, I don't think I'd give it to *you*, or to any other man from Illinois." Indianapolis correspondence by C. A. P., 30 Apr. 1865, *New York Tribune*, 4 May 1865, p. 1, c. 5. Dubois protested bitterly about the way Lincoln ignored his appeals on behalf of friends. Dubois to Lincoln, Springfield, 27 Mar. and 6 Apr. 1861, AL MSS, DLC; Dubois's undated interview with Jesse W. Weik, Weik Papers, IHi.

35. AL MSS, DLC. In *Abraham Lincoln: A History*, Nicolay and Hay gave this as a letter from Simon Cameron to Scott, written by Lincoln (3:379). Basler stated that "the original has not been located." *Collected Works of Abraham Lincoln*, 4:280n.

36. JGN MSS, DLC.

37. During the Civil War, other White House secretaries and clerks, including Gustave Matile and Nathaniel S. Howe, were similarly employed in the Interior Department. See Ronald Rietveld, "The Lincoln White House Community," *Journal of the Abraham Lincoln Association* 20 (summer 1999): 31–32.

38. JGN MSS, DLC.

39. JGN MSS, DLC.

40. JGN MSS, DLC.

41. JGN MSS, DLC.

42. OMH MSS, IHi.

43. Elizabeth Todd Grimsley (1825–95) had come to Washington to help her cousin Mary Todd Lincoln adjust to conditions in the capital. She remained in the White House for six months. Lincoln did not give her the postmastership because he had appointed many of the First Lady's other relatives to office, along with several Illinois friends of Senator Lyman Trumbull. Roy P. Basler, *President Lincoln Helps His Old Friends* (Springfield: Abraham Lincoln Association, 1977), 7–11. Cf. Lincoln to John Todd Stuart, Washington, 30 Mar. 1861, in Basler, *CWL*, 4:302; John Todd Stuart to Lincoln, Springfield, 3 Apr. 1861, and Elizabeth Todd Grimsley to Lincoln, Springfield, 22 Nov. 1864, AL MSS, DLC. When the speaker of the Illinois House of Representatives, Shelby M. Cullom, asked Lincoln in March

for control of the postmastership and the revenue collectorship of Springfield, the president replied, "Now you can have the collectorship, but the Post Office I think I have promised to old Mrs. *[Seymour]* Moody for her husband. I can't let you have the Post Office, Cullom; take the collectorship." "Now Mr. President," replied Cullom, "why can't you be liberal and let me have both?" "Mrs. Moody would get down on me," Lincoln said. "Lincoln as Senator Cullom Knew Him," unidentified newspaper clipping, LM. Cf. Mrs. Seymour Moody to Lincoln, Springfield, 19 July 1861, AL MSS, DLC. In July, Lincoln appointed John Armstrong postmaster in Springfield.

44. JGN MSS, DLC.

45. JGN MSS, DLC.

46. JGN MSS, DLC.

47. JGN MSS, DLC.

48. JGN MSS, DLC.

49. On 15 April, Lincoln issued a proclamation calling for seventy-five thousand militia to help suppress the insurrection. Basler, *CWL,* 4:331–32.

50. H. Nicolay, *Lincoln's Secretary,* 96.

51. James H. Lane (1814–66) represented Kansas in the U.S. Senate (1861–66). When Virginia adopted a secession ordinance on 17 April, authorities in Washington, fearing for the safety of the capital, took emergency measures. After consulting with Gen. Winfield Scott and Secretary of War Simon Cameron, Maj. David Hunter, in charge of security for the president, appealed to Senator Lane to organize a special White House guard. Lane immediately gathered a force of fifty to one hundred men, dubbed them the Frontier Guard, and led them to the Executive Mansion. Later, Nicolay and Hay described the scene: "[a]fter spending the evening in an exceedingly rudimentary squad drill, under the light of the gorgeous gas chandeliers, they disposed themselves in picturesque bivouac on the brilliant-patterned velvet carpet—perhaps the most luxurious cantonment which American soldiers have ever enjoyed. Their motley composition, their anomalous surroundings, the extraordinary emergency, their mingled awkwardness and earnestness, rendered the scene a medley of bizarre contradictions,—a blending of masquerade and tragedy, of grim humor and realistic seriousness,—a combination of Don Quixote and Daniel Boone altogether impossible to describe." *Abraham Lincoln: A History,* 4:107. According to the 19 April issue of the *Washington Evening Star,* the company "goes on duty at the Executive Mansion every night at 8:30 o'clock, and will continue to guard the White House until there is no danger of an attack upon the city." "The Soldiers of Kansas: The Frontier Guard at the White House, Washington, 1861," *Kansas Historical Collections,* 10:420. The Guard disbanded on 3 May. A member of the Guard sent the following description home:

This well-known resort is one of the most beautiful and magnificent halls in the country. Such a post of honor, on such an emergent occasion—for the President had heard the rumor that day that himself and General Scott were in danger of assassination from a Virginia party that night—was no ordinary compliment. Other companies, of no little notoriety and experience, were in the city, but this distinction was reserved for Kansas.

That night, Kansas had supreme possession of the White House, and fifty of her "Old Guard" slept sweetly on the President's rich Brussels *[carpet]*, with their arms stacked in martial line down the center of the hall, while two long rows of Kansas ex-Governors, Senators, Judges, Editors, Generals and Jayhawkers were dozing upon each side, and the sentinels made regular beats around them.

These guardians, instructed not to allow anyone into the East Room without giving the password, refused admission to Lincoln! "Even the President, when he attempted to enter the hall, accompanied by his lady and some members of the Cabinet, was pricked with the sharp steel of the sentinel, and told,—perhaps jocosely— that *he could not possibly come in!*" The President thanked them at a brief White House ceremony on 26 April. *Kansas State Journal* (Lawrence), 9 May 1861, quoted in Edgar Langsdorf, "Jim Lane and the Frontier Guard," *Kansas Historical Quarterly* 9 (Feb. 1940): 16, 17, 20–21. According to Ward Hill Lamon, the president said that "language was incapable of expressing how great an obligation he and the people all over this country are under to this little patriotic band of men, for their timely services in preventing, as they undoubtedly did prevent, this capital from falling into the hands of the enemy." *Washington Evening Star*, 24 May 1890, p. 8, cc. 4–5.

52. JGN MSS, DLC.

53. Thomas H. Hicks (1798–1865) was governor of Maryland (1858–62). George William Brown (1812–90) was mayor of Baltimore. The telegram from Hicks and Brown, dated Baltimore, 19 Apr. 1861, is in the AL MSS, DLC.

54. The clerk was John Philip Sanderson (1818–64) of Philadelphia, a good friend of Simon Cameron. Later in the war, he became provost marshal general of the Department of Missouri.

55. The president was trying to spare General Scott, who suffered from gout, any unnecessary pain.

56. JGN MSS, DLC.

57. At Harper's Ferry, Lt. Roger Jones commanded but forty-three men. When pickets announced that six hundred hostile Virginians were approaching, he ordered the buildings burned and marched with his men thirty miles to Hagerstown, Maryland.

58. The *Pawnee* was a twin-screw, 1,289-ton steamer built in Philadelphia between 1858 and 1860. Criticized as clumsy, it nevertheless did good service in the South Atlantic Blockading Squadron. In 1864, Adm. S. F. Du Pont praised her highly: "Her light draft, heavy armament, and comfortable and healthy quarters made her a very superior vessel in the inland waters of my station." John D. Hayes,

ed., *Samuel Francis Du Pont: A Selection from His Civil War Letters,* 3 vols. (Ithaca, N.Y.: Cornell University Press for the Eleutherian Mills Historical Library, 1969), 1:31n.

59. During the riot on 19 April, at least nine citizens of Baltimore and four Massachusetts soldiers were killed.

60. In *Abraham Lincoln: A History,* Nicolay and Hay supply the word "designs," which is missing from Nicolay's letter (4:124).

61. Lincoln's Illinois friend Ward Hill Lamon (1828–93) was marshal of the District of Columbia.

62. In May 1861, Dorothea L. Dix (1802–87), a crusader to reform society's treatment of the insane, became superintendent of the Union nursing corps.

63. JGN MSS, DLC. This is a continuation of the document reproduced above, whose first entry was dated 19 April.

64. Lincoln's telegram is in Basler, *CWL,* 4:341.

65. Undated document, "L—— Mem.," Nicolay-Hay Papers, IHi.

66. Detective Allan Pinkerton (1819–84), who warned Lincoln of an assassination plot in Baltimore in February, became head of intelligence for the Army of the Potomac under George B. McClellan.

67. Son of Lincoln's good friend William Butler of Springfield, Speed Butler was made commissary of subsistence in Illinois and in September 1861 became a major in the 5th Illinois Cavalry.

68. The Jefferson Barracks were located in St. Louis County, Missouri.

69. Nathaniel Lyon (1818–61) was the leader of the Union military forces in Missouri.

70. JGN MSS, DLC. This is continuation of the document reproduced above that begins with the events of 19 April.

71. In *Abraham Lincoln: A History,* Nicolay and Hay give a different version of the president's words: "If I grant you this concession, that no troops shall pass through the city, you will be back here to-morrow demanding that none shall be marched around it" (4:127).

72. JGN MSS, DLC.

73. Along with Seward and Scott, Secretary of the Navy Gideon Welles (1802–78) apparently dissented. An aide of Welles's reported a year later that "[a]t the Cabinet meeting after the Balt. troubles, the President was for letting the matter slide—taking no steps then or hereafter to straighten things by opening a passage for Northern troops. Mr. Welles jumped up, swung his hat under his arm and hastily walked out, telling them that if that was their policy <u>he</u> would have no responsibility in the matter. He was so mad that he don't remember exactly what he did say." William Faxon often spoke with Welles and acted as a kind of secretary to forward to Mark Howard what Welles wanted him to know. William Faxon to Mark Howard, Washington, 12 May [1862], Mark Howard Papers, Connecticut Historical Society, Hartford.

74. On 20 April, the Gosport yard, near Norfolk, Virginia, was abandoned and burned by Union forces.

75. Among those resigning was navy captain Franklin Buchanan, who in 1862 commanded the CSS *Virginia* (formerly, the USS *Merrimack*).

76. Seward's letter to Hicks read:

Sir: I have the honor to receive your communication of this morning, in which you inform me that you had felt it to be your duty to advise the President of the United States to order elsewhere the troop*[s]* then off Annapolis, and also that no more may be sent through Maryland; and that you have further suggested that Lord Lyons *[British minister to the U.S.]* be requested to act as mediator between the contending parties in our country, to prevent the effusion of blood.

The President directs me to acknowledge the receipt of that communication, and to assure you that he has weighed the counsels it contains with the respect which he habitually cherishes for the chief magistrates of the several States, and especially for yourself. He regrets, as deeply as any magistrate or citizen of this country can, that demonstrations against the safety of the United States, with very extensive preparations for the effusion of blood, have made it his duty to call out the forces to which you allude.

The force now sought to be brought through Maryland is intended for nothing but the defense of the capital. The President has necessarily confided the choice of the national highway which that force shall take in coming to this city to the lieutenant-general commanding the army of the United States, who, like his only predecessor, is not less distinguished for his humanity than for his loyalty, patriotism, and distinguished public services.

The President instructs me to add that the national highway thus selected by the lieutenant-general has been chosen by him, upon consultation with prominent magistrates and citizens of Maryland, as the one which, while a route is absolutely necessary, is farthest removed from the populous cities of the State, and with the expectation that it would therefore be the least objectionable one.

He cannot but remember that there has been a time in the history of our country when a general of the American Union, with forces designed for the defense of its capital, was not unwelcome anywhere in the State of Maryland, and certainly not at Annapolis, then, as now, the capital of that patriotic State, and then also one of the capitals of the Union.

If eighty years could have obliterated all the other noble sentiments of that age in Maryland, the President would be hopeful, nevertheless, that there is one that would forever remain there and everywhere. That sentiment is, that no domestic contention whatever that may arise among the parties of this republic ought in any case to be referred to any foreign arbitrament, least of all to the arbitrament of a European monarchy.

John G. Nicolay and John Hay, eds., *Complete Works of Abraham Lincoln,* 12 vols. (New York: Tandy, 1905), 6:252–54.

77. Lincoln's letter to Scott is in Basler, *CWL,* 4:344.

78. Robert Milligan McLane (1815–98) represented a Maryland district in the U.S. House of Representatives (1847–51, 1879–83).

79. Gideon Welles Papers, DLC. Gideon Welles of Connecticut was Lincoln's secretary of the navy (1861–65).

80. OMH MSS, IHi.

81. Amos Tuck (1810–79) of New Hampshire, naval officer for the port of Boston, wrote urging the appointment of Solomon McNeal and assuring the president that New England stood by him in resisting treason. Tuck to [Nicolay?], Boston, 20 Apr. 1861, and Tuck to Nicolay, Boston, 17 July 1863, OMH MSS, IHi.

82. JGN MSS, DLC.

83. JGN MSS, DLC.

84. JGN MSS, DLC.

85. Copy, AL MSS, DLC.

86. Caldwell's letter, dated Wellsburg, Va., 25 Apr. 1861, is in the AL MSS, DLC.

87. On 1 May, John Hay recorded the following entry in his diary:

> Yesterday I read a letter from prominent Unionists of Western Virginia, asking help from the Government in resisting the coercion of the Eastern & rebellious portion of the State. Their plan is to endeavor to remove the State Government from Richmond west of the mountains, or failing in that to cut themselves off from the Eastern District, or rather by remaining in the Union let the Eastern portion cut itself off. The letter was signed by G. W. Caldwell. Nicolay answered it cautiously today, leaving the door open for future negotiations. This morning some of the same men called upon the President. Loyalty will be safer in Western Virginia than rebellion will be on the Eastern slopes of the Blue Ridge.

Michael Burlingame and John R. Turner Ettlinger, eds., *Inside Lincoln's White House: The Complete Civil War Diary of John Hay* (Carbondale: Southern Illinois University Press, 1997), 15. According to a journalist, a committee of delegates from Butler County, Virginia, had "long and satisfactory interviews with Messrs. Lincoln and Cameron" on the night of 1 May. "Their object," the reporter noted, "was to induce the Administration to pledge itself to support them if, at the coming election, the loyal citizens of that county showed need of protection. They are determined to assert the rights of citizenship, to resort to arms in self-defense, if attacked, and then, being backed by a Governmental force, they feel sure of success. No written pledges were given them, but such assurances as made them confident of ultimate triumph and entire impunity." Washington correspondence, 2 May 1861, *New York Tribune,* 3 May 1861, p. 5, c. 2. Several important men, including William E. Dodge, urged the president to honor the Virginians' request for

$100,000 and five thousand rifles. Washington correspondence, 3 May 1861, *New York Tribune,* 4 May 1861, p. 5, c. 1.

88. JGN MSS, DLC.

89. John Hay recorded the president's remarks more fully:

"For my own part," he said, "I consider the central idea pervading this struggle is the necessity that is upon us, of proving that popular government is not an absurdity. We must settle this question now, whether in a free government the minority have the right to break up the government whenever they choose. If we fail it will go far to prove the incapability of the people to govern themselves. There may be one consideration used in stay of such final judgement, but that is not for us to use in advance. That is, that there exists in our case, an instance of a vast and far reaching disturbing element, which the history of no other free nation will probably ever present. That however is not for us to say at present. Taking the government as we found it we will see if the majority can preserve it."

Hay diary, 7 May 1861, in Burlingame and Ettlinger, *Inside Lincoln's White House,* 20.

90. On 3 May, the governors convened at Cleveland.

91. JGN MSS, DLC.

92. Cf. diary of John Dahlgren, 9 May 1861, extracts, JGN MSS, DLC; Robert V. Bruce, *Lincoln and the Tools of War* (Indianapolis: Bobbs-Merrill, 1956), 17–18; *Washington Star,* 10 May 1861; *Washington Sunday Chronicle,* 12 May 1861.

93. JGN MSS, DLC.

94. JGN MSS, DLC. Nicolay went to Fort Monroe on 17 May and returned to Washington on 21 May.

95. Mattie McCook was the daughter of Daniel McCook (1798–1863) of Ohio. Seventeen members of that family fought for the Union cause, four of them as generals. Mattie McCook's brothers who served in the Union army included George (1821–77), Robert (1827–62), Alexander (1831–1903), Daniel (1834–64), Edwin (1837–73), Charles (1843–61), and John (b. 1845). Five of her cousins served in the Union army.

96. JGN MSS, DLC.

97. JGN MSS, DLC.

98. JGN MSS, DLC.

99. Nicolay left Washington on 5 June and returned on 18 June. He spent most of that time in Illinois. He described his travels to Therena Bates in letters dated Springfield, 7 and 14 June, JGN MSS, DLC.

100. JGN MSS, DLC.

101. "At present we have not much news here. The war remains as before and everyone awaits the reconvening of Congress. But our troops across the river are

close to those of the enemy and it would not be surprising to hear news of a battle at any moment."

102. Elmer E. Ellsworth Papers, IHi. Charles H. Spafford, a banker in Rockford, Illinois, was Elmer Ellsworth's father-in-law-to-be. Both his letter to Nicolay of 27 May and a response to this letter by Ephraim D. Ellsworth, dated 26 June, are in the JGN MSS, LM. In mid-April, Ellsworth resigned his commission as a lieutenant in the army and hastened to New York to recruit a regiment from the fire departments of that metropolis. Caroline M. Spafford (b. 1842) was Ellsworth's fiancée.

103. John A. Dahlgren (1809–70) commanded the Washington Navy Yard.

104. JGN MSS, DLC.

105. Fanny Campbell Eames (?–1890), wife of Charles Eames, was one of the foremost hostesses in Washington. After her death, a newspaper ran the following description of her accomplishments:

> During the twenty-eight years of her married life in Washington Mrs. Eames's house was one of the favorite resorts of the most conspicuous and interesting men of the nation; it was a species of neutral ground where men of all parties and shades of political opinion found it agreeable to foregather. Though at first in moderate circumstances and living in a house which rented for less than $300 a year, there was no house in Washington except, perhaps, the President's, where one was sure of meeting any evening throughout the year so many people of distinction.
>
> Mr. and Mrs. *[William L.]* Marcy were devoted to Mrs. Eames; her *salon* was almost the daily resort of Edward Everett, Rufus Choate, Charles Sumner, Secretary *[James]* Gutherie, Governor *[John A.]* Andrew of Massachusetts, *[Henry]* Winter Davis, Caleb Cushing, Senator Preston King, N. P. Banks, and representative men of that ilk. Mr. *[Samuel J.]* Tilden when in Washington was often their guest. The gentlemen, who were all on the most familiar terms with the family, were in the habit of bringing their less conspicuous friends from time to time, thus making it quite the most attractive *salon* that has been seen in Washington since the death of Mrs. *[James]* Madison, and made such without any of the attractions of wealth or luxury. . . . [D]uring her residence there she was intellectually quite the most accomplished woman in Washington.

Marian Gouverneur, *As I Remember: Recollections of American Society during the Nineteenth Century* (New York: D. Appleton, 1911), 178–79; *Washington Evening Star,* 1 May 1890.

106. Charles Eames (1812?–67), who graduated from Harvard in 1831 and achieved renown as an admiralty lawyer, was chief counsel for the navy department. In the 1840s, he had served as chief correspondence clerk of that department and as associate editor of the *Washington Union.* President Polk assigned him to negotiate a treaty with the Hawaiian Islands, and President Pierce named him minister to

Venezuela. Gouverneur, *As I Remember,* 171–73; *Washington Evening Star,* 1 May 1890.

107. JGN MSS, DLC.

108. Robert Patterson (1792–1881) commanded the department encompassing Pennsylvania, Delaware, Maryland, and the District of Columbia. On 2 July, he led forces across the Potomac and chased Stonewall Jackson's troops.

109. George B. McClellan (1826–85), commander of the Department of the Ohio, was to command the Army of the Potomac (1861–62).

110. JGN MSS, DLC.

111. Illinois senator Orville H. Browning (1806–81) was a good friend of Lincoln's.

112. Browning recorded in his diary an account of this visit with the president:

> [A]s he had just finished his message, he said he wished to read it to me, and did so. . . . I remained a while in conversation with him when the reading was concluded. He told me that the very first thing placed in his hands after his inauguration was a letter from Maj[o]r Anderson announcing the impossibility of defending or relieving Sumter. That he called the Cabinet together, and consulted Genl. Scott—that Scott concurred with Anderson, and the cabinet, with the exception of himself and P M Genl. Blair were for evacuating the Fort, and that all the troubles and anxieties of his life had not equalled those which intervened between this time and the fall of Sumter.

Theodore Calvin Pease and James G. Randall, eds., *The Diary of Orville Hickman Browning, 1850-1881,* 2 vols. (Springfield: IHi, 1925, 1933; Collections of the IHi, vols. 20 and 22), 1:475–76 (entry for 3 July 1861).

113. JGN MSS, DLC.

114. The Garde di Garibaldi (39th New York Regiment) consisted of Hungarians, Germans, Italians, Algerians, French Foreign Legionnaires, Cossacks, Sepoys, English, Swiss, Turks, Croats, Bavarian Dutch, Spaniards, Portuguese, and Platt Deutsch.

115. JGN MSS, DLC.

116. A New York businessman called the levee "a sham," attended by an "array of richly tho' badly dressed persons." He was "much surprised in Mrs. Lincoln. I expected to see a pretty & a tasty woman—the newspapers said so—they told a lie— . . . . She is small[,] rather fat & dumpy. The expression of her face is not pleasing nor does it indicate power or energy of character. She is not at home in the 'White House.' . . . The President looks better than he did—his face indicated great kindness of heart." Gideon J. Bull to his mother, Washington, 18 July 1861, *The Collector* 80.6–8 (1967): item A–358.

117. Irvin McDowell (1818–85), who commanded the Army of Northeastern Virginia, was to lead Union forces to defeat at Bull Run on 21 July.

118. JGN MSS, DLC.

119. A native of South Carolina, the journalist James E. Harvey wrote for the *New York Tribune* and edited the *Philadelphia North American*. In 1861, Lincoln appointed him U.S. minister to Portugal.

120. Solomon Foot (1802–66) was a senator from Vermont.

121. Charles Sumner (1811–74) was a senator from Massachusetts.

122. James R. Doolittle (1815–97) was a senator from Wisconsin.

123. Andrew Gordon Magrath (1813–93), secretary of state of South Carolina, had resigned his U.S. district judgeship in South Carolina when his state seceded. Toward the end of the war, he was chosen governor of South Carolina. He passed on James Harvey's message to the Confederate secretary of war in Montgomery.

124. In 1861, John Archibald Campbell (1811–89) resigned from the U.S. Supreme Court and became assistant secretary of war in the Confederacy.

125. Harvey had asked Magrath if South Carolina would obstruct the withdrawal of Union forces should Fort Sumter surrender. When Magrath replied that the state would not, Harvey passed the message on to Seward. Harry J. Carman and Reinhard H. Luthin, *Lincoln and the Patronage* (New York: Columbia University Press, 1943), 90–92.

126. Francis Wilkinson Pickens (1805–69) was governor of South Carolina (1860–62).

127. Orville H. Browning recorded in his diary on 13 July: "At night I went to the Presidents and had a long talk with him and Mr Seward Sec: of State about Harvey. . . . They do not want Harvey recalled." Pease and Randall, *Diary of Orville Hickman Browning,* 1:481. The following day, Senator Lyman Trumbull of Illinois told his wife: "The Republicans in caucus appointed a committee to express to him their want of confidence in Harvey. . . . Mr. Lincoln and Mr. Seward informed the committee that they were aware of the worst dispatch to Governor Pickens before he left the country, but not before he received the appointment, and they did not think from their conversation with Harvey that he had any criminal intent, and requested the committee to report the facts to the caucus, Mr. Lincoln saying that he would like to know whether Senators were as dissatisfied when they came to know all the facts. The caucus will meet to-morrow and I do not believe will be satisfied with the explanation." Horace White, *The Life of Lyman Trumbull* (Boston and New York: Houghton Mifflin, 1913), 155–56. Cf. Howard K. Beale, ed., *Diary of Gideon Welles, Secretary of the Navy Under Lincoln and Johnson,* 3 vols. (New York: W. W. Norton, 1960), 2:248 (entry for 22 Feb. 1865). Years later, Montgomery Blair claimed that Harvey had "telegraphed Gov[ernor] Pickens for Seward to apprise him of the sailing of the expedition to relieve Sumpter." Blair to Gideon Welles, Washington, 18 June 1870, Welles Papers, Connecticut Historical Society.

128. JGN MSS, DLC.

129. During the night of 11–12 July, Col. Schuyler Hamilton, military secretary to Gen. Winfield Scott, called on the president five times with news of the battle.

Hamilton later remembered that when, around 4 A.M., he knocked for a sixth time on the president's bedroom door, Lincoln

appeared, exhibiting some little vexation, in a red flannel shirt, which, out of modesty, he was holding down in front. He said, "Colonel, do you ever sleep?" The reply was, "Mr. President I was about to ask you the same question." He said, "I have not slept much since this civil war began." The rejoinder was, "Indeed, Mr. President, I regret to have to disturb you so often . . . but you know, Mr. President, I am under authority, and must obey General Scott's orders without question." "Oh, Colonel, I understand that very well. I have been disturbed at every hour of the night to-night, and poor Mrs. Lincoln also. . . . She is now asleep, and I hated to disturb her, but she has got my dressing-gown twisted around her feet, so I have had to come out in my red shirt. Either I have grown too long or the shirt has grown too short. I know not which."

But I said: "Mr. President, the telegram I hold in my hand will give you the greatest pleasure; it is the announcement of the first victory of the Union army." "But, Colonel, what am I to do?"

"Oh, Mr. President, I think we can manage that. If you will allow me for once in my life to turn my back on the President of the United States, you can let go and I can pass the telegram over my shoulder." "Do so, Colonel," said he. I faced about, and passed the telegram over my shoulder. He read it, pondered it, read it aloud. "Colonel," he asked, "is there anything in corroboration of this telegram?" "A great deal, Mr. President," was the reply.

"Colonel," and there was a happy rhythm in his voice, a ripple of merriment and satisfaction; "Colonel, if you will come to me every night and every hour of every night, with just such telegrams as that, I will come out not only in my red shirt, but without any shirt at all. Tell General Scott so." He handed me back the telegram over my shoulder, to be duly placed on file, and bade me good night.

Hamilton, "A True Story of President Lincoln," *New York Sun,* n.d., reprinted in an unidentified newspaper clipping in the LM.

130. On 11 July, some two thousand Union troops under William S. Rosecrans (1818–98) defeated Confederate forces under John Pegram (1832–65) at Rich Mountain in western Virginia.

131. Robert S. Garnett (1819–61) was the first Confederate general to be killed in the war.

132. McClellan's report, dated Beverly, Va., 12 July 1861, is in Stephen W. Sears, ed., *The Civil War Papers of George B. McClellan: Selected Correspondence, 1860–1865* (New York: Ticknor and Fields, 1989), 51–52.

133. H. Nicolay, *Lincoln's Secretary,* 108.

134. JGN MSS, DLC.

135. JGN MSS, DLC.

136. JGN MSS, DLC.

137. Simon P. Hanscom wrote for the *New York Herald* early in the war; later he became editor of the *Washington National Republican*. Many years after the war, Ben: Perley Poore recalled that Lincoln's "favorite among the Washington correspondents was Mr. Simon B. *[sic]* Hanscom,—a shrewd Bostonian, who had been identified with the earlier anti-slavery movements, and who used to keep Mr. Lincoln informed as to what was going on in Washington, carrying him what he heard, and seldom asking a favor." Poore, "Recollections of Abraham Lincoln," in James Parton, ed., *Some Noted Princes, Authors, and Statesmen of Our Time* (New York: Crowell, 1885), 352. In 1865, another journalist observed, "Every day the irrepressible Hanscom, of the *Republican,* comes after news, and brings the gossip of the day. The *Republican* is the President's favorite paper, and he gives it what news he has, but very rarely reads it or any other paper." *Philadelphia Sunday Dispatch,* 25 March 1865. In 1863, Noah Brooks reported that Hanscom, "a pushing and persevering man, has managed to so ingratiate himself with the President that he has almost exclusive access to the office of the Executive, and there obtains from our good-natured Chief Magistrate such scanty items of news as he is willing to give out for publication, and so the enterprising editor gets up his daily column of 'official intelligence,' much to the annoyance and jealousy of the New York and other Washington correspondents whose dependence is upon the current news of the day, which must be gained before a single hour has blown upon its freshness." Washington correspondence, 14 Oct. 1863, in Burlingame, *Lincoln Observed,* 69–70.

138. Nicolay did not record Lincoln's response to the bad news from Bull Run, but he was told about it by George P. Goff twenty-eight years later. An assistant to John D. Defrees, Goff often heard his boss describe visits to the White House during the Civil War. The day after the first battle of Bull Run, Defrees reported to Goff that he found Lincoln agitated, pacing the floor. On seeing his visitor, the president, "with intense feeling," said: "John, if Hell is *[not]* any more than this, it has no terror for me." Enclosure in Goff to Nicolay, Washington, 9 Feb. 1889, JGN MSS, DLC.

139. JGN MSS, DLC.

140. Gilder-Lehrman Collection, Pierpont Morgan Library, New York, N.Y. James Lesley, Jr., had been a correspondent for the *North American and U.S. Gazette* of Philadelphia.

141. JGN MSS, DLC.

142. JGN MSS, DLC.

143. Charles Morris McCook was killed. His brother was Alexander McDowell McCook of the 1st Ohio.

144. A. D. Bache Papers, DLC. An eminent physicist, Alexander D. Bache (1806–67) was vice president of the United States Sanitary Commission.

145. A Unitarian clergyman, Henry W. Bellows (1814–82) founded and presided over the United States Sanitary Commission.

146. JGN MSS, DLC.

147. Prince Napoleon (1822–91), cousin of the French emperor Napoleon III, was known as "Plon-Plon" because he had been a fat baby.

148. Marie Clotilde, the wife of Prince Napoleon, was the daughter of King Victor Emanuel of Italy.

149. JGN MSS, DLC.

150. Telegram, AL MSS, DLC. In poor health and suffering from the heat in the capital, Nicolay left Washington on 9 August for a vacation at Newport, R.I., where he remained until 31 August.

151. John A. Andrew (1818–67) was governor of Massachusetts (1861–66).

152. JGN MSS, DLC.

153. Butler Papers, DLC. Benjamin F. Butler (1818–93) of Massachusetts was a prominent political general.

154. On 27 August, Union forces under Butler and Commo. Silas H. Stringham attacked the forts guarding Hatteras Inlet on North Carolina's Outer Banks. The Confederates abandoned Fort Clark without a fight on 27 August; Fort Hatteras, after a heavy pounding by Stringham's ships, surrendered the next day.

155. Lawrence A. Gobright (1816–79) represented the Associated Press in Washington for a third of a century.

156. JGN MSS, DLC.

157. JGN MSS, DLC.

158. Joseph Holt Papers, DLC. Joseph Holt of Kentucky (1807–94) was judge advocate general of the army (1862–75).

159. JGN MSS, DLC.

160. JGN MSS, DLC.

161. JGN MSS, DLC.

162. John Charles Frémont (1813–90) commanded the Western Department (July–Nov. 1861). He had been the Republican presidential candidate in 1856.

163. Hamilton R. Gamble (1798–1864) was the Unionist governor of Missouri (1861–64).

164. A leading St. Louis Unionist, James O. Broadhead (b. 1819) had studied law with Attorney General Bates and served in the Missouri state senate (1850–54); in 1861 he served as U.S. district attorney for Missouri.

165. Among the letters about Frémont were James O. Broadhead to Montgomery Blair, St. Louis, 3 Sept. 1861, and Samuel T. Glover to Montgomery Blair, on board a steamer in the Mississippi River, 2 Sept. 1861, AL MSS, DLC.

166. The correspondence between Lincoln and Frémont is in Basler, *CWL,* 4:506, 517.

167. Montgomery C. Meigs (1816?–92) was quartermaster general of the Union Army.

168. Blair's letter, dated St. Louis, 14 Sept. 1861, is in the AL MSS, DLC.

169. JGN MSS, DLC.

170. François-Ferdinand-Philippe-Louis-Marie d'Orléans, Prince de Joinville (1818–1900), drew on his experiences with McClellan's staff to write *The Army of the Potomac: Its Organization, Its Commander, and Its Campaign* (New York: Randolph, 1862).

171. While serving on the staff of General McClellan, Louis Phillippe Albert d'Orléans, Comte de Paris (1838–94), and Robert Louis Eugene Ferdinand d'Orléans, Duc de Chartres (1840–1910), were known respectively as "Captain Perry" and "Captain Chatters."

172. JGN MSS, DLC.

173. JGN MSS, DLC.

174. JGN MSS, DLC.

175. Gurley was perhaps John A. Gurley (1813–63) of Cincinnati, who served in the U.S. House of Representatives (1859–63); in 1863, Lincoln appointed him governor of Arizona.

176. Lincoln had assigned Lorenzo Thomas (1804–75), adjutant general of the army, to investigate Frémont's command.

177. JGN MSS, DLC. Nicolay left Washington on 10 October and returned on 13 November.

178. AL MSS, DLC.

179. Otterville was a village thirteen miles east of Sedalia. John Pope (1822–92) commanded the 2nd Division of the Army of Southwest Missouri.

180. Tipton was a village in Missouri, 162 miles west of St. Louis.

181. Confederate general Sterling Price (1809–67) commanded the Missouri State Guard.

182. AL MSS, DLC.

183. Col. James Mulligan (1830–64) surrendered Lexington, Missouri, to Confederate forces on 20 September. Gustav P. Koerner (1809–96), a German-born Republican leader from Belleville, Illinois, had served as lieutenant governor (1852–56).

184. AL MSS, DLC.

185. Ninian Witt Edwards (1809–89), husband of Mary Lincoln's sister Elizabeth, was appointed commissary of subsistence on 8 August 1861. When he awarded a contract to former governor Joel Matteson, Republicans in Springfield protested, alleging that Edwards had made $15,000 on the deal. Bowing to such pressure, the president removed his brother-in-law from the office on 22 June 1863.

186. JGN MSS, DLC.

187. John Watt (1824–92), the White House gardener, collaborated with Mary Todd Lincoln to defraud the U.S. government by padding expense accounts and payrolls. Burlingame, "Mary Todd Lincoln's Unethical Conduct as First Lady," in *At Lincoln's Side*, 185–203.

188. According to Thomas Stackpole, a White House doorman, Mary Todd Lincoln pinched the salary of Mrs. Jane Masterson Watt. He alleged that "Watt's wife was now nominally stewardess at a salary of $100 p[e]r month, all of which by private arrangement, went into Mrs. Lincoln's pocket." Orville H. Browning diary, 3 Mar. 1862, IHi.

189. JGN MSS, DLC.

190. JGN MSS, DLC.

191. Copy, Nicolay-Hay Papers, IHi.

192. Thirty-five years later, Nicolay recalled that Lincoln this day "rode with General McClellan on his right hand and General McDowell on his left, and I was one of the cavalcade of the staff-officers who followed, and during that ride of two hours at a continuous and rapid gallop over all sorts of ground, I had full opportunity to observe his horsemanship, which suffered nothing in comparison with the two generals beside him." Nicolay to James Grant Wilson, Washington, 19 July 1896, copy, JGN MSS, DLC.

193. JGN MSS, DLC.

194. Thomas A. Scott (1823–81) was an officer of the Pennsylvania Railroad.

195. JGN MSS, DLC.

196. To his wife, General McClellan described Hermann's appearance at the White House: "The most striking feature of the performance was that the Magician asked the Presdt for his handkerchief—upon which that dignitary replied promptly, 'You've got me now, I ain't got any'!!!!" George B. McClellan to Mary Ellen McClellan, Washington, 21 Nov. 1861, in Sears, *Civil War Papers of George B. McClellan*, 137. On 24 November, John Hay reported that

> Herrmann is a genius—a bright-eyed, black-moustached, quiet, handsome and inscrutable German Jew. He evinced great power and originality in choosing a name to be known by, of such stupendous proportions that it has to be pronounced by installments. His brother, who always accompanies him, is a precocious boy about a dozen years, who, always ready and never obtrusive, is, in fact, the explanation of most of his wonderful tricks. The physical sleight which enables him to pull Canary birds from a spectator's ear, or Guinea pigs from a lady's porte monnaie, is very wonderful, but not to be compared to his masterly feats of mathematical combinations in cards and clairvoyant vision. The other evening at the President's, he asked Gen. Mcclellan to think of a card, not mentioning it. He then gave him a pack of cards and told him to look for the card he had in his mind. It was not there. "Give me the pack," said Herrmann. He took it, and springing the cards from one hand to the other, a card came to the top. It was the one the General had thought of. He will allow a dozen persons to select each a card from a pack and return them without his seeing them. Taking the pack in one hand and one card, selected seemingly at random, in the other, he will, without apparently bringing his hands near each other, cause the

single card to assume successively to each of the dozen persons the appearance of the card they had selected. One goes from his *soirees* with faith confirmed and strengthened in the father of lies, and a general impression left on the mind of the truth of those lines in which Horatio Smith embodies the substance of Byron's philosophy,

Thinking is but an idle waste of thought,
And naught is everything, and everything is naught.

Michael Burlingame, ed., *Lincoln's Journalist: John Hay's Anonymous Writings for the Press, 1860–1864* (Carbondale: Southern Illinois University Press, 1998), 149.

197. Copy, AL MSS, DLC.

198. John M. Schofield (1831–1906) commanded the district of St. Louis.

199. JGN MSS, DLC.

200. On 8 November, Charles Wilkes (1798–1877), commander of the USS *San Jacinto,* seized Confederate diplomats James M. Mason and John Slidell from the decks of the *Trent,* a British mail steamer.

201. JGN MSS, DLC.

202. JGN MSS, DLC.

1862

1. JGN MSS, DLC.

2. JGN MSS, DLC.

3. Unsigned and marked "Not sent," AL MSS, DLC.

4. William P. Dole of Indiana was assistant secretary of the interior.

5. Charles Sumner Papers, Harvard University.

6. JGN MSS, DLC.

7. A Pennsylvania attorney, Stanton (1814–69) had been Buchanan's attorney general (1860–61) and served as secretary of war (1862–68).

8. JGN MSS, DLC.

9. JGN MSS, DLC.

10. Gen. Ambrose E. Burnside (1824–81) of Rhode Island was to command the Army of the Potomac briefly (1862–63). On 11 January, with approximately fifteen thousand men, Burnside sailed from Hampton Roads, Virginia, for North Carolina. Two days later, the army reached Hatteras Inlet, where crossing the bar proved difficult. Finally on 7 February, Burnside's troops, assisted by Commo. Louis M. Goldsborough's warships, stormed Roanoke Island, whose defenders capitulated the next day.

11. JGN MSS, DLC.

12. At Mill Springs on 19 January, Union forces under Gen. George H. Thomas defeated Confederates under Gen. George B. Crittenden. Confederate general Felix

K. Zollicoffer (1812–62) was killed in the battle, the most significant engagement fought in Kentucky, with the exception of Perryville (8–9 October 1862).

13. Telegram, Nathaniel P. Banks Papers, DLC. Nathaniel Prentiss Banks (1816–94), former governor of Massachusetts (1858–61), commanded a division in the Army of the Potomac. In March, he took charge of the V Corps of that army.

14. JGN MSS, DLC.

15. JGN MSS, DLC.

16. The event took place on 5 February. See *infra,* letter to Therena Bates, 6 February 1862. William O. Stoddard described some of the maneuvers that people resorted to in order to get tickets for "the Lady President's Ball":

> I had some fun with it. It was a rigidly formal or rather official affair. The invitations were limited to certain kinds or species of men and women. Senators, Congressmen, Judges of the Supreme Court, members of the Cabinet, generals and high naval men. . . . [F]rom all over the country there came to prominent Washington men urgent applications for invitations, as if these were but free tickets to "the Greatest Show on Earth." To have granted any of these requests, by favoritism, would have given just offence to the multitude who could not be gratified. The first applicants to be disappointed and to get mad about it were the local representatives of the great northern journals, nearly all of whom appeared to consider themselves sufficiently official or military or naval or judicial or diplomatic to be entitled to tickets. Nicolay and Hay were masters of the situation but for some reason, perhaps because it was disagreeable and I was young, it was shunted over upon my shoulders, in part, and I found all explanations in vain. A certain number, of course, could be admitted as "reporters" but when I mentioned that fact the fat was all in the fire. In the language of one excited scribe, "If we cannot come as gentlemen, we will not come at all!"—Which was hard upon any fellow who ceased to be a gentlemen when he became a reporter. I was in my room, one day, when Nicolay sent Hay to see me, in hot haste. Two of Mrs. Lincoln's favorite Congressmen, one of whom was my old friend Caleb Lyon, of Lyonsdale, New York, and the other my especial friend Gen. Daniel E. Sickles, had asked for tickets for two New York litterateurs, an editor of the Herald, a daily paper, and Mr. George Wilkes of the Spirit of the Times, both of which journals had been anything but complimentary to Mr. Lincoln.
>
> "Stoddard!["] exclaimed poor Nicolay. "I can't do anything! It will make all sorts of trouble. 'She' is determined to have her own way. You will have to see to this. 'She' wouldn't listen to me."
>
> "Give me the tickets," I said, "and I'll attend to it."
>
> Down to the Red Room I went and there were present all the parties to the case and Mrs. Lincoln was smilingly expecting the cards which she had sent for under the pernicious beguilement of Dan Sickles and Caleb Lyon. They also smiled at me, as I came in.

"May I see you for a moment, Mrs. Lincoln?" I said, and she could see that I was boiling over, wild mad about something, furious but restraining myself, and she followed me into the Blue Room as once. "What is it, Mr. Stoddard?"

"Mrs. Lincoln! O! But won't I give it to Dan and Caleb!"

"Why? What for? What have they done?"

"Why, Mrs. Lincoln, I suppose you have a right to *know*. They have demanded of Mr. Nicolay invitations for those two fellows in there that have been abusing you, personally, and Mr. Lincoln, as though you were both pick-pockets. If we are to give out extra cards, we had better send them to our friends, not to our enemies. Besides, it would offend some of the best friends we have. I wish you would put your foot down on this and stop it. They can't have the invitations."

"Of course they can't!" she said, "I'll go right in and tell them so."

"And I'll give Sickles and Caleb a wigging!" I declared.

Into the Red Room she went again, to say very firmly:

"Gentlemen, Mr. Stoddard, who has absolute charge of this business, tells me that I cannot give you the invitations. I am sorry, of course, but I must abide by his decision."

There was no help for it and they had to give it up, but I did have an interesting little mill with Caleb and the General in the vestibule. As for Mrs. Lincoln, I had felt sure of her. She never really went back on me and she was wide awake to any attack upon her husband. Nicolay and Hay were ready to pat me on the back when I went up stairs, and they expressed much wonder as to how I did that thing. At all events, in this case as in some other, all the ugly part of it fell on me and sometimes I was not making friends. . . .

William O. Stoddard, typescript of memoirs, Stoddard Papers, Detroit Public Library, 2:346–48.

17. Col. Michael Corcoran (1827–63) of the New York State Militia was a captive in Confederate hands who faced a death sentence in case the North should punish Confederate privateers as pirates. In August 1862, he was exchanged and offered a generalship by Lincoln.

18. Joseph Jackson Grimshaw (1820–75), an Illinois lawyer and Republican politician, had practiced law in Pittsfield (1843–57), then moved to Quincy, where he ran unsuccessfully for Congress in 1856 and 1858.

19. Reuben B. Hatch of Meredosia, Illinois, brother of Lincoln's close friend Ozias M. Hatch, had been appointed assistant quartermaster of volunteers for the district of southeast Missouri, on Ulysses S. Grant's staff, in August 1861, and served in that capacity at Cairo, Illinois. In February, Hatch was charged with fraud and speculation but was released because General Grant feared that a court-martial might tie up too many officers who were needed in the field. Hatch was freed in April but rearrested soon thereafter. In August, a war claims commission cleared

Hatch of all charges. See Jackson Grimshaw to Ozias M. Hatch, Cairo, Ill., 11, 13, 18, 20 July 1862, OMH MSS, IHi. Hatch later served on the staff of Gen. Benjamin M. Prentiss and became a lieutenant colonel. Lincoln wrote to Gen. Montgomery C. Meigs about the case, but his letter is no longer extant. Entry for 21 Aug. 1862, register of quartermaster general records, p. 262, S 1014, War Records, National Archives.

20. JGN MSS, DLC.

21. One guest, a U.S. senator, condemned the First Lady's sartorial taste: "The weak minded Mrs Lincoln had *her bosom* on exhibition, and a flower pot on her head, while there was a train of silk or satin dragging on the floor behind her of several yards in length. As I looked at her I could not help regretting that she had degenerated from the industrious and unpretending woman that she *was* in the days when she used to cook Old Abes dinner, and milk the cows with her own hands, now her only ambition seems to be to exhibit her own milking apparatus to the public gaze. . . . It is a great pity particularly in these times that the wife of the President could not have brought something like republican simplicity to the White House." James W. Nesmith to his wife, Washington, 5 Feb. 1862, photocopy, James G. Randall Papers, DLC.

22. AL MSS, DLC. Schurz (1829–1906) of Wisconsin was a leading German American political figure and a general in the Union army.

23. Henry Wager Halleck (1815–72), commander of all Union forces in the west, was slowly advancing on Corinth, Mississippi, which the Confederates evacuated on 30 May.

24. The *St. Louis Anzeiger des Westens* was edited by Heinrich Boernstein (1805–92) and Carl L. Bernays (1815–79). Bernays was a friend of Lincoln, who in 1861 had appointed him U.S. consul in Zurich. The following year the president made him a paymaster in the army to help him financially while he continued to edit the newspaper. Lincoln counted on the *Anzeiger* to counteract the Radicalism of the *St. Louis Westliche Post,* edited by Emil Preetorius. Lincoln had named Boernstein consul to Bremen in 1861 but in 1862 recalled him so that he could continue to edit the *Anzeiger.* On 1 August 1862, Frank P. Blair, Jr., said that "Boernstein has acted more nobly and done glorious work since his return. I have no doubt that he has done more to reconcile the Germans to the Administration than any other man of that race is capable of doing in so short a time." A. E. Zucker, ed., *The Forty-Eighters: Political Refugees of the German Revolution of 1848* (New York: Columbia University Press, 1950), 281. German-born Franz Sigel (1824–1902) commanded the First Division of the Army of Southwestern Missouri. Like many other German papers, the *Anzeiger* was critical of the Lincoln administration's treatment of Sigel. Carl Wittke, *The German-Language Press in America* (Louisville: University of Kentucky Press, 1957), 150. The enclosed papers were seven letters to and from Franz Sigel.

25. JGN MSS, DLC.

26. On 20 February, William Wallace ("Willie") Lincoln (b. 1850) succumbed to "bilious fever" after a long illness. Thomas ("Tad") Lincoln (1853–71) survived the illness that afflicted him at the time that his brother was fatally stricken.

27. JGN MSS, DLC.

28. Gen. Ulysses S. Grant's forces captured Fort Donelson on 16 February.

29. Benjamin F. Wade Papers, DLC.

30. JGN MSS, DLC.

31. Ulysses S. Grant (1822-85) commanded the Department of Missouri.

32. Basler, *CWL,* 5:135.

33. Confederate general John B. Floyd (1806–63), who had served as secretary of war (1857–60), was nearly captured when Fort Donelson fell.

34. Jacob Thompson (1810–85) had been secretary of the interior (1857–61).

35. JGN MSS, DLC.

36. Andrew Hull Foote (1806–63), known as the "Gunboat Commodore," had captured Fort Henry on 6 February.

37. JGN MSS, DLC.

38. JGN MSS, DLC.

39. In 1872, Browning described Lincoln's reaction to the death of Willie: "At the time of his little son Willie's death, Mrs Browning and I were out of the city, but returned to Washington on the evening of the same day of his death. The President and Mrs Lincoln sent their carriage for us immediately upon learning that we were in the city, and we went to the White House, and remained with them about a week. His son Tad was also very ill at the time, and I watched with him several consecutive nights. The President was in the room with me a portion of each night. He was in very deep distress at the loss of Willie, and agitated with apprehensions of a fatal termination of Tad's illness." Browning to Isaac N. Arnold, Quincy, Ill., 25 Nov. 1872, Arnold Papers, Chicago Historical Society.

40. JGN MSS, DLC.

41. JGN MSS, DLC.

42. JGN MSS, DLC.

43. McClellan's dispatches to Stanton are in Sears, *Civil War Papers of George B. McClellan,* 191–92.

44. Randolph B. Marcy (1812–87) was McClellan's father-in-law and chief of staff.

45. Nicolay added an explanatory note: "As one of the facilities and precautions, arrangements had been made to build a bridge of canal-boats (permanent) across the Potomac, and a large number of canal boats had been gathered for that purpose." Later, Nicolay told Jay Linn Torrey, who commanded a "Rough Rider" regiment in the Spanish-American War, that the only time he had heard Lincoln swear was in response to this fiasco. When he learned of it, the president banged his fist on a table and exclaimed: "Why in hell didn't he measure first!" Unidentified newspaper clipping, "Anecdotes of Abraham Lincoln," Lincoln Shrine, A. K. Smiley Li-

brary, Redlands, Calif. Others confirmed Nicolay's observation. When given the bad news, Lincoln was, according to Horace White, in "a h[el]l of a rage" and "swore like a Phillistine." H[orace] W[hite] to [Joseph] Medill, Washington, 3 Mar. 1862, and White to Charles H. Ray, Washington, 3 Mar. 1862, Ray Papers, Huntington Library. White House secretary William O. Stoddard "never knew Mr. Lincoln so really angry, so out of all patience, as when it was reported impossible to obey his celebrated order for a general advance of the army on the 22d of February, 1862." Stoddard recalled the scene vividly: Lincoln

> was alone in his room when an officer of General McClellan's staff was announced by the door-keeper and was admitted. The President turned in his chair to hear, and was informed, in respectful set terms, that the advance movement *[against Winchester]* could not be made.
> "Why?" he curtly demanded.
> "The pontoon trains are not ready—"
> "Why in hell and damnation *ain't* they ready?"
> The officer could think of no satisfactory reply, but turned very hastily and left the room. Mr. Lincoln also turned to the table and resumed the work before him, but wrote at about double his ordinary speed.

Stoddard, *Abraham Lincoln: The True Story of a Great Life* (New York: Fords, Howard, & Hulbert, 1884), 285. On 1 March, Lincoln "angrily" described to Charles Sumner the canal boat fiasco, which "excited him very much." The president said he had "made up his mind to talk plainly" to McClellan. Charles Sumner to John A. Andrew, Washington, 2 Mar. 1862, in Beverly Wilson Palmer, ed., *The Selected Letters of Charles Sumner*, 2 vols. (Boston: Northeastern University Press, 1990), 2:103.

46. Pope captured New Madrid, Missouri, on 13 March.

47. JGN MSS, DLC.

48. McClellan to Lincoln, Sandy Hook, 28 Feb. 1862, in Sears, *Civil War Papers of George B. McClellan,* 193.

49. JGN MSS, DLC.

50. Federal troops led by John White Geary (1819–73) captured Leesburg on 8 March.

51. On 6 March, Lincoln had sent Congress a message recommending a program of gradual, compensated emancipation. Basler, *CWL,* 5:144–46.

52. Lincoln to Henry J. Raymond (1820–69), editor of the *New York Times,* Washington, 9 Mar. 1862, in Basler, *CWL,* 5:152–53.

53. Garrett Davis (1801–72) represented Kentucky in the U.S. Senate (1861–72).

54. Peter H. Watson, the shrewd and energetic assistant secretary of war, was a prominent patent lawyer.

55. John E. Wool (1784–1869) commanded the Department of Virginia.

56. The formidable ironclad CSS *Virginia* was converted from the captured USS *Merrimack*.

57. The *Cumberland* was a sloop with twenty-four guns.

58. The *Congress* was a frigate with fifty guns.

59. The *Minnesota* was a screw frigate with forty guns.

60. The CSS *Yorktown* and CSS *Jamestown* were side-wheel river steamers that had been converted into gunboats. They assisted the *Merrimack* in the attack on the Union fleet.

61. Fortress Monroe was the Union stronghold at the confluence of the York and James Rivers in Virginia.

62. Joseph G. Totten (1788–1864) was chief engineer of the U.S. Army.

63. Joseph Smith (1790–1877) was chief of the Bureau of Navy Yards and Docks.

64. Gustavus V. Fox (1821–83) was assistant secretary of the navy.

65. Joseph Hooker (1814–79) commanded a division in the Army of the Potomac; from January to June of the following year, he was to command that entire army.

66. The CSS *George Page* was a side-wheel river steamer with two guns.

67. Confederate forces abandoned Manassas and Centerville on 9 March. McClellan's dispatch to Lincoln and Stanton is in Sears, *Civil War Papers of George B. McClellan*, 200.

68. JGN MSS, DLC.

69. JGN MSS, DLC.

70. On 7 April, Pope captured Island No. 10 in the Mississippi River.

71. JGN MSS, DLC. Nicolay left Washington on 28 March and returned on 30 April.

72. Salmon P. Chase Papers, DLC.

73. Allen A. Hall (1803?–67) had been a prominent Whig, editor of Nashville newspapers, and an assistant secretary of the treasury (1849–50). In 1863, Lincoln appointed him minister to Bolivia.

74. Federal troops under Gen. Don Carlos Buell (1818–98) occupied Nashville on 25 February.

75. JGN MSS, DLC.

76. The Confederates abandoned Yorktown on 3 May.

77. JGN MSS, DLC.

78. The president left Washington on 5 May, arrived at Fort Monroe the following day, and returned to the capital on 12 May. On the 7th he visited the *Monitor*, whose paymaster wrote a description of the event: "We received a visit today from President Lincoln in company with Secretaries Chase and Stanton and other dignitaries, attended by General Wood [Wool], and staff in full uniform. Mr. Lincoln has

a sad, care-worn and anxious look, in strong contrast with the gay cortege by which he was surrounded." William F. Keeler to his wife, on board the *Monitor,* 7 May 1862, in "Battle of Monitor Is Told in Letters," unidentified clipping, LM.

79. On 25 April, David Farragut's fleet captured New Orleans.

80. JGN MSS, DLC.

81. AL MSS, DLC. Lee (1830–84) was judge advocate general of the Union army.

82. George H. Thomas (1816–70) commanded the Army of the Tennessee.

83. In an endorsement on this document, Lee explained that Reuben Hatch, brother of Lincoln's close friend Ozias M. Hatch, had been charged with fraud and speculation. See *supra,* letter to Therena Bates, 2 Feb. 1862.

84. JGN MSS, DLC.

85. This engagement near Richmond, known as the battle of Drewry's Bluff, took place on 15 May.

86. Halleck was closing in on Corinth, Mississippi, which the Confederates abandoned on 29 May.

87. JGN MSS, DLC.

88. JGN MSS, DLC.

89. On this day, Confederate forces under Stonewall Jackson defeated the Union troops of Nathaniel P. Banks at the battle of Winchester.

90. JGN MSS, DLC.

91. On 24 May, Lincoln ordered Frémont to march southeast to Harrisonburg; instead he went northeast to Strasburg.

92. JGN MSS, DLC.

93. The Battle of Fair Oaks (Seven Pines) took place on 31 May and 1 June.

94. Jackson evaded the Union pincers movement of Frémont and Shields on 2 June.

95. Copy, AL MSS, DLC.

96. Lee's letter to Nicolay (Washington, 4 June 1862, copy, AL MSS, DLC) stated that the president may not unilaterally reinstate an army officer after he has been dismissed from the service by a duly constituted court-martial.

97. On 4 June, Lincoln had sent Lee an order returning Capt. George W. Cothran of Battery M, 1st New York Artillery, to service after he had been dismissed by McClellan on 6 March in keeping with the sentence of a court-martial.

98. JGN MSS, DLC.

99. Confederate general Pierre Gustave Toutant Beauregard (1818–93) commanded the Army of the Mississippi.

100. At the Battle of Fair Oaks (Seven Pines) on 31 May and 1 June, the Confederates suffered 6,134 casualties and the Union forces 5,031.

101. JGN MSS, DLC.

102. Also known as Fort Pillow, Fort Wright on the Mississippi River was abandoned by the Confederates on 3–4 June.

103. Fort Randolph was in Tennessee, sixty miles north of Memphis on the Mississippi.

104. Memphis fell to Union forces on 6 June.

105. The Reverend Dr. Smith Pyne was the pastor of St. John's Episcopal Church in Washington. Located across the street from the White House, it had a socially prominent congregation. Smith was known for his warmth and wit. Gouverneur, *As I Remember,* 195–96.

106. JGN MSS, DLC.

107. In the last battles of Stonewall Jackson's valley campaign, the Confederates defeated Union forces under Frémont and Gen. James Shields (1810–79), commanding a division in the Department of the Shenandoah, at Cross Keys on 8 June and at Port Republic on 9 June.

108. JGN MSS, DLC.

109. Located outside the District of Columbia on a hilltop, the Soldiers' Home, a facility for disabled troops, was far cooler than the White House and thus became the Lincolns' summer retreat. In 1862, 1863, and 1864, the president and his family spent the summers in a stone cottage on this site.

110. JGN MSS, DLC.

111. On 16 June, about 2,500 Confederates under Gen. Nathan G. Evans decisively repulsed an attack by 6,600 Federal troops under Gen. Henry W. Benham at Secessionville, South Carolina, on James Island.

112. In March 1862, a convention in Illinois adopted a new constitution, which the voters rejected overwhelmingly.

113. Yates Family Papers, IHi.

114. Count Adam Gurowski (1805–66), who had been a Polish revolutionary, worked in the State Department as a translator.

115. JGN MSS, DLC.

116. On 24–25 June, Lincoln traveled to West Point to consult with General Scott.

117. Baron Munchausen was an eighteenth-century German adventurer and soldier renowned for exaggerating his heroics.

118. JGN MSS, DLC.

119. In the Seven Days Battles (25 June–1 July), Lee thwarted McClellan's attempt to capture Richmond.

120. JGN MSS, DLC.

121. In the Seven Days Battles, Confederate casualties exceeded twenty thousand, while Union casualties totaled about sixteen thousand.

122. In the summer of 1864, Lincoln told a caller, "when the Peninsular campaign terminated suddenly at Harrison's Landing, I was as nearly inconsolable as I could be and live." Henry C. Deming, *Eulogy of Abraham Lincoln* (Hartford: A. N. Clark, 1865), 40. Lincoln believed that if McClellan had seized the initiative after the battle of Malvern Hill on 1 July, he could have taken Richmond.

123. JGN MSS, DLC.

124. Chase Papers, DLC.

125. Andrew G. Curtin (1815–94) was governor of Pennsylvania.

126. JGN MSS, DLC.

127. John Hunt Morgan (1825–64) led Confederate cavalry raiders through Kentucky from 4 July to 1 August 1862.

128. Lincoln left Washington on 7 July and returned on 10 July.

129. JGN MSS, DLC.

130. JGN MSS, DLC.

131. Copy, AL MSS, DLC.

132. AL MSS, DLC.

133. Yates had asked that Col. William R. Morrison be given a leave of absence to restore his health. Yates to Nicolay, Springfield, 20 July 1861, AL MSS, DLC.

134. OMH MSS, IHi. Nicolay left Washington for Minnesota on 27 July and returned in September.

135. Maj. John J. Mudd served in the 2nd Illinois Cavalry. See *infra,* Nicolay to John Hay, 4 Aug. 1862.

136. Strother Grigsby was an active Republican organizer in Pittsfield. See Grigsby to John A. McClernand, Pittsfield, 21 Sept. 1864, OMH MSS, IHi.

137. In the 1863 and 1865 editions of the *Official Register of the United States,* Amos C. Babcock is listed as the assessor of the 9th District of Illinois.

138. OMH MSS, IHi.

139. AL MSS, DLC.

140. Ozias M. Hatch and Jesse K. Dubois had recommended Strother Grigsby for assessor. Hatch and Dubois to Lincoln, Springfield, 12 July 1862, OMH MSS, IHi. Mudd declined the offer, saying he would rather continue serving in the army. Mudd to Ozias M. Hatch, Jackson, Tenn., 11 Aug. 1862, OMH MSS, IHi.

141. Telegram, also signed by William P. Dole and Morton S. Wilkinson, AL MSS, DLC.

142. The Sioux uprising in Minnesota began on 17 August and ended on 23 September.

143. AL MSS, DLC.

144. JGN MSS, DLC.

145. JGN MSS, DLC.

146. From 2 October to 4 October, Lincoln visited McClellan in Maryland and inspected the Army of the Potomac.

147. Pinkerton to McClellan, Washington, 12 Oct. 1862, copy, quoted and paraphrased, Allan Pinkerton Papers (privately held by Howard Swiggert), copy, Allan Nevins Papers, Columbia University.

148. JGN MSS, DLC.

149. At the battle of Perryville on 8 October, General Buell, commander of the Army of the Ohio, repulsed Braxton Bragg's invasion of Kentucky.

150. Confederate general James Ewell Brown ("Jeb") Stuart (1833–64) commanded the cavalry of the Army of Northern Virginia. Between 9 and 12 October, Stuart made his second ride around McClellan's army, destroying much property in Chambersburg, Pennsylvania.

151. JGN MSS, DLC.

152. Unlike Ohio and Pennsylvania, Iowa went Republican on 14 October.

153. Confederate general Braxton Bragg escaped Buell on 22 October. Two days later, Lincoln dismissed Buell.

154. In April, Benjamin M. Prentiss (1819–1901) had been captured on the first day of the battle of Shiloh and was exchanged by the Confederates in October.

155. JGN MSS, DLC.

156. Cassius M. Clay Papers, Lincoln Memorial University, Harrogate, Tenn. Clay noted on this document, "Got personal leave of absence October 22."

157. Harwood Family Papers, Stanford University.

158. Fox endorsed this note thus: "Will Comd Harwood please put this vigorous youth whom the Presdt is interested in on board the Georgia and give him a month's advance." Another undated endorsement states that "Jesse Pratt was shipped accordingly drew his advance and 'skedaddled.'" Andrew A. Harwood was chief of the Navy Bureau of Ordnance and Hydrography.

159. JGN MSS, DLC.

160. The Quaker group was led by Joseph J. Gurney and his wife, Eliza.

161. JGN MSS, DLC.

162. William Henry Seward Papers, University of Rochester.

163. AL MSS, DLC.

164. The editor and proprietor of the *Missouri Statesman* (Columbia), Switzler had been nominated as an army paymaster. Nicolay apparently doubted his loyalty, based on articles that appeared in his newspaper. Switzler denied that he had written the pieces, which were published while he was away acting as military secretary to Governor Phelps in Arkansas. In 1863, Colonel Switzler became the provost marshal of the 9th congressional district in Missouri. Cf. Switzler to Nicolay, Columbia, 22 Apr. 1863, AL MSS, DLC. Lincoln had appointed John Smith Phelps (1814–86) military governor of Arkansas in July 1862. Switzler had been appointed military secretary to Governor Phelps on 4 August 1862. Amos F. Eno to Nicolay, Helena, Ark., 18 Nov. 1862, AL MSS, DLC.

165. JGN MSS, DLC.

166. JGN MSS, DLC.

167. McClellan was relieved on 7 November; two days later Ambrose E. Burnside was named as his replacement.

168. This editorial, published in the *Washington Daily Morning Chronicle*, 12 Nov. 1862, was pasted into Nicolay's scrapbook of his own writings. JGN MSS, DLC.

169. JGN MSS, DLC.

170. S. F. B. Morse Papers, DLC.

171. In the AL MSS, DLC, Morse's letter of 14 November is incorrectly filed 14 May 1862.

172. JGN MSS, DLC.

173. JGN MSS, LM.

174. AL MSS, DLC. Lucius Eugene Chittenden (1824–1902) of Vermont was register of the U.S. Treasury (1861–65).

175. Chittenden's letter was a printed form letter (Washington, 9 Oct. 1862, AL MSS, DLC).

176. JGN MSS, DLC.

177. JGN MSS, DLC.

178. William O. Stoddard (1835–1925) assisted Nicolay and Hay in the White House (1861–64). At first, he served as the "Secretary to the President to Sign Land Patents." After the war began, as Nicolay recalled, "business became very slack so that he had scarcely any official work to do. He was therefore assigned to duty as one of my clerks at the White House, being able just as well to sign there the few Land Patents which were issued from time to time. Also on one or two occasions when Hay and I were both absent, he carried a message to Congress. So that you see he . . . was not in any proper sense either a real or acting Presidents Private Secretary*[.]*" Nicolay to Paul Selby, Washington, 11 Mar. 1895, draft, JGN MSS," DLC. Also present were Senators Ira Harris and Orville H. Browning, Congressman Isaac N. Arnold, and Supreme Court Justice David Davis. Pease and Randall, *Diary of Orville Hickman Browning,* 1:592 (entry for 7 Dec. 1862).

179. Copy, AL MSS, DLC. Henry Hastings Sibley (1811–91) joined the army in the midst of the Sioux uprising and helped put it down. He had been governor of Minnesota before the war.

180. Thomas S. Williamson was a missionary to the Sioux. See Williamson to Lincoln, Washington, 27 Apr. 1864, AL MSS, DLC.

181. JGN MSS, DLC.

182. JGN MSS, DLC.

183. Nicolay left Washington to visit Burnside on 12 December. On that day, Edwin M. Stanton, secretary of war, and his assistant Peter H. Watson, issued Nicolay passes to visit the headquarters of the Army of the Potomac.

184. JGN MSS, DLC.

185. Republican senators, frustrated by the Union defeat at Fredericksburg and incited by Salmon P. Chase, held a caucus and demanded that Seward be removed from the cabinet. On 18 and 19 December, Lincoln finessed them with a clever strategy, and the crisis passed with the cabinet remaining intact.

186. A copy of this item, clipped from the *Washington Daily Morning Chronicle,* appears in Nicolay's scrapbook of his own writings. JGN MSS, DLC.

187. Lincoln's note to Chase and Seward is in Basler, *CWL,* 6:12–13.

188. JGN MSS, DLC.

189. A skirmish took place at Dumfries on 27 December.

190. Between May 1862 and June 1864, the Confederate commerce raider *Alabama*, commanded by Capt. Raphael Semmes, wreaked havoc on the American merchant marine, destroying or capturing sixty-nine ships. When on 7 December 1862 the *Alabama* captured Commo. Vanderbilt's steamer *Ariel*, Captain Semmes was disappointed to find no gold in the safe. He let his prize go only after Captain Jones of the *Ariel* gave him a ransom bond.

191. Photocopy, box 19, James G. Randall Papers, DLC.

192. Lincoln Collection, Brown University. Nicolay sent an identical message to Henry Raymond of the *New York Times*.

1863

1. A clipping of this editorial from the *Washington Daily Morning Chronicle*, 2 Jan. 1863, p. 2, cc. 1–2, is pasted in Nicolay's scrapbook of his own writings. JGN MSS, DLC.

2. JGN MSS, DLC.

3. William S. Rosecrans commanded the Army of the Cumberland. The battle of Murfreesboro (Stone's River), part of the struggle for control of central Tennessee, began on 31 December and ended on 2 January. After much carnage, resulting more or less in a draw, the Confederates fell back thirty-five miles and went into winter quarters.

4. When the *Monitor* sank on the night of 30–31 December, sixteen of the crew drowned and forty-seven were rescued.

5. JGN MSS, DLC.

6. On 23 December, William T. Sherman's assault on Chickasaw Bluffs failed. On 2 January, Sherman abandoned this part of the Vicksburg campaign.

7. JGN MSS, DLC.

8. JGN MSS, DLC.

9. Gen. John A. McClernand (1812–1900), commander of the XIII Corps of the Army of the Tennessee, had captured Arkansas Post on 11 January.

10. JGN MSS, DLC.

11. Fitz-John Porter (1822–1901) had commanded the V Corps of the Army of the Potomac at the Second Battle of Bull Run. For his conduct there, he was cashiered. Lincoln shared Nicolay's view. Robert Todd Lincoln recalled seeing his father plainly exhibit distress "when he learned of General Fitz-John Porter's conduct." Robert Todd Lincoln to Isaac Markens, Manchester, Vt., 13 July 1918, Robert Todd Lincoln Papers, Chicago Historical Society. To Orville H. Browning, Lincoln declared "that he knew no reason to suspect any one *[involved in the Second Battle of Bull Run]* of bad faith except Fitz John Porter, and that . . . at present he believed his disobedience of orders, and his failure to go to Popes aid in the battle

. . . had occasioned our defeat, and deprived us of a victory which would have terminated the war." Pease and Randall, *Diary of Orville Hickman Browning*, 1:589 (entry for 29 Nov. 1862). After signing the order to dismiss the general, Lincoln remarked that he should have been shot. John Hay to [C. C.] Buel, [Nov. 1888?], Lincoln File, Huntington Library; memorandum by Rush C. Hawkins, Hombourg-les-Bains, Prussia, 17 Aug. 1872, Rush Hawkins Papers, Brown University.

12. On 19 January, Burnside ordered the Army of the Potomac to begin yet another attempt to cross the Rappahannock. Heavy rains forced him to abandon his plans, however, and the troops returned to their original camp on 23 January after an ignominious "mud march."

13. JGN MSS, DLC.

14. Moncure D. Conway (1832–1907), editor of the *Boston Commonwealth*, was a leading anti-slavery spokesman.

15. On 25 January, Burnside demanded the removal of some of his corps commanders; Lincoln responded by replacing Burnside with Joseph Hooker.

16. JGN MSS, DLC.

17. The Blackwater River is in Virginia.

18. JGN MSS, DLC.

19. Hooker took command of the Army of the Potomac in January.

20. Simon Cameron Papers, Dauphin County Historical Society, Harrisburg, Penn.

21. John S. Gittings of Baltimore was president of the Chesapeake Bank. Gittings to Lincoln, Baltimore, 8 Aug. 1864, AL MSS, DLC.

22. Holt Papers, DLC.

23. JGN MSS, DLC.

24. Charles Sherwood Stratton (1838–83), a midget known as General Tom Thumb, married Lavinia Warren (1841–1919) on 10 February; the wedding received much press attention.

25. Galusha A. Grow (1823–1907) of Pennsylvania was speaker of the U.S. House of Representatives (1861–63).

26. AL MSS, DLC. Col. James B. Fry (1827–94) was an assistant adjutant general; the following month he became provost marshal general.

27. In an endorsement on the back of this letter, Fry replied that Henry King had not been nominated as commissary of subsistence.

28. Copy, AL MSS, DLC. There is no enclosure to indicate what Nicolay refers to.

29. JGN MSS, DLC.

30. Edwin M. Stanton Papers, DLC.

31. Samuel D. Sturgis (1822–99) commanded the 2nd Division of the IX Corps. On 19 March, he was transferred from the Army of the Potomac to the Army of the Ohio, in charge of its cavalry.

32. John G. Parke (1827–1900) had been General Burnside's chief of staff and

was to become, on 19 March, commander of the IX Corps of the Army of the Potomac.

33. JGN MSS, DLC.

34. On 5 March, Union troops under Col. John Coburn of the 33rd Indiana lost badly when they fought Confederates under Earl Van Dorn near Spring Hill, south of Franklin.

35. JGN MSS, DLC.

36. Hay left on 4 April and did not return until early June.

37. A copy of David D. Porter's telegram to Gideon Welles, dated Yazoo River, 10 Mar. 1863, is in the AL MSS, DLC. Porter (1813–91) commanded the Mississippi squadron. The Confederates captured the ram *Indianola* on 24 February and scuttled it two days later. Quaker guns were logs painted to resemble cannons. At Manassas, such artificial artillery had intimidated McClellan in 1861 and 1862.

38. JGN MSS, DLC.

39. David G. Farragut (1801–70) had captured New Orleans the previous year. On 19 March, Farragut sailed the *Hartford* and the *Albatross* past Confederate artillery posted just below Vicksburg. The USS *Mississippi*, however, was destroyed, and the *Monongahela* and the *Richmond* were forced to turn back.

40. JGN MSS, DLC.

41. The Democrats had triumphed at the polls in Illinois the preceding November.

42. Daniel Ullman Papers, New-York Historical Society. Gen. Daniel Ullman (1810–92) was in New Orleans organizing and training black troops.

43. Milton Smith Littlefield (1830–99) later assumed command of the 21st U.S. Colored Troops. During Reconstruction, he achieved notoriety as a corrupt railroad lobbyist in North Carolina and Florida.

44. JGN MSS, DLC.

45. JGN MSS, DLC.

46. The Lincolns returned to Washington on 10 April.

47. Grant had dispatched troops to get at the rear of Vicksburg via the Yazoo, Coldwater, and Tallahatchie Rivers; the expedition failed.

48. In mid-March, Admiral Farragut's fleet passed the Confederate fort at Port Hudson, Louisiana, and General Banks made demonstrations against the fort. Not until 8 July did it fall to Union forces.

49. The Union ironclads that assaulted Fort Sumter in Charleston harbor on 7 April were repulsed.

50. JGN MSS, DLC.

51. *Washington Chronicle,* 3 Mar. 1864.

52. JGN MSS, DLC.

53. Seward Papers, University of Rochester.

54. JGN MSS, DLC.

55. Adm. Samuel F. Du Pont (1803–65), commander of the South Atlantic

Blockading Squadron, led the assault on Charleston. Of the nine Union ironclads that attacked Charleston on 7 April, five were disabled by Confederate batteries; one (the *Keokuk*) sank the following day.

56. In mid-April, Nicolay wrote a letter to Maj. Edward Wright of Hunter's staff. On 25 April, Charles G. Halpine responded with a long defense of Du Pont:

> Our friend, Major Wright, showed me one paragraph of your letter to him, in which you referred, apparently with surprise, to the fact that the attack on Charleston by the iron-clads should have been discontinued "when so few casualties had occurred." This is so obvious a reflection, on the first hasty view of the affair, and one so radically unjust when we look calmly at the facts, that, in Major Wright's absence (he has gone down the posts along the Florida coast on a tour of inspection) I will venture to occupy your time a few moments on the subject.
>
> In ordinary warfare the amount of casualties will give a fair idea of the strength of the resistance and the power and persistency of the attack. With wooden vessels, your remark, as previously quoted—and I know it to be an all but universal one—would apply with truth; and it is because we have all become so accustomed to measure battles on land or sea by the amount of slaughter and maiming inflicted, that we are apt to err in judging an utterly uncommon and unprecedented battle by the ordinary or common standard. Let me also add that this standard is both a vulgar and false one. McClellan's victory at Yorktown was a bloodless one, but, nevertheless, a triumph of the highest importance in its results. Of Halleck's siege and capture of Corinth, the same may be said—that victory, although a bloodless one, having thrown open the doors of the entire South-West to the conquering advance of our armies.
>
> And now, let me submit to you, more in detail, some few hasty reflections on the subject of the recent operations for the capture of Charleston: —
>
> 1. It is to be borne in mind that this (so far as the navy was concerned) was purely an experiment as to the possibility of taking a city by machinery. The Monitors might be called blood-saving instruments, with this penalty attached to them: that whenever the loss of life should begin, it would involve the almost certain destruction of every man on board. The number of men in the whole iron-clad squadron was less than a regiment; and these few hundred men, rushing against thirty or forty thousand behind powerful fortifications, were to have no other part in the fight than to supply the necessary power for working the machines. If Charleston were to fall, it was by machinery; and the moment the experiment was tested to the point of proving that the machines were inadequate to their work, it was wisdom to withdraw them, and would have been dangerous foolhardiness to have held them longer exposed.
>
> 2. The experiment was fully prosecuted up to this point, with a magnificence of gallantry before which every generous and just spectator, not directly involved

in the attack, must have bowed in reverence. The machines were untried, and the conflict was the first practical test we have ever had of the power of the new kinds of ordnance and ordnance material employed against them. I refer to the Blakely and Whitworth English guns, firing bolts and steel-pointed shot. The warfare was almost as new to Admiral Du Pont and his Captains as it would have been to you or myself—new kinds of projectiles raining on them from above; vast torpedoes *[mines]* known to be underneath their keels, and every channel of entrance blocked up with triple rows of torpedo-armed obstructions.

3. After less than an hour's conflict, five out of the eight Monitors were disabled—the Keokuk sinking. Behind the forts, calmly waiting their opportunity, lay three of the enemy's iron-clads in plain view: vessels not able in fair fight to live an hour before one of our Monitors; but held in readiness to cruise out and capture any Monitor disabled by the artillery practice of the forts and batteries. This should not be let out of sight.

4. With two or three of our vessels of this kind disabled, captured, repaired, and in the enemy's service, what force would it require to maintain the blockade of Charleston? Wooden vessels—our gunboats and steam-sloops—would be useless; and our iron vessels could not live outside of Charleston bar in rough weather. Nor, even if they could, unless we had enough of them to cross-fire over every inch of the mouth of the harbor permanently, could a blockade be maintained against the fast clipper steamers built as blockade-runners in English shipyards. In a word, the enemy, with a single Monitor of ours, could drive every wooden boat from the blockade: and the blockade would thus practically be raised.

5. Could we afford to have Charleston a free port—the greatest free port in the world, when viewed as the only outlet and inlet for the commerce of eight millions of people; with arms and all other requisites pouring into it unmolested, and cotton, tobacco, naval stores, and so forth, pouring out? Would not such an event of necessity—a moral and political necessity—compel France, and perhaps other wavering foreign Powers, to acknowledge the Confederacy? Are we in a position lightly to hazard these consequences?

6. Bear in mind that the weakness of the Monitor-turrets was increasing in geometrical ratio under the force of each concussion. Each bolt started, each plate cracked, each stancheon bent by the first ball, left weaker protection against the second; and the second transmitted this deterioration, increased by its own impact, to the third. Thus onward—the element of the calculation being that three hundred guns, worked with every advantage of space and fixity, were arrayed against thirty-two guns cramped up in delicate machines, and requiring to be fired just at the exact right moment of turretal rotation.

7. Fort Sumter itself, we should not forget, was but the fire-focus of two long, converging lines of forts and batteries; and while, for aggressive purposes, and from its position, its armament was more to be dreaded than that of any other

work,—the fort itself, being built of masonry, fully exposed to fire, was the most pregnable point in the harbor. Nor would its fall have terminated the contest, nor given any further ease to the iron-clads, than the withdrawal of so many guns from against them. Their work would still lie before them, in silencing the other forts and removing the triple line of powerful and cunningly devised obstructions.

The foregoing, my dear Nicolay, are only a few of the most prominent suggestions to be used in forming a right estimate of the struggle. Busy and overworked as I am, this explanation has appeared necessary to my conscience as a point of duty: insomuch that I could not rest until my very utmost was done to let you see this affair from the standpoint of a deeply interested spectator, who had given some thought and observation to the problem, and who certainly has no other interest in this matter than to see that no injustice is done to brave, true patriots whom he honors—honors with his whole heart and soul.

How I should have felt if in the Weehawken, commanded by John Rodgers, who had the post of honor in the van, I do not know; but suppose that pride and the busy sense of duty and responsibility would have held me firm to my work. Only a spectator, however, with no immediate cares to distract my attention, I am not ashamed to say that I trembled like a leaf for the gallant souls on board the Weehawken, when she first steamed into the hell-made-visible fronting and around Fort Sumter.

The chief officers, as you know, who took part in this fight were Admiral Du Pont, Commodore *[John W.]* Turner, Fleet Captain *[Christopher]* Raymon*[d]* Rodgers, Dupont's chief of staff; and Commanders John Rodgers, *[Percival]* Drayton of South Carolina, brother to General *[Thomas F.]* Drayton of the Confederate army; George W. Rodgers, Daniel Ammen, *[John A.]* Down*[e]*s, *[Donald M.]* Fairfax, *[John L.]* Worden, who commanded the original Monitor in her fight with the Merrimac in Hampton Roads; and *[Alexander C.]* Rhind who, with rash gallantry, ran his vessel, the Keokuk, right under the walls of Fort Sumter, in which position she was so badly riddled and ripped up with bolts and percussion shells, that she sank next morning, despite all efforts to keep her afloat and send her down for repairs to Port Royal. I record these names because it gives me pleasure to write them. It is with names such as these that the future crown of the Republic will be most brightly jewelled. . . .

Before concluding this letter—hastily written, but containing points, it seems to me, which you might do the country a service by bringing to the notice of Mr. Lincoln—let me call attention to the manifest impolicy of further increasing our fleet of Monitor built iron-clads. These vessels, admirable perhaps for attacking fortified places along our coasts—although they have been badly repulsed at Forts McAlister and Sumter—are manifestly unfit to cross the ocean, except when a guaranty-deed of "dead calm" shall have been obtained from the Clerk of the Weather; and are just as manifestly unfit for human beings to live in for any length of time. Besides, it is clear, that, with the reduction of Charleston and Mobile, all the work for which this class of vessels is peculiarly fitted will have been accomplished.

I know it is said that they could be used as floating batteries with which to defend our harbors; but ask the men best competent to judge of their capacities as against vessels like the Warrior, Guerrière, La Gloire, etc., and this illusion will be dissipated. In the judgment of men who have commanded these little, low-lying, two-gun, slow sailing, floating batteries, one of the vast iron-clad frigates of France or England could receive the fire of any two of them—eight or ten guns at most—and then run right over them, the vast ploughs which such frigates carry in front, beneath the water, ripping the whole lower skin of the Monitor-hulls to pieces, and their tall prows moving on undisturbed over the little circular towers and pilot-houses, which would go down in eddying whirlpools beneath their irresistible weight and impetus.

Believe me, my dear Nicolay, that we need iron-clad frigates; and fast vessels to fight fast vessels. There is not one of our grass-grown Monitors to-day that can make, to save her life, even in tideless water, over five miles an hour, if so much; while the mailed frigates of France and England make from seven to eleven and a half. In this respect also, the Roanoke is a failure, only making six knots per hour; and our only safeguard against invasion, and our only means of aggression in case of a foreign war, must be looked for in such vessels as Mr. *[William Henry]* Webb, of New York, is now constructing.

Cannot the Navy Department be made to realize these obvious facts? Cannot Mr. Assistant Secretary Fox—whose abilities and zeal are highly spoken of by many who are in the best position to judge—cannot he be brought to comprehend that all vessels-of-war must be in their nature a compromise between the best shape and construction for the immediate purposes of battle—occurring, mayhap, once in several years; and the necessity for having such accommodations, ventilation, comforts, etc., as will preserve the health of the men and officers forming the respective crews? These questions are asked by every unprejudiced naval officer at this station; and it is important that the matter should receive the prompt attention of all who are interested in city property along the Atlantic and Pacific seaboards.

Charles G. Halpine, *Life and Adventures, Songs, Services, and Speeches of Private Miles O'Reilly* (New York: Carleton, 1864), 11–24.

57. JGN MSS, DLC.

58. JGN MSS, DLC.

59. John Hay had similar experiences. One day a gentleman insisted that he must see Lincoln immediately. "The President is engaged now," replied Hay. "What is your mission?" "Do you know who I am?" asked the caller. "No, I must confess I do not," said Hay. "I am the son of God," came the answer. "The President will be

delighted to see you when you come again. And perhaps you will bring along a letter of introduction from your father," retorted the quick-witted secretary. John W. Starr, "Lincoln and the Office Seekers," typescript dated 1936, addenda, p. 6, Lincoln files, "Patronage" folder, Lincoln Memorial University, Harrogate, Tenn.

60. JGN MSS, DLC.

61. JGN MSS, DLC.

62. Hooker fought the battle of Chancellorsville between 1 and 4 May.

63. Gen. John Sedgwick (1813–64) commanded the VI Corps of the Army of the Potomac.

64. In December 1862, Gen. E. V. Sumner (1797–1863) had commanded the Right Grand Division at the battle of Fredericksburg.

65. Hiram G. Berry (b. 1824), commanding the 2nd Division of the III Corps of the Army of the Potomac, was killed on 3 May.

66. OMH MSS, IHi.

67. Telegram, OMH MSS, IHi.

68. Benjamin F. Westlake became provost marshal for the 9th District of Illinois.

69. JGN MSS, LM. Alexander Hamilton Bowman (1803–65) was superintendent of West Point (1861–64).

70. JGN MSS, DLC.

71. Lincoln left for Falmouth on 6 May and returned the following day.

72. Gen. George Stoneman (1822–94), commander of the cavalry of the Army of the Potomac, made a raid on Richmond that virtually denied Hooker any cavalry during the battle of Chancellorsville.

73. The Confederates lost 12,764 men all told (killed, wounded, and missing), while the Federals lost 17,287.

74. Grant had crossed the Mississippi on 30 April and was winning battle after battle as he closed in on Vicksburg. The battle of Port Gibson took place on 1 May. Grant forced the Confederates to evacuate Grand Gulf on 3 May. On 6 May, David Dixon Porter's flotilla took Alexandria, Louisiana.

75. JGN MSS, DLC.

76. Ohio senator Benjamin F. Wade (1800–78) and Michigan senator Zachariah Chandler (1813–79) were leading members of the Joint Congressional Committee on the Conduct of the War and were prominent Radical Republicans.

77. JGN MSS, DLC.

78. In late April and early May, Grant fought successful battles at Port Gibson, Grand Gulf, Jackson, Raymond, Champion's Hill, and Big Black River Bridge; on 18 May he began the siege of Vicksburg, which culminated in the surrender of that town on 4 July.

79. JGN MSS, DLC.

80. Hay's letter read:

I take advantage of a transient boat to send a line.

On my return from a week at Beaufort & the Sea Islands, I learned that the General had sent Arthur Kinzie to Washington to bear a letter begging that the Govt. would release him from the orders which bind him to the dead body of the Navy here & would permit him to organize an expedition of his own into the Interior. I was very sorry that the letter had been dispatched in my absence as I should have preferred to use what influence my position would give me to bring the matter at once before the President and Secretary of War. There is positively nothing to hope for from the Navy at present. The Admiral so dreads failure that he cannot think of success. If anything is to be done here, General Hunter must, in the present aspect of affairs do it himself. The enemy are hurrying every available man away from the coast, to reenforce their great armies in the interior. Now is our time to strike them while & where they are weak. If the matter is not already settled, I hope you will exert yourself, for the good of the country to have it done.

Another thing about which I wrote before. Why is not authority given to Genl. Hunter to organize Negro Regiments? He very much needs it. He has written twice for it, and has gotten no answer. I wish you would, simply *pro bono publico,* have some resurrection made of the matter. Negroes are coming in, slowly as yet. But when our expeditions get on the Main he will be very much embarrassed for authority to do this.

I will start in a day or two. I write today because of the importance of the subject involved. The Arago is now lying at the wharf. I leave in her. But I thought a day or so might be gained by posting this today.

I am very sorry that I have to leave just as a prospect for some work opens. But I have been away as long as my conscience will permit to tax yr. forbearance.

Poor Charlie is in bad health. His lungs are affected. His physician thinks he must go North, which he flatly refuses to do as he thinks nothing ails him, and is only useful here now. I think I will bring him with me and send him home for a while.

Hay to Nicolay, Hilton Head, S.C., 24 May 1863, in Burlingame, *At Lincoln's Side,* 42–43.

81. Holt Papers, DLC.

82. JGN MSS, DLC.

83. Gen. N. P. Banks began the siege of Port Hudson on 21 May.

84. Confederate general Joseph E. Johnston (1807–91) commanded the Department of the West.

85. James R. Gilmore, *Personal Recollections of Abraham Lincoln and the Civil War* (London: John MacQueen, 1899), 151.

86. James R. Gilmore (1822–1903) was a journalist who had spoken with Gen-

eral Rosecrans in May about several things, among them a proposed insurrection by Southern blacks scheduled for 1 August. Rosecrans had been asked to support it, but he and his chief of staff, James A. Garfield, opposed it. Acting as a courier, Gilmore informed Lincoln of the matter. Gilmore, *Personal Recollections of Abraham Lincoln,* 142–53.

87. AL MSS, DLC.

88. An endorsement on this document stated that Foster had been confirmed but that his commission had not yet been issued. Foster worked for Follett and Foster, the Columbus, Ohio, company that had published the Lincoln-Douglas debates and William Dean Howells's campaign biography of Lincoln. In 1861, Salmon Chase had asked that some position be found for Foster. Basler, *CWL,* 4:556.

89. Draft, AL MSS, DLC.

90. The *Tribune* had been harshly critical of Lincoln, who responded by refusing to see its editor, the Radical Joseph Medill, when he four times tried to call on him in May 1863.

91. AL MSS, DLC. Hebard was one of the editors of the *Rochester (N.Y.) Evening Express.*

92. The copperhead paper was the *Rochester Union & Advertiser.*

93. JGN MSS, DLC.

94. On 3 June, the Army of Northern Virginia began heading north in a campaign that culminated in the battle of Gettysburg on 1–3 July.

95. On 17 June, the Illinois Democrats convened in Springfield and adopted the following resolution: "That we are in favor of peace upon the basis of a dissolution of the Union, and for the accomplishment of which we propose a national convention to settle upon the terms of peace, which shall have in view the restoration of the Union as it was, and the securing by Constitutional amendments such rights to the several States and the people thereof as honor and justice demand." *Chicago Tribune,* 18 June 1863.

96. JGN MSS, DLC.

97. George Gordon Meade (1815–72) of Pennsylvania, commander of the V Corps of the Army of the Potomac, took charge of that entire army on 28 June.

98. JGN MSS, DLC.

99. Darius N. Couch (1822–97) of Massachusetts commanded the Department of the Susquehanna, primarily a militia force. He had commanded the II Corps of the Army of the Potomac from the fall of 1862 till late May 1863.

100. JGN MSS, DLC.

101. OMH MSS, IHi. Nicolay left Washington on 16 July to help negotiate a treaty with the Ute Indians.

102. OMH MSS, IHi.

103. Amos Tuck (1810–79) of New Hampshire was naval officer of the port of Boston (1861–65). On 17 July, Tuck wrote Nicolay saying: "The Collector, Mr. Goodrich, knowing my anxiety to oblige those who took an interest in retaining

Mr. McNeal, has placed in my hands the enclosed letter, which he thinks correctly sets forth Mr. McNeal's merits as a public officer. I have told him to forbear action till I could confer with you, and ascertain, if you, the President or Mr. Hatch, would still wish his retention in the service of the Custom House. OMH MSS, IHi.

104. Hay Papers, Brown University.

105. Conejos is a town in southwest Colorado.

106. Col. John Evans (1814–97) was territorial governor of Colorado (1862–65).

107. Telegram, AL MSS, DLC.

108. *Pike County Press* (Pittsfield, Ill.), 6 Nov. 1974. Seeley was the surgeon on the 21st Illinois Volunteers. He practiced medicine in Pike County, of which his father, Col. James Seeley, was one of the first settlers.

109. AL MSS, DLC. Solomon A. Meredith (1816–74) was a prisoner-of-war exchange agent at Fortress Monroe.

110. Born in Kentucky in 1814, attorney Daniel H. Gilmer served as states attorney in Pike County (1860) and was the partner of Milton Hay for a time. He was a leading Republican in Pittsfield. He died at Chickamauga.

111. JGN MSS, DLC.

112. Schuyler Colfax of Indiana was speaker of the U.S. House of Representatives. Conservative Unionist Emerson Etheridge (1819–1902), a slaveholder from west Tennessee, was clerk of the U.S. House of Representatives. He hoped to disqualify many Republican Representatives on a technicality.

113. Lincoln sent his letter to Senators James W. Grimes, Zachariah Chandler, and Jacob Collamer as well as to Vice President Hannibal Hamlin. Basler, *CWL,* 6:546–50. Cf. Nicolay and Hay, *Abraham Lincoln: A History,* 7:390–91.

114. JGN MSS, DLC.

115. Gen. John G. Foster (1823–74) commanded the XVIII Corps, which was supporting Burnside in east Tennessee. On 9 December, he replaced Burnside. Confederate general James Longstreet (1821–1904) commanded the Department of East Tennessee.

116. JGN MSS, DLC.

117. On 30 September 1863, seventy delegates from Missouri called on Lincoln to protest against administration policies and appointments in their state.

118. Wendell Phillips (1811–84) of Massachusetts was a leading abolitionist.

119. Lincoln's letter to Charles D. Drake et al., Washington, 5 Oct. 1863, is in Basler, *CWL,* 6:499–504.

120. JGN MSS, DLC.

121. Edward McManus, a servant in the White House, was described by William O. Stoddard as a "short, thin, smiling, humorous-looking elderly Irishman . . . who has been so great a favorite through so many administrations. He is as well liked by his seventh President *[Lincoln]* as he was by even General Taylor. There is no end of quiet fun in him as well as intelligence, and his other name is Fidelity. He

is said to have been the first man met in the White House by Mr. Lincoln who succeeded in making him laugh." Stoddard, *Inside the White House in War Times,* 3. For unclear reasons, he was dismissed in January 1865, evidently at the behest of Mary Lincoln, who called him a "serpent." Justin E. Turner and Linda Levitt Turner, eds., *Mary Todd Lincoln: Her Life and Letters* (New York: Knopf, 1972), 200–202. In March 1865, his replacement, Cornelius O'Leary, was fired after being caught peddling influence to obtain pardons. It was alleged that he shared with Mary Lincoln the illegal fees he received. Noah Brooks, Washington dispatch, 12 Mar. 1865, in Burlingame, *Lincoln Observed,* 171-74.

122. Fernando Wood (1812–81) was mayor of New York. Cf. Nicolay and Hay, *Abraham Lincoln: A History,* 7:394–95.

123. Clement L. Vallandigham (1829–71) of Ohio, a leading Peace Democrat, had been exiled to the Confederacy after being arrested by General Burnside for sedition.

124. JGN MSS, DLC.

125. Seward Papers, University of Rochester.

126. JGN MSS, DLC.

127. The *Philadelphia Inquirer* was run by Jesper Harding and his son William W. Harding. Jay Cooke and Company, headed by Jay Cooke (1821–1905) of Philadelphia and his brother Henry (1825–81), worked on Chase's behalf, planting favorable stories about him in the press and contributing money to his campaign. The Cooke brothers, along with other Chase backers, raised $13,500 to buy a newspaper that would support Chase. The negotiations were handled by Chase's son-in-law, William Sprague. Ellis Paxson Oberholtzer, *Jay Cooke: Financier of the Civil War,* 2 vols. (Philadelphia: George W. Jacobs & Co., 1907), 1:364–65.

128. Lincoln's Secretariat Collection, LM. Joshua Ballinger Lippincott (1813–86) established his publishing firm in 1836 in Philadelphia.

1864

1. JGN MSS, DLC.

2. AL MSS, DLC.

3. Holt's endorsement of 9 January states that on 11 June 1863, his office sent Lincoln a report on the case of George H. Mitchell, which report should still be with the president. Mitchell was the assistant surgeon of the 88th Pennsylvania Volunteers.

4. Seward Papers, University of Rochester.

5. JGN MSS, DLC.

6. A reference to Rhode Island senator William Sprague and his wife, Kate Chase Sprague.

7. A reference to Secretary of the Treasury Salmon P. Chase.

8. Denmark and Germany had long contended for dominance in the two "Elbe duchies" of Schleswig and Holstein. The crisis reached a head on 15 November 1863 with the death of King Frederick IV of Denmark, who had no male heir. The complex dispute threatened to provoke a general European war.

9. During a speech in the House of Representatives on 16 January, the Radical abolitionist Anna E. Dickinson (1842–1932) was denouncing the president's reconstruction policy when Lincoln arrived. She abruptly changed course and urged his reelection.

10. Photocopy, JGN MSS, DLC. Alvord was a special commissioner who in 1864 helped negotiate a treaty with Indian tribes in Michigan. Basler, *CWL,* 8:219–20.

11. JGN MSS, DLC.

12. The "subs" were Edward D. Neill, Gustave Matile, and Nathaniel S. Howe.

13. Jesse K. Dubois (1811–76) was a Springfield friend and neighbor of Lincoln's.

14. Gantt's address was *Address of E. W. Gantt, of Arkansas (Brigadier General in the Confederate Army) in Favor of Re-union in 1863,* which urged Arkansans to quit the war, reorganize the state, and bring it back into the Union. Edward Walton Gantt (1812–83), repenting his secessionism, told Lincoln he wanted "to induce the withdrawal of my State from its allies in rebellion and its reentry into the Federal Union." Nicolay and Hay, *Abraham Lincoln: A History,* 8:410. Cf. *New York Times,* 6 Feb. 1864. On 11 December, it was reported that Lincoln "has signed the pardon, exempting E. W. Gantt of Arkansas, from the penalty of treason of which he is accused by accepting and exercising the office of Brigadier General in the service of the rebels. The pardon also reinstates General Gantt in all his rights of property excepting those relating to slaves." Washington correspondence, 11 Dec. 1863, *Chicago Tribune,* 12 Dec. 1863.

15. JGN MSS, DLC.

16. The next day, Lincoln ordered the immediate replacement of the stable. The commissioner of public buildings stated that it "is very necessary for the convenience of the President, that it should be rebuilt as soon as possible. At an interview with him, early this morning, he expressed a desire that I would bring the matter to the attention of Congress to-day, if possible, that measures might be taken to have it rebuilt." Benjamin Brown French to John H. Rice, Washington, 11 Feb. 1864, copy, Records of the Commissioner of Public Buildings, National Archives.

17. Holt Papers, DLC.

18. Holt had urgently requested that the president meet with him to finish up work on court-martial cases. Holt to Nicolay, Washington, 13 Feb. 1864, AL MSS, DLC.

19. Draft, AL MSS, DLC. Thaddeus Stevens (1792–1868) of Gettysburg, Pennsylvania, represented his district in the U.S. House (1849–53, 1859–68). He chaired the House Ways and Means Committee (1861–65).

20. JGN MSS, DLC.

21. Quincy A. Gillmore (1825–88) commanded the Department of the South.

22. The pamphlet, "The Next Presidential Election," was, according to one source, the handiwork of Anna Ella Carroll, who "has written grossly and personally abusive of Mr. Lincoln." This document "has been published by the copperheads, together with an *addendum* containing articles also abusive of Mr. Lincoln, by [George] Wilkes, of the New York *Spirit of the Times.*" Washington correspondence, 23 Feb. 1864, *Chicago Tribune,* 27 Feb. 1864. It may have been written by James M. Winchell, New York agent of both the Union Pacific and the Kansas Pacific Railroads, or by Edmund C. Stedman, a poet and former clerk of Attorney General Bates. Several hundred copies were distributed to newspaper editors and other influential public figures. John Niven, *Salmon P. Chase: A Biography* (New York: Oxford University Press, 1995, 359–61. Kansas senator Samuel C. Pomeroy (1816–91) was the author of the "Pomeroy Circular." Based on the pamphlet "The Next Presidential Election," it denounced Lincoln and called for Chase's nomination. It was distributed to scores of political leaders and published in press. The full text can be found in Nicolay and Hay, *Abraham Lincoln: A History,* 8:319–20.

23. Maryland congressman Henry Winter Davis (1817–65), a leading Radical critic of Lincoln, had, according to a Washington journalist, a large "organ of combativeness," was "always spoiling for a fight," and seemed "to be ever wandering about dragging an imaginary coat upon the floor of the House and daring any one to tread upon it." Early in 1864, "his favorite object of attack" became Lincoln, who said: "Well, well, it appears to do him good, and as it does me no injury, (that is I don't feel that it does) what's the harm in letting him have his fling? If he did not pitch into me he would into some poor fellow whom he might hurt." Washington correspondence, 28 Feb. 1864, *Chicago Tribune,* 3 Mar. 1864.

24. John D. Defrees (1811–82), a leader of the Republican party in Indiana, was superintendent of public printing.

25. JGN MSS, DLC.

26. AL MSS, DLC.

27. JGN MSS, DLC.

28. The *National Intelligencer* of Washington first published the circular on 22 February.

29. Truman Seymour (1824–91) commanded the X Corps in Gillmore's army. On 20 February, he precipitated the battle of Olustee, a major defeat for Union arms.

30. Copy, AL MSS, DLC.

31. Governor Yates's telegram to Stanton (Springfield, 2 Mar. 1864, AL MSS, DLC) reported two clashes in Paris, Illinois, between Union men and copperheads that left several killed. He asked that troops to be sent to Paris to restore order.

32. JGN MSS, DLC.

33. Gen. Judson Kilpatrick (1836–81) led an unsuccessful cavalry raid on Richmond in late February and early March.

34. Ulric Dahlgren (b. 1842), son of Adm. John A. Dahlgren, had commanded a five-hundred-man force in Kilpatrick's raid.

35. JGN MSS, DLC. In 1897, Nicolay described this event to Rene Bache:

The incidents attending the first personal meeting of President Lincoln and General Grant were as simple and impressive as the characters of the two men. On the 29th of February 1864 the President signed the Act passed by Congress reviving the grade of Lieutenant General; and immediately nominated General Grant to that office to command the armies of the United States. On the 3d of March the new General was ordered to Washington, where he arrived on the 8th. Though this was now the fourth year of the war, the two men had never yet seen each other. Neither however felt that they were strangers. Their strongly marked features were familiar not only to each other but to all the world from countless photographs, engravings and woodcuts, and the remarkable career of each had impressed upon the other a feeling of admiration and trust which left little to be added by the eye and voice.

Grant arrived in Washington on the evening of March 8th, and immediately proceeded to the White House. An unusually crowded public reception was in progress when he entered at about 9:30. A hum of eager whispered recognition and interest among the guests was the sole announcement of the victor of Donelson and Vicksburg, and as he approached the President the crowd instinctively fell back, and Lincoln warmly clasped the hand of Grant in an impressive silence of some seconds' duration. There followed a few words of casual greeting, then the General was introduced to Mrs Lincoln and next to Secretary Seward, who escorted him to the East Room crowded almost to suffocation, where cheer after cheer went up as soon as his presence was recognized. The General, blushing like a girl, was compelled to mount upon a sofa, from which height he shook hands with as many as could force their way to his side.

The reception closed promptly at eleven, after which the General again met the President and Secretary of War in the Blue Room to appoint an hour for the formal presentation of the new commission as Lieutenant General on the following day. At one oclock on the 9th this formal presentation took place in the presence of the entire Cabinet and sundry high officials. I was again present on this occasion, and in the general conversation which followed the formalities, heard General Grant ask Mr Lincoln what specific service was expected of him. The President replied that the country wanted him to take Richmond, and asked if he could do it, to which Grant said he could if he had the troops; and in turn the President assured him he should have the full support of the country and the Executive. . . .

Nicolay to Bache, Washington, 19 Apr. 1897, copy, JGN MSS, DLC. Cf. Frederick D. Grant's recollections in the *National Republican,* 22 Feb. 1923.

36. JGN MSS, DLC.

37. The texts of Grant's and Lincoln's remarks are in Basler, *CWL,* 7:234, and John Y. Simon, ed., *The Papers of Ulysses S. Grant,* vol. 10 (Carbondale: Southern Illinois University Press, 1982), 195.

38. James C. Hall was a state senator from Toledo. Chase's letter to Hall (Washington, 5 Mar. 1864) is in Jacob W. Schuckers, *The Life and Public Services of Salmon Portland Chase* (New York: D. Appleton, 1874), 502–3.

39. Charles G. Halpine Papers, Huntington Library. Halpine (1829–68), an Irish-born New York journalist, served as assistant adjutant to General Hunter as well as liaison with the press. Written under the pen name of Miles O'Reilly, his contributions to the *New York Herald* were popular. Joseph R. Hawley described him as "a beautiful hater of . . . [the] swindlers" who infested Florida. Joseph R. Hawley to Charles Dudley Warner, St. Augustine, 14 July 1863, in Arthur L. Shipman, ed., "Letters of Joseph R. Hawley," typescript dated 1929, p. 154, Connecticut Historical Society, Hartford.

40. JGN MSS, DLC.

41. Lyman Stickney observed that "Maj Hay was greatly excited at the notice taken of his Florida mission by the Herald." Stickney to Salmon P. Chase, 2 Mar. 1864, Chase Papers, DLC. On 23 February 1864, the *New York Herald* reported that

> a curious development of Executive intermeddling with military movements has been developed by inquiries about the recent Florida expedition. It is said that upon hearing of it General Halleck was quite taken by surprise, and wrote to General Gillmore to know what he was doing at Jacksonville, a place that had been two or three times in our possession and was not considered worth holding, and asking how he came to go there, not only without orders but without the knowledge and contrary to the positive instructions of the Secretary of War and General Halleck. In reply General Gillmore is said to have enclosed a letter of instructions from the President, transmitted to him by Mr. Hay, late private secretary of Mr. Lincoln, directing the movement to be made. Since this statement has been in circulation it is rumored that the expedition was intended simply for the occupation of Florida for the purpose of securing the election of three Lincoln delegates to the National Nominating Convention, and that of John Hay to Congress. The cost of the operation to the government is estimated at about one million of dollars.

42. Telegrams Collected by the Office of the Secretary of War, 1861–1882, Record Group 473, reel 1, National Archives.

43. JGN MSS, DLC. Nicolay left Washington for New York on 25 March and returned 6 April.

44. AL MSS, DLC.

45. Thurlow Weed (1797–1882) was a New York newspaper editor, political savant, and alter ego of William Henry Seward. Lincoln's letter to Weed is in Basler, *CWL,* 7:268.

46. Weed had lamented to Davis that "[n]early all the Office-holders appointed through our enemies, are now Mr. Lincoln's Enemies. My Friends, though 'out in the cold,' are the Friends of the President." He begged Davis to tell Lincoln "distinctly and emphatically, that if this Custom House is left in custody of those who have, for two years, sent 'aid and comfort' to the enemy *his* fitness for President will be questioned." Willard L. King, *Lincoln's Manager: David Davis* (Cambridge: Harvard University Press, 1960), 216. Davis told Weed that it "pains him [Lincoln] when you are not satisfied with what he does. . . . I think he ought to act & act promptly. But his mind is constituted differently from yours and mine. We will have to await the slowness of his movement. . . . I wish the *power* in relation to such things was in my hands." King, *Lincoln's Manager,* 216. In November 1863, Weed had told Lincoln "that the infamies of the Appraiser's Office required the Removal of [John T.] Hogeboom and Hunt, men whose appointments, originally, we in vain resisted. . . . It is not alone that these men are against Mr. Lincoln, but they disgrace the office—a Department everywhere spoken of as a 'Den of Thieves.' Mr. Lincoln not only spurns his friends . . . but *Promotes* an enemy who ought to be removed!" Weed told David Davis that "[a]fter *this* outrage and insult I will cease to annoy him; and tho' ever remembering how pleasant my acquaintance is with you, I will no more trouble you with matters which make us both unhappy." Weed to Davis, 29 Mar. 1864, in King, *Lincoln's Manager,* 216–17. Davis replied that Lincoln "spoke of you in the highest terms: of your ability & disinterested patriotism & of the great friendship that you had always shown him." King, *Lincoln's Manager,* 217.

47. Hiram Barney (1811–95) was a New York attorney, anti-slavery leader, and collector of the port of New York (1861–64).

48. Rufus F. Andrews was surveyor of customs in the New York Custom House.

49. John T. Hogeboom, a friend of Salmon Chase and a member of the Old Democrat faction in New York politics, was appointed general appraiser in the New York Custom House. In June 1864, Lincoln explained to Chase that the appointment of Hogeboom "brought me to and has ever since kept me at, the verge of open revolt" by his friends in New York. Basler, *CWL,* 7:413–14.

50. Thomas McElrath (1807–88), a business partner of Horace Greeley's, had quit his post as appraiser-general, which he had assumed in 1861, to devote full time to publishing the *New York Tribune.*

51. AL MSS, DLC.

52. There is an undated four-page memorandum filed with Nicolay's letter, AL MSS, DLC. In September 1863, en route to Tennessee from Virginia with the XI Corps, Schurz ordered that the train be halted so that he could rejoin his division.

Since any delay might allow the Confederates to capture Rosecrans's besieged army, Stanton was furious and Schurz was put on the shelf.

53. AL MSS, DLC.

54. Col. Gotthilf de Bourry belonged to the 63rd New York Volunteers. The undated memorandum about Bourry was by Carl Schurz, who supported the colonel's appeal of a conviction for drunkenness.

55. AL MSS, DLC.

56. An editorial entitled "The Presidency" urged that the Republican national convention be postponed until after the scheduled 7 June date.

57. Sydney Howard Gay (1814–1888) was managing editor of the *New York Tribune*.

58. On 4 April, the Metropolitan Fair, which was held to raise funds for the U.S. Sanitary Commission, opened in New York.

59. On 29 January 1864, Leavitt Hunt of 34 Wall Street, New York, N.Y., wrote to Nicolay asking for original documents signed by Lincoln that might be auctioned at the Metropolitan Fair in April. AL MSS, DLC. E. D. Webster was a fourth-class clerk in the State Department.

60. By this date, Lincoln had issued four Thanksgiving proclamations. Nicolay evidently refers to the one of 3 October 1863. See Basler, *CWL*, 6: 496–97.

61. JGN MSS, DLC.

62. Telegrams Collected by the Office of the Secretary of War, 1861–1882, Record Group 473, reel 1, National Archives. Dennison (1815–82) was governor of Ohio and would later in 1864 become Lincoln's postmaster general.

63. On behalf of a friend who wished to speculate in southern cotton, Dennison had asked the president to write a letter urging U.S. authorities to assist the speculator. Dennison to Lincoln, Columbus, 28 Mar. 1864, AL MSS, DLC.

64. Copy, AL MSS, DLC.

65. Chase's letter of 8 April requested that Lincoln suspend an order forbidding the export of salted provisions, for the order would affect foreign trade and hence the public finances, which depended in part on import duties. Chase wished to be consulted about such an order. AL MSS, DLC.

66. JGN MSS, DLC.

67. Democrat Alexander Long (1816–86) represented an Ohio district in the U.S. House (1863–65).

68. Benjamin Gwinn Harris (1805–95) represented a Maryland district in the U.S. House (1863–67). In 1865, he was convicted of disloyal conduct and forbidden to hold any U.S. office, but President Andrew Johnson remitted his sentence.

69. Copy, AL MSS, DLC.

70. On behalf of General Rosecrans, Gilmore had two interviews with Lincoln in May 1863 about a projected slave insurrection on 1 August and about a furlough for Colonel Jacques. Gilmore to Lincoln, Boston, 25 Mar. 1864, AL MSS, DLC. Cf. Gilmore, *Personal Recollections of Abraham Lincoln*, 148–66.

71. Holt Papers, DLC.

72. JGN MSS, DLC.

73. On 12 April, the Confederates captured Fort Pillow on the Mississippi. When Union troops threw down their arms and surrendered, their captors killed some of them in cold blood, including many black troops.

74. Butler Papers, DLC. Nicolay pasted into the body of this letter a clipping from an unidentified newspaper.

75. In the spring of 1864, Martha Todd White, Mary Lincoln's half-sister, called at the White House, where the First Couple would not see her. The president did, however, send her a pass for travel back to the South. She returned it, asking for special permission to have her luggage exempt from inspection. When Lincoln refused, Mrs. White dispatched emissaries to plead her case. To one of those gentlemen, Lincoln said that "if Mrs. W[hite] did not leave forthwith she might expect to find herself within twenty-four hours in the Old Capitol Prison." Lincoln did, however, grant Mrs. White a pass to travel south. Beale, *Diary of Gideon Welles,* 2:21 (entry for 29 Apr. 1864). Cf. Mrs. H. C. Ingersol to the editor, 1 June 1875, *Springfield (Massachusetts) Republican,* 7 June 1875, p. 4, c. 6; Elizabeth Todd Grimsley, "Six Months in the White House," *Journal of the Illinois State Historical Society* 19, nos. 3–4, (1926–27): 56–57. See *infra,* letter to Horace Greeley, 25 Apr. 1864.

76. Small Manuscript Collection no. 1107, IHi.

77. The National Convention of the Union (that is, Republican) party was held in Baltimore on 7–8 June.

78. Missouri senator B. Gratz Brown (1826–85), a Radical Republican disenchanted with Lincoln, was to sign the call for the Cleveland Convention, which nominated Frémont for president.

79. Holt Papers, DLC.

80. Greeley Papers, DLC.

81. The acccount was printed in the *New York Tribune* as follows:

We have the highest authority for the following statement in connection with the story that Mrs. M. Todd White (a sister of Mrs. Lincoln) was permitted by the President to carry contraband goods south: Mrs. White went south with only the ordinary pass which the President gives to those persons whom he permits to go. The President's pass did not permit Mrs. White to take with her anything but ordinary baggage, nor did she attempt to take anything more. The President's pass *did not* exempt her baggage from the usual inspection; and her baggage *did* undergo the usual inspection. Gen. Butler found *no* contraband goods or letters in her baggage. She did not insult or defy Gen. Butler; nor was there anything in her words or actions which led him to suspect that she was either a Rebel spy or emissary, or that she was violating any of the rules under which persons are sent through the lines. As the Copperhead papers throughout the country are quoting The Tribune as authority in this matter, and using that authority to sustain assertions never made thorough our columns, we hope they will give this statement a speedy and wide publication.

"The Story about Mrs. White," *New York Tribune,* 27 April 1864.

82. "It is stated in best-informed circles that Mrs. J. Todd White, the sister of Mrs. Lincoln, did pass through our lines for Richmond via Fortress Monroe with three large trunks containing medicines and merchandise, so that the chuckling of the Rebel press over her safe transit with Rebel uniforms and buttons of gold was founded in truth. Gen. Butler is not wont to be a 'respecter of persons,' and it is considered here a legitimate inquiry why he permitted this woman to pass to the enemy with her great quantity of contraband property when he arrests all others." Washington correspondence, 27 Mar. 1864, *New York Tribune,* 28 Mar. 1864.

83. Copy, AL MSS, DLC.

84. Butler's letter to Nicolay (Fort Monroe, Va., 21 Apr. 1864) is in the AL MSS, DLC. In it, Butler denied at length the assertions in the *New York Tribune* story of 28 March about Mrs. White passing with impunity through Butler's lines with contraband.

85. Telegrams Collected by the Office of the Secretary of War, 1861–1882, Record Group 473, reel 1, National Archives.

86. James R. Fry of Philadelphia invited the president to address a Sanitary Fair in May. Lincoln's letter (in the hand of John Hay) declining the invitation is dated 30 April. Basler, *CWL,* 7:323–24.

87. JGN MSS, DLC.

88. Nicolay to Edgar T. Welles, Washington, 10 Apr. 1888, Miscellaneous Manuscripts (Welles), New-York Historical Society.

89. Welles did record in his diary Lincoln's request that all members of the cabinet submit opinions about how to respond to the Fort Pillow massacre. Beale, *Diary of Gideon Welles,* 2:23. Nicolay and Hay wrote an extensive account of the administration's response to the atrocity, which concluded that "Grant was about entering upon his Wilderness Campaign, and its rapid succession of bloody conflicts crowded out of view and consideration a topic so difficult and so hazardous as wholesale retaliation for the Fort Pillow barbarity, which, on one hand, strict justice demanded, and which, on the other, enlightened humanity forbade." *Abraham Lincoln: A History,* 6:483–84.

90. JGN MSS, DLC.

91. In the battle of the Wilderness (5–6 May), Grant suffered 17,666 casualties (including more than 12,000 wounded) and Lee about 7,500.

92. On 4 May, Butler's Army of the James began its move against Richmond from the southeast.

93. On 7 May, Sherman launched his campaign against Atlanta.

94. Copy, AL MSS, DLC. Albert Gallatin Riddle (1816–1902) of Cleveland,

who had served in the U.S. House of Representatives (1861–63), was an attorney in Washington.

95. In his letter to Nicolay (Cleveland, 7 May 1864, AL MSS, DLC), Riddle recalled an interview that he and Ohio congressman Rufus Paine Spalding (1798–1886) had had with the president on 29 February 1864 about Frank Blair. In response to Salmon Chase's request that he write out the interview, Riddle asked Lincoln if that would be agreeable to him. Riddle later published the interview. Riddle, *Recollections of War Times: Reminiscences of Men and Events in Washington, 1860–1865* (New York: G. P. Putnam's Sons, 1895), 270–76.

96. Copy, AL MSS, DLC.

97. In his letter to Lincoln (Boston, 4 May 1864, AL MSS, DLC), Burnham had requested free copies of Joseph Henry's "Contributions to Knowledge" series published by the Smithsonian Institution.

98. Joseph Henry (1797–1878) was director of the Smithsonian Institution in Washington.

99. Copy, AL MSS, DLC.

100. William Kellogg had been a judge of the state circuit court (1850–55).

101. William G. Greene (1812–94) of Petersburg, Illinois, an old friend of Lincoln's and a leading citizen of Menard County, was collector of internal revenue for the 9th District of Illinois.

102. In April, Hatch had written: "*If you can be a Delegate at all,* it must be from our old District. . . . *[Milton]* Hay is for it and will go to Pike day after tomorrow and will see *[William]* Grimshaw Ross &c. I think it can be done." Hatch to Nicolay, Springfield, 11 Apr. 1864, scrapbook, box 1, JGN MSS, DLC. Merchant and banker Col. William Ross (1792–1873) was a leading Republican who had served in the state legislature (1834–40), was vice president of the 1856 Bloomington convention that launched the Republican party of Illinois, and served as a delegate to the Chicago convention in 1860.

103. OMH MSS, IHi. Edward Davis Townsend (1817–93) was adjutant general of the army.

104. The enclosed note, dated Springfield, 9 May 1864, was from Ozias M. Hatch, forwarding a request from Francis Freitas, a soldier who wished to return to his regiment after recuperating from six months in a Confederate prisoner-of-war camp. Hatch recommended against granting the appeal. General Orders 191, dated 7 May 1864, dealt with the exchange of prisoners of war.

105. Townsend's undated reply, written on Nicolay's note, read: "G. O. 191 enclosed does cover the case."

106. JGN MSS, DLC.

107. On 8 May, Grant attacked Lee at Spotsylvania Court House, launching a series of battles that lasted through 21 May. When assaults on the 8th, 10th, and 12th failed, Grant swung around Lee's right and pressed south.

108. An undated document entitled "Grant," written in Nicolay's hand, may

quote Lincoln: "Whatever objection may be urged as to the talents, or culture, or sobriety and military skill of Grant, or his evident stubborn[n]ess of purpose, or his alleged recklessness of means, it must be confessed that after repeated trials and failures with other Generals, he alone had the faith, the confidence and the persistence to compel success." In the margin of the slip of paper on which this is written, Nicolay jotted "L Mem," which appears on many of Nicolay's memoranda of Lincoln's conversations. Nicolay-Hay Papers, IHi.

109. Copy, AL MSS, DLC.

110. Gilmore's article was "The 'Poor Whites' of the South," *Harper's Magazine,* June 1864, 115–24.

111. Perhaps an allusion to the black insurrection scheme discussed *supra,* in the note to Nicolay's letter of 14 June 1863.

112. JGN MSS, DLC.

113. Horace Greeley Papers, New York Public Library.

114. The Washington correspondent was probably Samuel Wilkeson, a native of Buffalo and a graduate of Union College, who headed the Washington bureau of the *Tribune.* Before the war, he had been an editor and part owner of Thurlow Weed's *Albany Evening Journal,* but after a falling-out with Weed, Wilkeson joined forces with Horace Greeley, Weed's nemesis in New York politics.

115. On 18 May, the president ordered the *New York World* and the *New York Journal of Commerce* suppressed. Basler, *CWL,* 7:347–48.

116. Jose A. Arguelles, a Spanish officer who had come to New York from Cuba, was turned over to Spanish authorities even though the U.S. had no extradition treaty with Spain.

117. JGN MSS, DLC.

118. AL MSS, DLC.

119. Burton C. Cook (1819–94), who was to represent an Illinois district in the U.S. House of Representatives (1865–71), nominated Lincoln at the 1864 Republican national convention in Baltimore. He was chairman of the Illinois Republican State Central Committee.

120. The original report of the Committee on Resolutions was tabled, a new committee was constituted, and a new set of resolutions, far more supportive of the Lincoln administration, was finally passed. *Chicago Tribune,* 26 May 1864.

121. Thomas J. Turner (1815–74) of Freeport, who had represented his district in the U.S. House of Representatives (1847–49), had been the temporary chairman of the Illinois Republican convention when it met on 25 May in Springfield.

122. Joseph Medill (1823–99) owned the *Chicago Tribune.*

123. Attorney Grimshaw (b. 1813) settled in Pike County, Illinois in 1833. A leading Whig and later Republican, he served as a delegate to the 1847 Illinois constitutional convention and to the 1856 and 1860 Republican national conventions. He practiced law with his brother Jackson from 1843 to 1857. See William A. Grimshaw to Lincoln, 14 June 1849, AL MSS, DLC.

124. Leonard Swett (1825–89) of Illinois, an old friend and political ally of Lincoln's, was a delegate to the Baltimore convention.

125. The convention voted 440 to 4 to seat only the Missouri Radicals. Those delegates at first cast their ballots for Grant as the party's presidential candidate but then moved that the nomination of Lincoln be made unanimous.

126. Whitelaw Reid (1837–1912) was the Washington correspondent for the *Cincinnati Gazette* and a champion of Salmon P. Chase.

127. In pencil, Lincoln endorsed this letter on its back: "Swett is unquestionably all right. Mr. Holt is a good man, but I had not heard or thought of him for V.P. Wish not to interfere about V.P. Can not interfere about platform—Convention must judge for itself —"

128. JGN MSS, DLC.

129. Henry T. Blow (1817–75) represented a Missouri district in the U.S. House (1863–67).

130. Hannibal Hamlin (1809–91) of Maine was Lincoln's vice president (1861–65).

131. Gen. John A. Dix (1798–1879), commander of the Department of the East, had served as secretary of the treasury at the end of the Buchanan administration.

132. Daniel S. Dickinson (1800–66), a prominent New York politician, was a delegate to the Republican national convention.

133. Robert J. Breckinridge (1800–71), a professor at Danville Theological Seminary in Kentucky, presided over the Baltimore convention.

134. JGN MSS, DLC.

135. AL MSS, DLC.

136. Captain Brown was perhaps James Nicholas Brown, of Island Grove, Illinois, an old friend and political ally of Lincoln's.

137. JGN MSS, DLC.

138. In 1864, Edward Duffield Neill (1823–93) of Minnesota replaced William O. Stoddard as the presidential secretary to sign land patents. Nicolay left Washington after the convention, returned, then departed again on 5 August and returned 17 September. He spent most of his time in Illinois and Colorado.

139. Edward D. Neill Papers, Minnesota Historical Society.

140. AL MSS, DLC.

141. Clinton B. Fisk (1828–90) commanded the Department of North Missouri. A militant abolitionist, he established Fisk University for the freedmen after the war.

142. Capt. Harry Truman was a native Missourian who escaped conviction in part because potential witnesses against him were slain and others refused to participate in the trial. Michael Fellman, *Inside War: The Guerrilla Conflict in Missouri During the American Civil War* (New York: Oxford University Press, 1989), 172.

143. AL MSS, DLC.

144. Willard Preble Hall (1820–82) was provisional lieutenant governor of Missouri (1861–64) before becoming governor (1864–65).

145. Sanderson claimed that the Order of American Knights had conspired to overthrow the government and that Clement Vallandigham was in charge of the northern half of the conspiracy.

146. The reference to coal oil lamps may be an allusion to the so-called dark lantern societies, secret political organizations disloyal to the Union (the Knights of the Golden Circle, the Order of American Knights, and the Sons of Liberty).

147. AL MSS, DLC.

148. Lincoln accepted Chase's resignation on 30 June and nominated as his replacement David Tod (1805–68), governor of Ohio (1862–64). Tod declined the offer.

149. JGN MSS, DLC.

150. AL MSS, DLC. This document was evidently written by Lincoln and signed by Nicolay. Basler, *CWL,* 7:483.

151. McMahon's telegram of 5 August, from Harmsbrook, Pennsylvania, said in part, "Equal Rights & Justice to all white men in the United States forever—White men is in Class number one & black men is in class number two & must be governed by white men forever." AL MSS, DLC.

152. JGN MSS, DLC.

153. On 7 August, Union forces took Fort Gaines in Mobile Bay; sixteen days later they captured the nearby Fort Morgan. They finally entered Mobile itself on 12 April 1865.

154. Copy, JGN MSS, DLC.

155. Telegrams Collected by the Office of the Secretary of War, 1861–1882, Record Group 473, reel 1, National Archives. George W. Bridges (1825–73) was a member of the 37th Congress and colonel of the 10th Tennessee Volunteers.

156. William R. Bridges was a Confederate lieutenant who had been sentenced to death for murder. George W. Bridges to Lincoln, telegram, 18 Aug. 1864, AL MSS, DLC.

157. AL MSS, DLC.

158. Baldwin wished to set up a bakery at City Point, Virginia, and asked Lincoln to write a letter to help facilitate his plan. Baldwin to Lincoln, City Point, 17 Aug. 1864, AL MSS, DLC.

159. Marsena R. Patrick (1811–88) was provost marshal general of the Army of the Potomac (1862–65).

160. AL MSS, DLC.

161. The enclosed letter (Elliott F. Shepard to Lincoln, New York, 13 Aug. 1864, AL MSS, DLC) urged that Seward stump New York in the election campaign.

162. Copy in the hand of E. D. Neill, Benjamin F. Butler Papers, DLC.

163. JGN MSS, DLC.

164. AL MSS, DLC. Attorney William Tod Otto (1816–1905) of Indiana, who had been appointed assistant secretary of the interior by John P. Usher after Caleb B. Smith retired, remained in that post until 1871.

165. Charles Henry Philbrick (1837–85), a resident of Griggsville, Illinois, and a graduate of Illinois College, became Nicolay and Hay's assistant in 1864. Clark E. Carr called him "a man of singularly sweet and gentle nature." Carr, *The Illini: A Story of the Prairies* (Chicago: A. C. McClurg, 1905), 140. In 1860, a young woman in Springfield described him as "a sweet little fellow," "short and rather stout," with "light [h]air and bright blue eyes with a small nose and the sweetest mouth I almost ever saw," "quite bashful, but intelligent," and, in sum, "a real true honest young man." Diary of Anna Ridgely Hudson, entry for 26 Feb. 1860, IHi. In that year, Philbrick replaced Nicolay as assistant to Illinois Secretary of State Ozias M. Hatch. Wayne C. Temple, "Charles Henry Philbrick: Private Secretary to President Lincoln," *Lincoln Herald* 99 (1997): 6–11.

166. Telegrams Collected by the Office of the Secretary of War, 1861–1882, Record Group 473, reel 1, National Archives.

167. In his letter, Greeley asked that the president grant an audience to an unnamed southern Unionist.

168. Telegrams Collected by the Office of the Secretary of War, 1861–1882, Record Group 473, reel 1, National Archives.

169. Rosecrans replied that Mills had deserted several times, that there were no mitigating circumstances, and recommended against clemency. Rosecrans to Nicolay, St. Louis, 30 Aug. 1864, telegram, AL MSS, DLC.

170. Seward Papers, University of Rochester.

171. Ward Hunt (1810–86) of Utica, New York, served as associate justice of the U.S. Supreme Court (1873–79).

172. In his letter of 9 August, Hunt complained to Lincoln that Seward had helped engineer the defeat of Republican congressman Roscoe Conkling in 1862. Lincoln replied to Hunt on 16 August that he supported the regular nominee of the party and that he admired Conkling. Basler, *CWL,* 7:498. The president also enclosed a letter from Seward.

173. Cameron Papers, DLC. This letter is in the hand of Edward D. Neill.

174. Cameron forwarded letters from Pennsylvanians complaining about unfair taxes, among other things. Cameron to Lincoln, Harrisburg, 22 Aug. 1864, AL MSS, DLC.

175. JGN MSS, DLC.

176. In addition to Sumner, other Radicals joined the movement to dump Lincoln. They included Parke Godwin, Theodore Tilton, George Wilkes, John A. Andrew, David Dudley Field, and Horace Greeley.

177. Draft, AL MSS, DLC. William Edward Dorsheimer (1832–88) was a New York lawyer and politician.

178. In his letter (Buffalo, New York, 24 Aug. 1864, AL MSS, DLC),

Dorsheimer suggested that Lincoln authorize him to act as a go-between to help expedite peace negotiations with Confederate agents in Canada.

179. Neill Papers, Minnesota Historical Society.

180. Neill Papers, Minnesota Historical Society.

181. JGN MSS, DLC.

182. Henry J. Raymond's letter to Lincoln, dated New York, 22 Aug. 1864, is in the AL MSS, DLC.

183. William Pitt Fessenden (1806–69) of Maine was secretary of the treasury.

184. Telegrams Collected by the Office of the Secretary of War, 1861–1882, Record Group 473, reel 1, National Archives.

185. On 27 August, Johnson had telegraphed inquiring about the cases of four men condemned to be hanged as spies (William H. Rodgers, John R. H. Embert, Branton Lyons [or Braxton Lyon], and Samuel Hearn). Gen. Lewis Wallace (1827–1905) commanded the VIII Corps of the Army of the Potomac. Lincoln ordered the commutation of their sentences. Lincoln to Lew Wallace, Washington, 28 Aug. 1864, in Basler, *CWL*, 7:522.

186. Telegrams Collected by the Office of the Secretary of War, 1861–1882, Record Group 473, reel 1, National Archives.

187. Gwynn, counsel for four condemned men, urged that a respite be given before they were executed, which was to happen on the following day. Lincoln complied. Gwynn to Montgomery Blair, Baltimore, 28 Aug. 1864, telegram, AL MSS, DLC.

188. AL MSS, DLC.

189. Isaac Sherman (1818–81) was a New York businessman and active member of the Union League Club. *New York Times,* 23 Jan. 1881.

190. Simeon Draper (1804–66), a prominent New York auctioneer and Republican leader, became collector of the port of New York in September 1864.

191. Moses Hicks Grinnell (1803–77) was a New York merchant.

192. Congressman Reuben E. Fenton (1819–85) was the Republican candidate for governor of New York. See Fenton's recollections about Nicolay's mission to New York in Allen Thorndike Rice, ed., *Reminiscences of Abraham Lincoln by Distinguished Men of His Time* (New York: North American Review, 1888), 68–70.

193. AL MSS, DLC.

194. Edward Delafield Smith (1826–78) was district attorney for the southern district of New York (1861–65).

195. William M. Evarts (1818–1901) was a prominent attorney and Republican politician in New York.

196. Abram Wakeman (1824–89) was postmaster of New York.

197. Republican Lot M. Morrill (1813–83) represented Maine in the U.S. Senate (1861–76).

198. Preston King (1806–65) of New York served in the U.S. House of Representatives (1843–47, 1849–53) and the U.S. Senate (1857–63).

199. James Kelly, treasurer of the New York Republican State Central Committee, had for two years chaired that committee. Kelly to William Henry Seward, New York, 12 Aug. 1864, AL MSS, DLC.

200. AL MSS, DLC.

201. In his letter to Nicolay (New York, 31 Aug. 1864, AL MSS, DLC), Rufus Andrews agreed to resign whenever the president asked him to, but only if the president told him the true reason for making the request. Andrews's relations with Thurlow Weed were badly strained. See Andrews to Weed, New York, 10 Dec. 1864, *New York Tribune*, 12 Dec. 1864.

202. At the urging of his Springfield friend Robert Irwin, Lincoln had overruled Treasury Secretary Chase and appointed George Denison (sometimes spelled Dennison) naval officer for the port of New York in 1861.

203. AL MSS, DLC.

204. JGN MSS, DLC.

205. Sherman's army captured Atlanta on 2 September.

206. At the end of August, the Democrats adopted a platform denouncing the war as a failure and nominated George B. McClellan for president and George H. Pendleton for vice president.

207. Seward Papers, University of Rochester.

208. Miscellaneous Manuscripts (Nicolay), New-York Historical Society. Tilton (1835–1907), editor of the *New York Independent,* had opposed Lincoln's renomination.

209. In reply to this letter, Tilton said that he was so cheered by the capture of Atlanta and so outraged by the Democratic platform that he would vigorously promote Lincoln's reelection. Tilton to Nicolay, New York, 6 Sept. 1864, AL MSS, DLC.

210. JGN MSS, DLC.

211. Lincoln used the expression about the husband and bear in his final debate with Stephen A. Douglas in 1858. It alludes to the tale of a long-suffering Kentucky wife who observed her husband and a bear locked in hand-to-paw combat. From the sidelines she shouted, "Fair play! fair play!" When others tried to separate the contestants, she objected: "No—no—let them fight! for it is the first fight I ever saw, that I did not care which whipped." *The Humorist's Own Book* (Philadelphia: Key and Biddle, 1834), quoted in P. M. Zall, ed., *Abe Lincoln Laughing: Humorous Anecdotes from Original Sources by and about Abraham Lincoln* (Berkeley: University of California Press, 1982), 20.

212. Grant to E. B. Washburne, City Point, Va., 16 Aug. 1864, *New York Times,* 9 Sept. 1864, p. 4, c. 3.

213. Draft, AL MSS, DLC. James Cook Conkling (1816–99) of Illinois was a friend and neighbor of Lincoln's.

214. A call for a convention to meet in Cincinnati on 28 September to choose an alternative to Lincoln was sent out under the signature of John Austin Stevens.

Conkling believed that the movers intended to nominate Benjamin Butler. The disgruntled Republicans who gathered in New York on 30 August to plot a strategy for dumping Lincoln found their case undermined by the fall of Atlanta on 2 September and the Democratic party's adoption on 30 August of an unpopular platform declaring the war a failure. On 5 September, they called off their effort. Frémont withdrew his candidacy on 22 September.

215. Cameron Papers, DLC.

216. Cameron asked Nicolay to have Carl Schurz come speak in Pennsylvania. Cameron to Nicolay, Philadelphia, 13 Sept. 1864, AL MSS, DLC.

217. Taggart was perhaps David Taggart, former speaker of the Pennsylvania state senate and a political ally of Cameron.

218. Greeley Papers, DLC.

219. The letter enclosed was Absalom Hanks Markland to John G. Nicolay, Louisville, Ky., 14 Sept. 1864, AL MSS, DLC. A Kentucky native, Markland (b. 1825) was appointed special post office agent in 1861 and two years later took charge of the mails for the Army of Tennessee. On 14 September, Markland told Montgomery Blair that arrangements had been made to distribute papers and documents to troops in the Richmond campaign. Markland to Blair, Washington, 14 Sept. 1864, AL MSS, DLC.

220. Greeley to Nicolay, New York, 4 Sept. 1864, AL MSS, DLC.

221. Frederick A. Conkling (1816–91), colonel of the 84th New York Volunteers, then stationed in Baltimore on provost-guard duty, complained to Greeley that Lincoln had wrongfully spared a convicted spy caught by one of his men. Conkling to Greeley, Great Falls, Md., 3 Sept. 1864, AL MSS, DLC.

222. William A. Phillips (1824–93) was colonel of the 3rd Indian Regiment. According to an endorsement in the hand of Edward D. Neill, these papers related to charges against people in the District of the Frontier, commanded by Gen. John Milton Thayer (1820–1906).

223. JGN MSS, DLC.

224. Copy, Hay Papers, Brown University. Leonard Grover (1835–1926), proprietor of the National Theater in Washington, was also an actor and playwright.

225. AL MSS, DLC. Nicolay left for New York around 19 September and returned to Washington on 26 September.

226. Hay responded: "Your despatch was just brought in. I took it to the President & he told me to tell you you had better loaf around the city a while longer. You need some rest & recreation & may as well take it in N.Y. as anywhere else." Hay to Nicolay, Washington, 24 Sept. 1864, in Burlingame, *At Lincoln's Side*, 95.

227. Draft, AL MSS, DLC. William Eaton Chandler (1835–1917) was the speaker of the New Hampshire state assembly. His loyal support of Lincoln's candidacy led the president in March 1865 to appoint him solicitor and judge advocate general of the Navy Department.

228. On 16 September, Chandler wrote to Nicolay from Concord, New Hampshire, asking: "Have you any objection to preparing and forwarding me a certificate substantially like the form enclosed? Our judges now have the question whether our soldiers voting bill has become a law, before them, and I am confident of a favorable decision, but wish to give the Justices all the light that can be obtained.

"If the President could find time to glance at the certificate I should like it; and if any stronger statement can be made it would be desirable." AL MSS, DLC. The enclosed certificate read:

I, John G. Nicolay, Private Secretary of President Lincoln certify and say that the customary mode of presenting to the President bills which have passed Congress is substantially as follows:

Some member of the Congressional Committee on Engrossed Bills brings the bills to the President's House and is admitted to the Room in which the office business of the President is transacted. If the President is in the room the bills are either handed to him, or laid upon his table and his attention called to them. If the President is absent the bills are laid upon his table and the attention of the Secretary or some other person called to them.

There is no formality of presentation; the day on which the bills are brought to the President's House is always taken as the day of presentation without inquiry as to the exact time when they met the eye of the President; and I am not aware and cannot learn that any question has arisen upon the subject.

229. Hay Papers, Brown University. Risley, a special treasury department agent "for the purchase of products of insurrectionary states on behalf of the Government of the United States," wrote to Nicolay on 29 September asking if the papers he had left at the White House on 28 September had returned from the War Department. "We only await the order of the Secretary of War to set the Cotton mills running." AL MSS, DLC. Cf. Basler, *CWL*, 8:185–86, and Roy P. Basler, ed., *The Collected Works of Abraham Lincoln: Supplement, 1832–1865* (Westport, Conn.: Greenwood, 1974), 268–69.

230. JGN MSS, DLC.

231. Gen. Philip H. Sheridan (1831–88) defeated Confederate forces under Jubal Early on 19 September at Winchester and three days later at Fisher's Hill.

232. On 29–30 September, Grant fought battles at Peebles' Farm and at Fort Harrison.

233. JGN MSS, DLC.

234. Greeley Papers, DLC.

235. On 19 September, Greeley had written Nicolay from New York:

I thank you heartily for your note of the 15th and enclosure. I am glad to hear that *you,* at least, are alive.

The McClellanites are very active and strong here, working and pushing night and day, while our people are mainly engaged in squabbles about paltry offices, &c.

Now will you please consider that we are dying for a short, sharp, clear, concise statement . . . of *why there is no general exchange of prisoners,* what is the [precise?] hitch, &c. Won't you understand that the McClellanites are making capital on this point, and that they ought to be stopped if they *can* be.

[P.S.] If the vote were to be taken to-morrow, McClellan would carry this city by 40,000. We can improve this if we can stop these detestable feuds and go to work.

AL MSS, DLC.

236. Message written on a business card, Hay Papers, Brown University. The Planters House was a hotel in St. Louis. Capt. Edward Geer Bush (1838–92), a personal friend of Nicolay's from Pittsfield, Illinois, was the son of Daniel Brown Bush, editor of the *Pike County Journal* and brother-in-law of Ozias M. Hatch. He graduated from West Point in 1859, served in the 2nd Brigade, 2nd Division of the V Corps under General Sykes, and was wounded at Gettysburg.

237. AL MSS, DLC. Nicolay left Washington on 7 October and returned on 30 November.

238. AL MSS, DLC.

239. On 11 July 1861, Rosecrans led two thousand Union troops to victory at Rich Mountain in western Virginia.

240. McClellan claimed credit for the victory although Rosecrans truly deserved it, for he had successfully attacked the Confederates from the rear while McClellan bungled a frontal assault. On 15 June 1865, Rosecrans in his final report on his war service said: "My brigade after a march often hours over pathless mountains, gained the gap two miles and a half in the rear of the rebel entrenched camp, where he met and fought us with all the infantry and artillery he could spare from his camp, which General McClellan contrary to agreement and military prudence did not attack." William M. Lamers, *The Edge of Glory: A Biography of General William S. Rosecrans* (New York: Harcourt Brace, and World, 1961), 33.

241. AL MSS, DLC.

242. Conservative Missouri Republicans were called "Claybanks," while the Radicals were known as "Charcoals."

243. John F. Hume of the *Missouri Democrat* was a Radical Republican delegate to the Baltimore Convention in 1864. See Hume to James M. Edmunds, St. Louis, 2 July 1864, AL MSS, DLC.

244. Peter L. Foy was the postmaster of St. Louis.

245. Col. Thomas C. Fletcher (1827–99) served as governor of Missouri (1865–69).

246. On 10 June 1864, Samuel Knox (1815–1905) had entered the U.S. House

of Representatives, taking Frank Blair's seat. In November, his bid to retain that seat failed.

247. The *Missouri Democrat* (St. Louis) was a leading Radical newspaper.

248. Charles Philip Johnson (1836–1920) of St. Louis was a Missouri state legislator. A Radical, he was a member of the delegation of seventy that had called on Lincoln on 30 September 1863. Statement of Johnson to J. McCan Davis, 17 Dec. 1898, Ida M. Tarbell Papers, Allegheny College.

249. On 12 October, Rosecrans issued General Orders 195, which denied the franchise to anyone who had fought against the U.S., commanded the military to maintain order at the polls, and allowed Missouri soldiers to vote in the field.

250. The following month in Missouri, Lincoln received 72,991 votes to McClellan's 31,026.

251. In 1864, the Thirteenth Amendment abolishing slavery throughout the U.S. had passed the Senate by the requisite two-thirds majority but had failed to do so in the House. The lower chamber finally passed it on 31 January 1865.

252. In November, Democrat John Hogan (1805–92) won the election in the 1st congressional district. He served one term.

253. Telegram, AL MSS, DLC.

254. Telegram, AL MSS, DLC.

255. Telegram, AL MSS, DLC.

256. JGN MSS, DLC.

257. John W. Forney (1817–81) was secretary of the U.S. Senate and editor of the *Washington Chronicle* and *Philadelphia Press.*

258. JGN MSS, DLC.

259. Lincoln appointed Chase to the Supreme Court even though he would, to use his own language, "rather have swallowed his buckhorn chair" or "have eat[en] flat irons" than to have made such an appointment. William E. Chandler, quoting Lincoln, in Beale, *Diary of Gideon Welles,* 2:196 (entry for 15 Dec. 1864); Virginia Fox diary, quoted in Earl Schenck Miers et al., eds., *Lincoln Day by Day: A Chronology, 1809–1865,* 3 vols. (Washington: Lincoln Sesquicentennial Commission, 1960), 3:301 (entry for 10 Dec. 1864).

260. JGN MSS, DLC.

261. JGN MSS, DLC.

262. Sherman captured Savannah on 21 December.

263. At Nashville on 15–16 December, George H. Thomas's Army of the Cumberland demolished Confederate forces under John Bell Hood.

264. Banks Papers, DLC.

265. Congressman-elect Shelby M. Cullom (1829–1914) of Springfield had been the speaker of the Illinois House of Representatives.

266. JGN MSS, DLC.

267. Cameron Papers, DLC.

268. Nicolay had earlier consulted with William W. Seaton about purchasing the

Washington National Intelligencer. Joseph C. G. Kennedy to Nicolay, Washington, 5 Dec. 1864, scrapbook, box 1, JGN MSS, DLC. According to a *New York Tribune* correspondent, Nicolay and Hay had been trying to obtain control of other papers:

> I did everything I could to promote the sale of the *Chronicle.* It failed. The scheme in behalf of the youthful secretaries finally took the shape of a union of the *Intelligencer* and *Republican.* Seward sent for Forney, and felt him to see if he would consent to a diversion of the Government patronage from his papers to *[Simon]* Hanscom*[']s* pocket!! Forney in a profane rage told him the President might take his patronage and go to Hell with it—that if the scheme of starting a paper against him was persevered in, he would sell the *Chronicle* to an interest that voted indeed for Mr Lincoln, but despaired and dreaded his policy, and desired to resist it. Seward in alarm swore that the ambition of the youthful secretaries should be squelched and that the *Intelligencer* and *Republican* should swim as they might. [Samuel] Wilkeson to Horace Greeley, Washington, 24 Dec. 1864, Greeley Papers, New York Public Library.

269. JGN MSS, DLC.

270. JGN MSS, LM.

271. Copy, AL MSS, DLC. Gen. John M. Palmer (1817–1900), a leading Illinois Republican, was on the military sidelines; in February 1865 he became head of the Department of Kentucky.

272. Palmer had offered to resign his commission. Palmer to Nicolay, Carlinville, Ill., 22 Dec. 1864, AL MSS, DLC.

273. JGN MSS, DLC.

274. On 23–25 December, Benjamin F. Butler unsuccessfully attacked Fort Fisher at Wilmington, North Carolina.

1865

1. Seward Papers, University of Rochester.

2. George M. Dallas (b. 1792), vice president of the U.S. (1845–49), died on 31 December.

3. William L. Dayton (b. 1807), a New Jersey politician whom Lincoln had appointed minister to France in 1861, died on 1 December.

4. JGN MSS, DLC.

5. Telegrams Collected by the Office of the Secretary of War, 1861–1882, Record Group 473, reel 1, National Archives. Swift was the warden of the Missouri State Prison in Jefferson City.

6. JGN MSS, DLC.

7. Sherman captured Savannah on 21 December.

8. On 6 January, Congress began discussing the proposed constitutional amendment to abolish slavery throughout the nation.

9. JGN MSS, DLC.

10. James M. Ashley (1824–96) of Toledo, Ohio, represented his district in the U.S. House (1859–69).

11. The Camden & Amboy Railroad enjoyed a monopoly over the passenger traffic between New York and Philadelphia. The bill would have ended that monopoly.

12. Andrew Jackson Rogers (1828–1900), a Democrat who represented a New Jersey district in the U.S. House (1863–67), did not appear in the lower chamber on the day that the Thirteenth Amendment was voted on.

13. Charles Sumner was, according to a White House observer, "the only man, so far as my knowledge goes, to obtain the President's bitter dislike." Once, Lincoln's "intense antipathy" toward the Massachusetts senator prompted him to order the hall attendant, Elphonso Dunn, to deny him admission. William Henry Crook, "Lincoln as I Knew Him," ed. Margarita Spalding Gerry, *Harper's Magazine* 115 (June 1907): 45; Dunn, paraphrased in Margarita Spalding Gerry, ed., *Through Five Administrations: Reminiscences of Colonel William H. Crook, Body-Guard to President Lincoln* (New York: Harper and Brothers, 1910), 36–37.

14. JGN MSS, DLC.

15. Francis P. Blair, Sr. (1791–1876), a close advisor of President Jackson in the 1830s, offered counsel to Lincoln on many issues. He visited Richmond twice in January to promote a plan that would unite the North and South in an attempt to drive French forces from Mexico.

16. Telegram, AL MSS, DLC.

17. The Thirteenth Amendment abolished slavery throughout the United States. Eight members of the House abstained.

18. Telegrams Collected by the Office of the Secretary of War, 1861–1882, Record Group 473, reel 1, National Archives.

19. Wallace sent two telegrams on 31 January about Charles E. Waters, who had been tried and convicted in Washington, not Baltimore, where General Wallace was in charge. AL MSS, DLC.

20. Lincoln to Wallace, Washington, 31 Jan. 1865, in Basler, *CWL*, 8:251. Waters had been found guilty based on testimony provided by a blockade runner.

21. Telegrams Collected by the Office of the Secretary of War, 1861–1882, Record Group 473, reel 1, National Archives.

22. Telegrams Collected by the Office of the Secretary of War, 1861–1882, Record Group 473, reel 1, National Archives. Richard J. Oglesby (1824–99) was governor of Illinois.

23. Oglesby notified Lincoln on 1 February that the legislature had ratified the Thirteenth Amendment, abolishing slavery. Telegram, AL MSS, DLC.

24. JGN MSS, DLC.

25. Alexander H. Stephens (1812–83) of Georgia was vice president of the Confederacy.

26. Robert M. T. Hunter (1809–87) represented Virginia in the Confederate Senate.

27. John A. Campbell (1811–89) of Virginia was the Confederacy's assistant secretary of war.

28. Telegrams Collected by the Office of the Secretary of War, 1861–1882, Record Group 473, reel 1, National Archives.

29. Hoyt had requested a short presidential interview with a delegation from the New York Young Mens Republican Union, of which he was president. Hoyt to Lincoln, New York, 8 Feb. 1865, telegram, AL MSS, DLC.

30. Telegrams Collected by the Office of the Secretary of War, 1861–1882, Record Group 473, reel 1, National Archives.

31. On 9 February, Andrew had telegraphed Lincoln asking for a delay of execution for Hugh F. Riley. AL MSS, DLC.

32. JGN MSS, DLC.

33. Nicolay evidently alludes here to his poor relationship with Mary Lincoln.

34. Batchelder Autograph Collection, DLC.

35. Copy, AL MSS, DLC.

36. On 1 April 1861, Lincoln signed an order fitting out the USS *Powhatan* to head to sea under sealed orders prepared without the knowledge of the navy department. The warship, originally intended to escort the relief expedition to Fort Sumter, was diverted to the mission to Fort Pickens in Pensacola, Florida. For the files of the navy department, Fox had asked for a copy of the orders Lincoln gave to Porter. Fox to Nicolay, Washington, 22 Feb. 1865, AL MSS, DLC.

37. JGN MSS, DLC.

38. Charleston surrendered to Union forces on 18 February; Fort Anderson in North Carolina followed suit on 19 February; the North Carolina port of Wilmington did so on 23 February.

39. JGN MSS, DLC.

40. JGN MSS, DLC.

41. The salary, double what Nicolay received as private secretary to the president, would enable Nicolay to marry his fiancée.

42. Fuller Autograph Collection, Houghton Library, Harvard University. Charles Lush Wilson (1818–78) edited the *Chicago Journal*; earlier in the war he had been the secretary of the American legation in London.

43. JGN MSS, DLC.

44. Lincoln left Washington on 24 March to visit the Army of the Potomac and returned on 9 April. His wife went back to Washington on 1 April, only to return to the front on 5 April.

45. Small Manuscripts Collection no. 1107, IHi, Springfield. Journalist Charles A. Dana (1819–97) was assistant secretary of war (1864–65).

46. Cross was either Thomas H. Cross, a furnace man at the White House, or Thomas Cross, a doorkeeper.

47. Lincoln's Secretariat Collection, LM.

48. JGN MSS, DLC.

49. JGN MSS, DLC.

50. Andrew Johnson Papers, DLC.

51. Andrew Johnson Papers, DLC.

52. Lincoln's barber, Solomon James Johnson (1842?–85), had started the war as an employee of the quartermaster's department, then worked with a military company that served as a presidential bodyguard. In 1864, Lincoln helped him obtain a supplementary job as a laborer in the treasury department and to gain a promotion in 1865. After the war, he became a first-class clerk in that department. John E. Washington, *They Knew Lincoln* (New York: E. P. Dutton, 1942), 135–41.

53. JGN MSS, DLC.

54. Soon thereafter, while attending Lincoln's funeral in Springfield, Nicolay was described as looking "very much fatigued." His face "was the picture of despair." Octavia Roberts Corneau, "A Girl in the Sixties: Excerpts from the Journal of Anna Ridgely (Mrs. James L. Hudson)," *Journal of the Illinois State Historical Society* 22 (1929): 445 (entry for 7 May 1865).

Index

The following abbreviations are used throughout the index:
JN John G. Nicolay
AL Abraham Lincoln

Michael Burlingame is the May Buckley Sadowski Professor of History at Connecticut College. His previous books include *Inside Lincoln's White House: The Complete Civil War Diary of John Hay* (coedited with John R. Turner Ettlinger); *Lincoln's Journalist: John Hay's Anonymous Writings for the Press, 1860–1864; At Lincoln's Side: John Hay's Civil War Correspondence and Selected Writings;* and *An Oral History of Abraham Lincoln: John G. Nicolay's Interviews and Essays,* which won the 1995 Abraham Lincoln Association Prize. He is presently working on a multivolume biography of Abraham Lincoln.